Section and Party

GEOGRAPHICAL RESEARCH STUDIES SERIES
(Studies in Political Geography)

Series Editor: **Dr. Peter J. Perry**
Reader in Geography, University of Canterbury, New Zealand

Section and Party

A POLITICAL GEOGRAPHY OF AMERICAN
PRESIDENTIAL ELECTIONS, FROM
ANDREW JACKSON TO RONALD REAGAN

Dr. J. Clark Archer
Dartmouth College, New Hampshire, U.S.A.

and

Dr. Peter J. Taylor
University of Newcastle upon Tyne, England

RESEARCH STUDIES PRESS
A DIVISION OF JOHN WILEY & SONS LTD.
Chichester · New York · Brisbane · Toronto

RESEARCH STUDIES PRESS

Editorial Office:
8 Willian Way, Letchworth, Herts SG6 2HG, England

British Library Cataloguing in Publication Data:

Archer, J. Clark
    Section and Party: a political geography of American
    presidential elections from Andrew Jackson to Ronald
    Reagan.—(Geographical research studies series)
    1. Presidents—United States—Election—History
    2. Voting—United States—History
    I. Title   II. Taylor, Peter J., *1948—*
    III. Series

    ISBN 0 471 10014 5

Printed in the United States of America

For
    JILL
        JANET
              and
                  JASON
and
    ENID
        CARL
              and
                  CLARE

EDITOR'S PREFACE

This series comes into existence as the result of a
decade's experience of teaching political geography
at the undergraduate level. That experience has
convinced me that the scarcity of research monographs
in the field, by comparison with other branches of
geography and with what is now an abundance of text-
books and an adequacy of research papers, is an
obstacle to be overcome if this particular branch of
geography is to be well taught at any level. I come
to the series then not as myself a researcher but as
a teacher whose experience has armed him however with
the conviction that exposure of students to the
fruits of current research activity at an early stage
of their undergraduate career is an essential characteristic of university education. I am equally
convinced that the geographical dimension of current
affairs has too often been neglected in public
debate, at our peril and often by our default. The
missing contribution in otherwise well informed
analysis of the contemporary world in the media is
almost invariably that of the political geographer,
and its absence often serves seriously to weaken or
undermine the structures erected by historian,
economist, sociologist and political scientist. This
series possesses then a practical as well as an
academic aim and is directed towards a readership
outside as well as within the universities. The
study of political geography has its part to play not
only in the education of every geographer but in the
achievement of 'a just and lasting peace among
ourselves and with all nations'.

Peter Perry
University of Canterbury
Christchurch, N. Z.

PREFACE

On Tuesday November 4, 1980, at 9:45 p.m. Jimmy
Carter announced that "The People of the United States
have made their choice." Indeed they had. The
nation's fortieth President would be a Republican.
The Democratic incumbent won but six states,
including his home state of Georgia, plus the
District of Columbia. In Electoral College balloting
the outcome was an overwhelming 489 to 49 in favor of
Ronald Reagan.

Underlying Reagan's victory and Carter's defeat,
which for the nineteenth time transferred the
Presidency from the hands of one party to those of
another, is a geography of voting which will be
important as Republicans and Democrats challenge one
another for the Presidency once again in 1984. One
of the most notable features of the popular balloting
in 1980 was the devastating defeat of the Democratic
incumbent in the West. The mountains and plains
beyond the Mississippi River contain eight states
where less than thirty percent of the electorate
supported Carter. It seems that the solidly
Democratic South of a bygone era has been replaced by
a solidly Republican West of the present one. In
this book we consider and develop such ideas, not
just in terms of present patterns, but through a
broad historical perspective which extends back in
time to the founding of the Republic and the shifting
sectional alliances which have occurred since then.

Studies of the geography of voting have become
relatively common in recent years and in some ways
represent the convergence of two separate trends.
First is the rise of quantitative methods in
geography, the so-called quantitative revolution,
which led to elections becoming popular topics for
study as they presented readily available data for
analysis. Second is the more recent development of
interest in political aspects of geography which has
made elections of interest for quite different
reasons. The legacy of the quantitative trend was
only a sporadic growth of individual studies hardly
related one to another. Increasing awareness of the
political dimension in geography, however, has

prompted integration of the study of elections into a broader concern for the state and its role in making and unmaking geographies of well-being. This has been the essence of recent contributions in this field by Ron Johnston and we follow his lead in trying to set our concern for the geographies of presidential voting into a broader framework. This involves an interpretation of elections which places emphasis on political parties as moulders and manipulators of mass mobilisation and which finds the motives for such manipulation in the material base of American society as reflected in economic sectional differences. Hence, our main themes through which we study American Presidential elections are Party and Section.

The structure of our argument consists of four main chapters. The first is made up largely of a literature review plus a description of the methodology employed in the remainder of the book. Despite the existence of many interesting individual electoral geography studies of American contests, there exists no general pool of ideas and concepts for us to draw upon in this restricted area. Hence, the literature pool we are fishing in has been partly stocked by other students of electoral patterns. Our major sources are from history (e.g. F. J. Turner), political science (e.g. E. E. Schattsneider) and political sociology (e.g. A. Campbell). Although this monograph is breaking new ground as a comprehensive political geographical study of American Presidential elections, it is more generally following several research traditions within the broader realm of political studies.

Chapter two consists of a discussion of the rise of political parties within the context of the American federal system. Beginning with the 'anti-party' Constitution of 1789, we trace the emergence and consolidation of political parties before the Civil War. Particular emphasis is placed upon how the parties reacted with the sectional conflicts which underlay this whole period. In chapter three the post Civil War period to the present is considered when the link between party and section became quite explicit. In both of these chapters election results

for states are analysed to produce a new typology of
elections which confirms some previous studies while
emphasising new themes and structures. In chapter
four similar analyses are carried out separately for
the three major American sections: North, South and
West. A brief review of our findings and their
relations to previous literature is presented in a
short concluding chapter.

In carrying out this study perhaps our major
acknowledgment should be to the postal services of
Britain and America which made this trans-Atlantic
effort possible. Several people have read and
commented upon portions of the manuscript and we
should mention Dave Reynolds, Ron Johnston and Peter
Perry in this context. The credit for typing the
manuscript and preparing the diagrams reproduced
below go to Jill Archer and Olive Teasdale,
respectively. Finally we dedicate this book to our
families: Enid, Carl and Clare, and Jill, Janet and
Jason.

Peter J. Taylor and J. Clark Archer
Christmas, 1980

CHAPTER 1
American Presidential Elections as a Topic of Study

American presidential elections are probably the most exhaustively researched series of political events in the modern world. Why, therefore, are two political geographers offering an additional monograph on this theme? In what ways do we claim to add to this enormous preceding literature? Our answer is a simple one: American presidential elections are unique in two respects which elicit simultaneous concern for both temporal and spatial variation. First, American presidential elections have been the focus of a competitive two party politics involving the mass mobilization of voters for a century and a half. Second, these voters have been distributed over a large and increasing area which became continental in scope before the turn of the present century. It is the purpose of this monograph to explore the fundamental patterns underlying these unique ranges of variation over time and space.

This long time span and large geographical extent have, of course, been common themes in discussions of American presidential elections. Debates regarding the relative importance of local, sectional or national interests and the continuity or the discontinuity of voter behavior at different times in the evolution of the American political system abound in literature. Yet, with important and notable exceptions, these dual and related themes of variation in time and in space have commonly been treated separately. What we attempt is the design and execution

of a series of analyses which explicitly and systematically unify the temporal and spatial dimensions of
popular voting for the United States Presidency. As
well as asking, for example, when 'critical'
elections occurred, we also pose the question of
where they occurred since the American polity is as
diverse in its local or sectional interests as it is
in its private or group interests. Hence, whereas
Sundquist (1973) begins his study of the American
party system by asking "Party Realignment: What?
When? How?," we explicitly add the further question
'Where?' In short we derive the broad spatial and
temporal patterns for interpreting the politics and
geography of American presidential elections.
Whether this approach indeed yields additional interesting or worthwhile insight into the spatial and
temporal dynamics of American politics is a matter
for the reader's judgment.

  Although our methodology is novel in research on
American electoral behavior at national scale and
over an extended time horizon, we are clearly dependent upon the vast legacy of prior research on
American elections from which we draw concepts and
ideas. Our starting point must, therefore, be this
legacy. American electoral research falls into two
basic categories which we term the 'individual-
behavioral tradition' and the 'group-ecological
tradition.' The next two sections of this chapter
selectively review these two sets of literature and
identify concepts and findings which we use in our
subsequent analyses. These ideas are discussed and
their interrelationships drawn together in the final
section of the chapter where we propose the outlines
of a new electoral geography of American presidential
elections.

THE INDIVIDUAL-BEHAVIORAL TRADITION
Burnham (1974, p. 695) has pointed out that "survey
analyses of electoral behavior have more completely
dominated the mainstream of voting research in the
United States than in any other country." One of the
reasons he gives for this situation is "the overwhelming preoccupation with analyses at the individual scale" reflecting America's liberal tradition
in both polity and research. Although several recent

studies have attempted to relate individual-scale
research to analyses to larger scales, the major
thrust in American electoral research has dealt
explicitly and exclusively with the behavior of individual voters. This tradition can be traced back to
the very earliest development of an independent
political 'science' and has been continued in the
classical school of political sociology to which
Burnham is referring above.

The New Political 'Psychologists'
It is rather difficult to differentiate between different academic disciplines and their approaches to
electoral research before 1920. Until then work by
political historians and political scientists closely
reflected developments in one another's fields. In
fact the coalescence of political science as a separate discipline was not formally acknowledged by the
formation of a national professional organization
until 1903. At this time political scientists
"recognized explicitly the necessity of basing their
interpretations of the evolution of government forms
upon historical research" (Jenson, 1969, p. 1). By
the third decade of the twentieth century, however,
political scientists began to reject historical
analyses and instead turned towards sociology and
psychology (Jenson, 1969, p. 4).

Although the terms "behavioral" and "behavioralism"
did not become common currency until the 1960's
(Eulau, 1976, p. 119), the antecedents of this now
dominant paradigm can be traced back to the early
1920's (Jenson, 1969). The watershed events of the
decade transpired during a series of special confer-
ences on the "science of politics" conducted at the
University of Chicago in the summers of 1923, 1924
and 1925. The tenor of the times is captured by
Charles Merriam, a leading University of Chicago
political scientist, who charged that "we are in fact
coming into a new world, with new social conditions
and with new modes of thought and inquiry, and we may
well inquire what direction and form our politics
must take if it is to interpret and express these new
tendencies of the new world" (Merriam, 1925, p. 2,
cited in Jenson, 1969, pp. 3-4). A new paradigm was
sought after and 'scientific,' rather than

'historical,' methods seemed the most potentially
useful.

The second Chicago conference (1924) introduced
contemporary scientific psychology to political
science. The principal spokesman was Thurstone, now
well-known for his work on factor analysis, who "in
five days in September 1924 revolutionized political
science by converting virtually every leader of the
profession to the behavioral persuasion" (Jenson,
1969, p. 5). The paradigm Thurstone offered was that
of experimental psychometrics. The stumbling block
was that of identifying a suitable basic unit of
measurement which could serve a role perhaps analogous to those of money or utility in economics.

Thurstone proposed that the concept of attitude
could be adopted as the basic unit of analysis. To
him, attitude implied "the sum total of man's
inclinations and feelings, prejudice or bias, pre-
conceived notions, ideas, fears, threats and con-
victions about a specific topic" (Thurstone, 1928,
p. 520, cited in Jenson, 1969, p. 6). Although more
recent research has indicated that linkages between
attitudes and behavior are at best complex and at
worst tenuous and unpredictable, the potential
grounding of the study of politics upon scientif-
ically designed questionnaires and quantitatively
scaled opinions created great optimism at the time.
Rice's now classic Quantitative Methods in Politics,
first published in 1923, for example, was viewed by
its author as preparatory to, in his words, "a
behavioralistic political psychology" as a science
"concerned among other things with the nature,
content and distribution of attitudes among individuals, and with the manner in which they have
practical effect in the machinery of government"
(Rice, 1928, pp. 5, 8, cited in Silbey, Bogue and
Flanigan, 1973). For various reasons these expectations were not realized (Jenson, 1969, pp. 8-10).
The major difficulties involved in measuring
attitudes in the context of mass mobilization of
voters led some researchers such as Merriam towards
detailed studies of political elites--the "psycho-
biographies" of representative American statesmen
written in the 1920's and 1930's--and others towards

experimenting with the new techniques of psychometrics outside attitude-scaling contexts. Hence the
early pioneering work on the application of factor
analysis to ecological, as opposed to experimental,
data was carried out in the 1930's by Gosnell in
Chicago (Gosnell and Gill, 1935). This work belongs
to the ecological tradition dealt with in the next
section, however; the behavioralist tradition
continued and was developed by researchers from other
backgrounds in other places.

The Social Surveyors

During the 1940's and 1950's voting research merged
individual attitudinal orientation initiated by
Thurstone with survey methods pioneered by sociologists to create a series of highly influential works
on the subject of popular electoral behavior. At
Columbia University, Lazarsfeld, a sociologist, quite
by accident directed his attentions from consumer
behavior to electoral behavior and with his research
associates applied panel polling techniques to a
study of voter decisions during the 1940 election in
Erie County, Ohio. The People's Choice by Lazarsfeld, Berelson and Gaudet (1944) using the 1940
results was followed with Voting by Berelson, Lazarsfeld and McPhee (1954) using Elmira, New York, in
1948 as the setting. Together these provided a
variety of provocative generalizations concerning the
impact of the social-psychological context of an
individual upon voting behavior. These include the
two-step flow of information hypothesis (mass media
influence is modified by opinion leaders), the reference group hypothesis (voters are influenced by significant others such as friends or work associates),
and the cross-pressure hypothesis (overlapping group
membership reduced political interest and motivation)
(Eulau, 1976, pp. 120-121).

"The Social Psychology of Voting," as these
researchers referred to their work (Lazarsfeld,
Lipset, Barton and Linz, 1954), was back at the
centre of voting studies. Unfortunately, however,
panel techniques were not suited to large scale
investigation of electoral behavior because of the
huge costs involved in the data collection.

Once again a historical accident intervened.
Shortly before the upset election of Truman in 1948,
a poll conducted by the University of Michigan's
Survey Research Centre (associated with the Department of Agriculture at the time) on American foreign
policy included an incidental question on voting
intentions. Intrigued by conflicting explanations of
Truman's victory, social psychologist Campbell undertook another round of interviews in order to discover
how actual voting behavior had differed from pre-
election intentions. This led to the publication of
The Voter Decides (Campbell, Gurin and Miller, 1954),
a work which "introduced the trilogy of party identification, issue orientation and candidate image as
the variables that remain basic in voting research"
(Eulau, 1976, p. 121). But it was the publication of
The American Voter (Campbell, Converse, Miller and
Stokes, 1960) which revealed the full potential
contribution of survey research to an understanding
of electoral behavior. In many ways this was the
capstone effort "to account for a single behavior at
a fixed point in time" (Campbell, et.al., 1960,
p. 24). This particular way of describing electoral
behavior emphasizes the basic individualistic orientation of the social surveyors. Taken to its
extreme, the act of voting becomes an end in itself
with little or no concern for the wider political
context of which it is a part.
    Perhaps one of the best examples of the extreme
individualistic position can be found in the reju-
venated electoral geography which emerged from
geography's 'behavioral revolution' of the late
1960's (Johnston, 1979). The innovator in this field
was undoubtedly Kevin Cox who, as well as employing
survey methods to test community influences on voting
(Cox, 1970), set out to build a conceptual model of
the "Voting Decision in a Spatial Context" (Cox,
1969) which attempts "to relate the voting decision
of individuals to their location in an information
flow network," (Cox, 1969, p. 112). It is just such
studies which clearly illustrate Key and Munger's
(1959) fear of the behavioral approach taking the
politics out of electoral research and presumably
relates to Cox's more recent disenchantment with

electoral geography because of its omission of the broader political context (Cox, 1976).

We describe the research tradition to which Key belongs in the next section, but at this stage it is worth pointing out that this behavioral electoral geography does represent an extreme position in its continued emphasis on the individual voter. Both in The American Voter, and more particularly since 1960, the major trend has been to integrate the findings of the surveyors with the larger scale analyses we describe in the next section. This is explicitly illustrated in a volume of essays by Campbell and his associates dedicated to the memory of V. O. Key and suitably entitled Elections and the Political Order (Campbell, Converse, Miller and Stokes, 1966). In the final part of this section we draw on this volume to introduce concepts from the behavioral school which we will subsequently adapt for our own analyses.

The Concept of the Normal Vote

Although the survey approach may obtain large amounts of information about contemporary or recent elections it is not, by its very nature, really able to describe events over a long time horizon. Campbell and his associates were keenly aware of this limitation and looked forward to interchanges of ideas between studies of short-term and of long-term electoral change: "The firmer grasp of the underlying individual meaning...from current studies of individuals provides keys to unlock hidden meanings in the past record. At the same time, that record of past aggregative variation, if properly illuminated, can help to interpret the significance of limits in current or 'modern' variation" (Campbell, et.al., 1966, p. 8). The major contribution to bridging the gap between past and present, between aggregate and individual analyses, was Converse's concept of the normal vote.

As we have previously noted, Campbell and his associates' interest in voting was stimulated by Truman's surprise victory in 1948. Hence they started with explicit concern for changes in voting or 'the flow of the vote' as they term it, but only over a short time span. Converse (1966, p. 9) described this orientation as follows:

"In interpreting mass voting patterns, great importance is given to any signs of change that current
balloting may betray. Patterns established in the
past, even though they may nearly determine the
outcome of the election, tend to be taken for
granted, while results are eagerly scanned for
departures from these patterns. These departures
are then taken to represent the unique 'meaning' of
the electoral message."

It is just these short-term fluctuations which survey
methods can identify, but the past patterns which
'may nearly determine the outcome' are, by necessity
neglected.

In recognizing this problem in The American Voter,
the authors develop 'the funnel of causality' which
they describe as their 'structure of theory.' The
"funnel" represents the time dimension which termi-
nates at the actual act of voting. At the other end,
the 'funnel' is open ended so that there are a
multiple set of causes strung out in time before the
voting decision. Far back along the 'funnel' the
causes underlying the ultimate voting decision are
general societal scale forces, but as we come closer
to the day of decision, more immediate causes such as
those relating to a candidate or a campaign become
progressively more important. The final decision
at the end of the 'funnel' is the result of a convergence of these relevant causes.

The purpose of this analogy was to help derive "a
theory that will help us assess the current political
effects of remote events like the depression or the
'Civil War'" (Campbell, et.al., 1960, p. 25). These
ideas were never operationalized in the subsequent
analysis or discussion of the survey results, and it
was left to Converse, six years later, to propose a
way of incorporating past events in analysis of
current voting changes. In effect Converse (1966)
proposes dichotomising the funnel of causality along
its time dimension with 'past' causes producing a
'normal vote' and 'contemporary' causes producing
fluctuations around the normal vote.

Converse (1966) begins with the simple proposition that you cannot measure the extent of short-term changes unless you have a 'benchmark' against which to compare current voting decisions. Furthermore, such benchmarks are not measured for an individual alone, but for groups of individuals. Hence, operationalizing the benchmark leads Converse toward consideration of group characteristics and away from sole reliance upon the individual act of voting. It is, Converse (1966, p. 14) argues, "useful to consider any particular vote cast by _any particular group_ (our italics)--the nation as a whole or some subpopulation--as consisting of a long-term and a short-term component." He then goes on to describe the normal vote and deviations from it as follows:

"The long-term component is a simple reflection of the distribution of underlying loyalties, a distribution that is stable over substantial periods of time. In any specific election the population may be influenced by short-term forces associated with peculiarities of that election...to shift its vote now towards the Republicans, now towards the Democrats" (Converse, 1966, p. 14).

This construct was derived from the experience of the research on the 1952 and 1956 elections which elected a Republican president from an electorate dominated by Democrats. This can now be interpreted as a national normal vote with a Democrat majority, but with this potential Democratic vote eroded by short term forces associated with the attractiveness of the Republican candidate, Eisenhower.

Converse (1966) describes techniques for converting this theoretical construct into actual estimates of normal vote levels for subgroups of the American population using survey data on partisanship levels. The details of his methods do not concern us here and in fact we will suggest alternative modeling procedures for the concept in the final section of this chapter. What is of interest to us is that Converse explicitly extends application of the concept beyond its empirical derivation from survey data. He asserts that the normal vote "has increasingly become

an integral part of our thinking about the flow of
the vote registered across the history of American
elections" (Converse, 1966, p. 33). The normal vote
is to become the tool linking together the survey
school with more historically orientated research on
American elections. Thus Converse (1966, p. 33-34)
concludes

> "within the recent period for which sample survey
> measurements are available, the actual computation
> of normal votes under differing circumstances
> provides baselines which become crucial in assess-
> ing the meaning of electoral change....But even for
> the prehistory of survey research, where normal
> vote divisions can at best be crudely estimated
> from the general cast of election returns, the
> concept of an underlying normal vote remains
> crucial in finding new meaning in old statistics."

As we will illustrate below, we will very much be
applying this concept to elections which for the most
part are devoid of survey data. Like the Michigan
school, our foray into election history is built upon
ideas first developed systematically by V. O. Key.
It is now appropriate to consider this second
research tradition to which we have allocated Key in
our review and upon which we hope to build.

THE GROUP-ECOLOGICAL TRADITION
V. O. Key is in some ways a paradoxical figure in
the study of American elections. He most clearly
does not belong to the dominant behavioral school
described above and in fact has been a critic of
their concentration on the individual (Key and
Munger, 1959). Despite this position on the edge of
the major thrust in American electoral studies, one
recent reviewer has referred to Key as "probably the
most widely respected student of American politics in
the century" (Eulau, 1976, p. 116). The solution to
the paradox comes with Eulau's use of the phrase
'American politics' to describe Key's expertise.
Although Key has made major contributions to the
study of American elections, these contributions do
not treat elections or voting as ends in themselves.
Elections and those who participate in them are seen

as part of a wider political and social system.
Hence, emphasis moves from individual to group with
ecological data regarding actual voting returns playing a major part. Of course this group-ecological
tradition with its pluralistic theories and cartographic analyses predates the researches of Key so
that we will begin our consideration of this work by
turning to a political historian who in his day, at
the beginning of the century, was as influential as
Key has been to the last generation of researchers.

The Turnerian Historians
Before the rise of modern social science interest in
voting, the study of elections was largely a matter
for historians. Initially elections were treated as
unique expressions of the popular will at a given
historical juncture rather than as indicators of
deeper currents (Burnham, Clubb and Flannigan, 1978,
p. 50). As one critic recently noted:

> "We have as historians frequently been more
> impressed by what our subjects have said than by
> what they have done. As a group we have been
> unsystematic in our generalizations and too little
> interested in comparisons and categorization"
> (Bogue, 1968, p. 21).

The implication is not that the traditional narrative
is without appeal, but that the past rarely speaks to
the present in mutually comprehensible terms without
intervening interpretation.
    Intellectually grander schemes endeavoring to yield
a historical synthesis and incorporating an attrib-
ution of causal effects became more common in
historical research towards the close of the nineteenth century. This new political interpretation
came from the works of a group of researchers who are
now commonly referred to as the 'progressive
historians' (Hofstadter, 1968). They were greatly
influenced by other intellectual advances so that
"History was...linked not to romantic fiction or
romantic philosophy, but to other academic disciplines that were swept along in the Darwinian
current--to anthropology, geography, sociology,
economics" (Hofstadter, 1968, p. 39). They were also

influenced by Marx's emphasis upon economic motivation, and they form what may be termed a materialistic school of history. Their two most famous members were Charles A. Beard and Frederick Jackson Turner. The former's <u>An Economic Interpretation of the Constitution of the United States</u> (Beard, 1914) will be discussed in the next chapter. Here we concentrate on Frederick Jackson Turner who is best known for his <u>The Frontier in American History</u> (Turner, 1920) although we will focus more upon a collection of his political essays which span 1908 to 1926 and which were published posthumously as <u>The Significance of Sections in American History</u> (Turner, 1932).

Although Beard and Turner developed materialist historical interpretations, they were very different in the ways they chose to identify economic interests. For Beard economic interests are to be found in groups and classes; for Turner, they are expressed in the United States as sections:

"the United States has the problem of the clash of economic interests closely associated with regional geography on a huge scale....Economic interests are sectionalized" (Turner, 1932, p. 36).

Turner (1932, p. 183) places great emphasis upon this finding:

"The frontier and the section are two of the most fundamental factors in American history."

In fact Turner interprets the frontier as a 'mobile' section and much of his discussion involves emphasizing the importance of the West as a section alongside the more obvious North-South sectional conflict. His thesis is based upon the huge geographical expanse of the United States which makes sections both 'inevitable' (Turner, 1932, p. 45) and comparable in scale with the individual countries of Europe so that sections are "the shadowy image of the European nation" (Turner, 1932, p. 316). Hence, towards the end of his career Turner interprets American democracy with its political parties, drawing together alliances of sectional interests as a 'lesson' for Europe with its history of wars and conflicts (Turner, 1932, p. 318).

Turner's concern for electoral history was in part derivative of his interest in the American West and his hope for its persistence as a major region to rival the North and the South. Nevertheless, his painstaking research on American presidential elections set methodological standards which are only now being reachieved by historians. Rather than relying exclusively upon secondary interpretations based upon party platforms and political rhetoric, Turner advised his students to carefully examine "correlations between party votes, by precincts, wards, etc., nationalities and state origins of the voter, assessment rolls, denominational groups, illiteracy, etc. What kind of people tend to be Whigs, what Democrats or Abolitionists, or Prohibitionists, etc." (Jenson, 1969, p. 233). Following his own advice, Turner included detailed county-level election maps for the Presidential contests of 1836, 1876, 1888, 1892 and 1904 in a paper asking "Is Sectionalism in America Dying Away?" (Turner, 1932, pp. 287-314) presented in 1908. In this manner he was later to assert that "The areas of great geographical provinces are revealed by the map of votes" (Turner, 1932, p. 322) so that he can conclude:

"The more the reader will probe the distribution of votes...the more he will see that sectionalism was the dominant influence in shaping our political history upon all important matters" (Turner, 1932, p. 323).

Hence, the argument comes full cycle with electoral history confirming his sectional interpretation of political history while never forgetting that:

"Underneath the party sectionalism there is, of course, a sectionalism of material interests--of business, manufacturing, mining, agriculture, transportation" (Turner, 1932, p. 326).

Turner's use of maps and his interest in geographical regions brought him directly to the attention of geographers. Two of his major papers (Turner, 1914 and 1926), in fact, were published in geographical journals. After his death in 1932, J. K. Wright (1932a and 1932b) reintroduced Turner's work as the basis for the development of an electoral geography, but there seems to have been little support for the idea. The main reaction was criticism of Turner's occasional references to physical geography in his explanation of voting patterns by geographers who were then excessively sensitive to arguments smacking of 'environmental determinism' (Kollmorgen, 1936). Hence, Turner's work on elections has been almost entirely neglected by modern electoral geographers who prefer to trace their lineage to the more 'respectable' French school of geography and Andre Siegfried as the 'father' of electoral geography (Taylor and Johnston, 1979, p. 24). Strangely, Turner suffered a similar fate in his own field of political history.

One writer has identified twenty-eight researchers as "Turnerian historians of elections," though not all actually studied with their intellectual mentor (Jenson, 1969, p. 14). The last piece of research in this tradition seems to have appeared in 1941 as a study of the electoral cleavage which resulted in Lincoln's victory and precipitated the Civil War (Schafer, 1941, cited in Silbey, Bogue and Flanigan, 1978, p. 9). Perhaps because of the cumbersome nature of the technique of visual map comparison the Turnerian tradition of electoral research was only a transitory one. As a result, "interest in electoral analysis among historians almost died altogether as interest in other varieties of history increased. Whatever the reason, the historian's commitment to studying mass voting behavior by systematic quantitative means was suppressed during the twenties, not to reappear for several decades" (Silbey, Bogue and Flanigan, 1978, p. 9).

The recent revival of interest in electoral research by political historians has stemmed less from a rediscovery of the Turnerian tradition than from interdisciplinary influences emanating from the behavioral school described in the last section

(Jenson, 1969, p. 240). Turner's ideas did not
disappear altogether, however. Within political
science, the pluralistic school's interpretation of
the American polity could not avoid sectionalism as
one aspect of the electoral input to politics.
Hence, though watered down, sectionalism continued as
a topic of interest in American electoral analysis
largely through the work of V. O. Key.

Key and the Pluralist Group Model

Writing in 1926, Turner could claim with some justification that:

> "From Bacon's Rebellion to the La Follette revolt,
> there are almost continuous manifestations of the
> sectional contests of East and West, of the
> frontier and the older areas (Turner, 1932,
> p. 196).

In hindsight, we can see that Turner's faith here
in the West as a section was misplaced.
La Follette's presidential challenge of 1924 was in
fact the last of the major Western third party
revolts. Since 1924 it is the North-South sectional
cleavage that has dominated as the 'continuous
manifestation of American politics, albeit sometimes
in an unpredictable fashion. Hence, interest has
shifted from Turner's concern for the West to more
detailed consideration of the South and its role in
the American political system. The now classic
investigation on this theme is V. O. Key's (1949)
Southern Politics in State and Nation where direct
use was made of mapped voting returns in ways reminiscent of Turner. Some years before, however, Key
had produced what was to become the standard textbook
on American politics for two generations of students.
Politics, Parties and Pressure Groups (Key, 1964) was
first published in 1942 and went through five
editions and thirty-one printings up to 1969. It is
this book which located sectionalism in a broader
study of American politics.
    Key was only interested in elections in so far as
they were a means of distributing power within
society. Hence, emphasis moves away from the individual voting decision of the behavioral school and

towards the mobilization of these individuals by
interest groups and, in particular, by political
parties:

"Political parties constitute a basic element of
democratic institutional apparatus. They perform
an essential function in the management of
succession to power, as well as in the process of
obtaining popular consent to the course of public
policy" (Key, 1964, p. 9).

This pluralistic-group orientation extends to the
treatment of sectionalism. After pressure groups
such as agriculture, business and labour have been
considered, Key turns to the party system and devotes
a chapter to sectionalism and urbanization (Key,
1964, Chapter 9). Key interprets sectionalism in
economic-group interest terms:

"Sectionalism tends to mask territorially separated
interests. Sectional and regional loyalties--to
the South, to the West, to New England--are not
without strength....While such differences furnish
some basis for regional rivalries, the concentration of cotton growing in the South and of
manufacturing in the Northeast more persuasively
explains decades of sectional political competition
than does the fact that some people call themselves
southerners and others regard themselves as
northerners" (Key, 1964, p. 233).

Such economic differences across regions has, in
Key's interpretation, "constituted important building
blocks for the American parties" (Key, 1964, p. 229)
since the "sectional clusters of interest, founded on
economics, hardened by Civil War and reinforced by
subsequent events, formed the hard cores of the major
parties." Key goes on to discuss American presidential elections as reflecting North-South competition
for support of the West in securing the national
government and uses maps of electoral votes for the
contests in 1896 and 1920 as his evidence
(Key, 1964, pp. 235 and 237).

Key concludes by viewing sectionalism as being a rural and small town phenomena which will be eroded by increasing urbanization especially of the South (Key, 1964, p. 245). Nevertheless, enough of the flavour of Key's work has been given to illustrate a continuity of ideas from Turner although set within a much more sophisticated model of politics located alongside interest groups and as part of a theory of the role of political parties. This pluralistic approach was clearly at variance with the dominant behavioralist school of voting studies.

One strange position that the studies of individual voting decisions reached was that democracy in America was based upon a very fragile basis. Converse (1966b, p. 136) describes the problem succinctly:

"Not only is the electorate as a whole quite uninformed, but it is the least informed members within the electorate who seem to hold the critical balance of power, in the sense that alternations in governing party depend disproportionally on shifts in their sentiment."

And yet, paradoxically, the American political system survives and, in fact, operates in a quite predict-able manner for the most part. This paradox can only be resolved by bringing political variables into consideration--parties, constitutions, electoral systems etc.--which marshal these ill-informed wishes of the electorate. Such naivete in the behavioralist thinking has allowed Key (1966, p. 7) to assert:

"The perverse and unorthodox argument that voters are not fools. To be sure many individual voters act in odd ways indeed; yet, in the large the electorate behaves about as rationally and responsibly as we should expect, given the clarity of the alternatives presented to it and the character of the information available to it."

Since political variables such as parties and electoral systems have long and continual histories, then it follows that perhaps the continual success of the American polity in not

collapsing upon its fragile behavioral basis confirms
the importance of parties in relation to those
'uninformed' individuals. This argument is a major
debating point in the criticism of the behavioralist
school by the pluralists. In fact, the former have
explicitly recognised their vulnerability to this
logic by their development of the normal vote concept
as we described it at the end of the last section.
As we shall see, the social surveyors directly drew
upon Key's work in their search for a framework for
their own researches.

The Classification of Elections

V. O. Key is perhaps most well-known to current
researchers through his seminal paper on "A Theory of
Critical Elections" (1955). Critical elections were
identified as those for which "the decisive results
of the voting reveal a sharp alteration of the
preexisting cleavages within the electorate" (1955,
p. 5). The basic notion was one of rather rapid
change in voting patterns as new coalitions and
alliances formed in response to some new and
important issue. In particular, critical elections
relate to the crisis surrounding the slavery issue of
the 1850's and the economic depressions of the 1890's
and 1930's. In some ways Key neatly codified
previous loose formulations concerning 'generation
cycles' in American politics. Key's original
'theory' has been contested and refined in two
directions. First, there have been further empirical
studies to test and evaluate the original ideas.
Second, the concept itself has been developed into
a broader notion of realignment periods, as there is
general agreement that fundamental voting changes
take more than a single election to complete. Nevertheless, Key's general approach to viewing American
elections through a series of relatively abrupt party
transformations now dominates most writing in this
field (e.g. Chambers and Burnham, 1967; Burnham,
1970, 1974; Sundquist, 1973).

The importance of Key's concept of the critical
election is attested to by its use in the work of the
social surveyors. In fact, this provides a basic
link between the two traditions of research. In The
American Voter the penultimate chapter includes "A

Classification of Presidential Elections" which is
presented as "an extension of V. O. Key's theory of
critical elections" (Campbell, et.al., 1964, p. 274).
However, it is with the development of the concept of
the normal vote that interrelationships between
behavioral and ecological studies are fully
developed. Converse's (1966) normal vote is interpreted as the benchmark of support by a group for a
party between critical elections. The passing of a
critical election will permanently change allegiances
and so fundamentally alter the prior level of the
normal vote. Hence, after each critical realignment
a new normal vote will need to be calibrated.

This explicit link with the normal vote is made by
Campbell (1966). He extends Key's theory by devising
a scheme for categorising all elections into three
types--maintaining, deviating and realigning.
Maintaining elections are those in which the normal
vote or long term forces dominate. Deviating
elections, on the other hand, are those where short-
term forces are important and, hence, upset the
dominant coalition reflected in the normal vote.
Realigning elections are what Key defined as
'critical.' They differ from deviating elections
because the deviations from the old normal vote are
not temporary, but lead to a new normal vote to
replace the old. This typology has been further
extended by Pomper (1967) who distinguishes between
critical elections which produce new coalitions
reinforcing the old majority party and those which
lead to a new majority party. The former become
converting elections with the term realigning
elections reserved for the situation where the
majority party changes (Pomper, 1967, p. 538).
However, we will be less concerned with the partic
ular allocation of elections to types than with the
broad periodization of American elections which
results.

Despite much minor debate surrounding the critical
election idea, there has developed an approximate
consensus on the way in which American presidential
elections may be divided into different 'party
systems.' We will follow the outline used for the
essays in The American Party System (Chambers and

Burnham, 1967) and developed by Sundquist (1973).
Party systems are separated from one another by
realigning or converting elections. Five party
systems are usually identified:
   1.   The first party system of Federalists versus
   Jeffersonian Republicans was from the 1790's to the
   gradual elimination of the Federalists by the
   1820's.
   2.   The second party system of Democrats versus
   Whigs was from Andrew Jackson's election in 1828 to
   the disappearance of the Whigs in the 1850's.
   3.   The third party system of Democrats versus
   Republicans, sometimes known as the Industrial
   party system, was from the Civil War to the 1890's.
   4.   The fourth party system of Democrats versus
   Republicans of the progressive and city boss era
   was from the 1890's to the Great Depression.
   5.   The fifth party system of Democrats versus
   Republicans started as the New Deal political
   system developed by Roosevelt and arguably
   continued into the 1970's.
In each of the final three party systems, party
labels remained unchanged while the mix of coalitions
and alliances shifted to produce a new system. The
fifth party system has always caused the most
problems in this sequence, since claims that the New
Deal coalition has ended have now lasted a generation. In fact, it is a testimony to the influence
of Key's ideas on contemporary political research
that every new election is now scrutinized for signs
of realignment (Sundquist, 1973, pp. 1-3). Burnham
(1974, p. 720) thought that 1964 and 1968 might be
realigning elections and felt certain that "the 1972
election bore the marks of a critical turning point
in American history." Of course, many commentators
are equally certain that the 1980 election is a
critical turning point. In the original theory, it
was not expected that critical elections would form
the majority of elections. Clearly the whole notion
requires some rethinking, especially in its crude
application to contemporary events. In the final
part of this chapter we outline an alternative
periodization of American politics which encompasses
the current volatility of the electorate without

making critical elections ubiquitous. The general
sequence of five party systems will also be set
within a broader framework which we use for our own
quantitative analysis of presidential election
results.

TOWARDS A NEW ELECTORAL GEOGRAPHY
The discussion of two previous sections delineates
our major sources for concepts and ideas. The lack
of any electoral geography tradition to draw upon in
this area is only a trivial embarrassment to us, and,
hence, has been relegated to comment in the preface.
Nevertheless, it does behoove us to set out in a
clear and precise manner the framework in which this
exercise in the goegraphy of elections is carried
out. How are concepts such as 'normal vote' and
'critical election' to be handled in this
geographical study? This section answers just such
questions, but before we come to these issues of
calibration, we need to take a broader view of the
overall purpose of our research. The contrasts
between the political sociologists and political
scientists described above can be traced back to
differences in basic assumptions relating to the
purposes of their respective studies. In some ways
our basic purpose has less in common with these two
groups of researchers than with the earlier studies
of elections in political history. Let us consider
this seemingly unlikely admission!

Purpose: Electoral Geography and the State
The conflict between individual- and group-oriented
research reflects very general differences in
assumptions to be found in most areas of social
studies The behavioralist approach concentrates on
the individual and attempts to build 'upwards' to
produce social theory. From our comments in the
previous discussion, it will be clear that we reject
this approach for our electoral studies. Quite
simply, we do not interpret the act of voting as an
end in itself. Elections are not just about voting;
they have as their purpose the selection of government. As such we must add political variables as the
context within which the act of voting takes place.
This is the essence of Key's criticism of the social

surveyors, and it has been neatly summarized by
Giovanni Sartori when he equates the neglect of
political variables in voting studies to being "like
explaining an economic system as if there could be
buyers without sellers" (Sartori, 1969, p. 90).
However, we would go one stage further and argue that
the political system itself can only be adequately
understood within a materialist framework. Political
variables do not exist in an economic vacuum, but
derive from and feed back into the broader realm of
society and its economy. This position pervades the
work of Turner, and it is in this sense that we are
more closely following his tradition of research
than more modern studies.

Neither historians nor geographers have a disci-
plinary interest in such academic battles as that
between sociologists and political scientists over
electoral research because a more holistic stance
underlies our approach. Turner was concerned with
the unfolding spatial manifestation of material
interests as shown by elections. We share that
concern. In keeping with more recent developments,
however, we link such ideas to a more explicit treatment of the state. Hence, we do not consider
Turner's suggested anology between American sections
and European states as anything more than a mis-
specified comparison. States are sovereign institutions with the right of coercion over a specified
territory and the people who reside therein. In the
American case, the state was set up in 1789 to
include elections as a vital ingredient in the
legitimation of its right of coercion. The real
lesson of Turner's work is that on such a large
geographical scale as the United States, the
territory being ruled will exhibit different regional
material interests which inevitably leads to
sectional conflict over control of the state. In the
1860's this conflict was fought on the battlefield;
but at all other times the major arena has been
elections, especially presidential contests. In this
sense, sectional voting patterns are not shadowy
images of European nations, but rather reflect
material interests organized as geographical
competition over control of the state.

In a large territory such as that controlled by the
United States even in its earliest days, material
interests are based upon a spatial division of labour
due to regional economic specialization. In the
evolution of this specialization into sectionalism,
two processes operate simultaneously. First, there
are the internal policy issues concerning the nature
of the integration of the national space which relates
to the traditional theme of nation building. Second,
there are the external policy issues concerning the
relations between the state and the rest of the world
which relates to the more recent theme of the world
economy in political geography. We consider both sets
of issues in the following chapters since conflicts
such as those over internal transport improvements
and tariff policies both help to consolidate regional
material interests and to stimulate sectional
political responses.

There is, however, a further reason why competition
for control of the state has been expressed
geographically in American history. The American
state was set up in 1789 under a federal Constitution,
the salient features of which are described in the
next chapter. From the perspective of this study, the
important effect was that electoral politics was
decentralized, even for the presidential contest.
Hence, to control the state through election of the
President, different material interests had to marshal
their support within the individual states of the
federation. In this way, any electoral strategy
was forced to organize geographically, since that was
the way the contest was decided. It is the electoral
alliances and coalitions for control of the American
state as they are geographically represented in the
presidential contests which are the subject matter of
this monograph.

Analysis: Calibrating the Normal Vote

In any analysis, a key choice must be the units of
analysis to be employed, and this choice must derive
directly from the research purpose. In most
ecological analyses, the smallest available areal
units are used to lessen the problem of the
ecological fallacy of incorrectly drawing inferences

about individuals from aggregates.   Such a strategy is
common in electoral studies where precincts are used
at the urban scale and counties are commonly employed
at regional and national scales.   However, this
argument is attractive only when the purpose of the
analysis is to understand individual acts of voting.
In our discussion above, we have explicitly forsaken
that aim and have instead concentrated our attention
upon control of the state.   In this context,
presidential election outcomes are not the direct
result of individual voting decisions, but derive
from aggregate results for the separate states in the
federation.   In this sense, the basic units of
concern are these states or constituencies of the
larger federal state.   Not only does the formal
constitution recognize states as the basic units
through the electoral college system, but the
'informal' constitution of electoral practice also
reflects these units through national political
parties as rather loose coalitions of state-
organized parties.   Both of these topics are dealt
with more fully in the next chapter; here, we need
merely conclude that for our purposes, the units of
analysis will be the states within the union.
    The variable to be measured over these units is the
percentage of the total vote going to the Democratic
candidate for the Presidency.   This choice is based
upon the fact that there is a continuous sequence
of candidates using the Democratic label from Andrew
Jackson in 1828 through to Jimmy Carter in 1980.
This gives us for each state a true series of
Democratic percentages since 1828 or from whenever
it entered the union.   Burnham (1970) in fact used
a form of time-series analysis to smooth out election
trends in studying such data.   The problem with this
approach is that it is in effect searching for only
broad trends over the whole period.   In complete
contrast, Burnham at a later date, adopted the
practice of correlating adjacent pairs of elections
(Burnham, 1974, p. 667; Taylor and Johnston, 1979,
p. 126).   However, we would agree with Pomper (1967,
p. 544) that "Emphasizing single elections, even
critical ones, can be misleading."   He had earlier
proposed two major solutions to the problem, first
that of correlating each election with the mean of

four previous elections, and second that of
inspection of the complete correlation matrix in
which every election is related to every other
election. Our analyses are a development upon
Pomper's second solution. But, we replace his
inspection with a factor analysis of the correlation
matrix which considers all pairs of correlations
simultaneously.

Although the use of factor analysis on Chicago
voting returns constitutes one of the earliest
applications of the technique outside its psychology
origins (Gosnell and Gill, 1935), it is generally
true that "applications of factor analysis (to
election data) have not searched for overtime
patterns," and therefore, "few historians have, as
yet, ventured into the world of factor analysis at
all" (Silbey, Bogue and Flanigan, 1978, p. 26). In
the discussion below, we show how factor analysis can
be applied in just this way to calibrate the concept
of the normal vote.

One obvious reason why many previous researchers
have stopped short of studying all correlations
between all elections has to do with the sheer
magnitude of the task. Such correlation analyses are
usually arranged into a correlation matrix--a square
box arraying elections by elections with the values
in the cells being the correlation coefficients. If
we were studying a series of twenty elections the
matrix would hold four hundred (20 x 20)
correlations. Because we are not interested in self-
correlations (i.e. how the 1932 election correlates
with itself) there are only 380 relevant correlations; also, because correlations are symmetrical
(i.e. the correlation between 1932 and 1936 is the
same as that between 1936 and 1932 the total number
of distinct relevant correlations is 190. This is a
large reduction from the original 400 cells in the
matrix, but it still represents a huge amount of
information on inter-election relations which is
difficult to comprehend and assimilate in any
coherent interpretation and discussion. A major role
of all factor analytic techniques is to distill such
correlation information into a smaller matrix where
the original variables are combined on the basis of

their correlations into patterns or general
'factors.'

In the analyses that follow we employ the common
factor model which shares the parsimonious property
of all factor analytic techniques. It further
involves modelling the data in such a way that the
technique may be interpreted as a new way of
measuring the concept of the normal vote. In fact
Converse's language in deriving his concept is
closely associated with notions underlying factor
analysis. He suggests, for instance, "a means of
splitting the actual vote cast by any part of the
electorate into two components: (1) the normal or
'baseline'...and (2) the current deviation from that
norm" (Converse, 1966, p. 11). In factor analysis
terminology these two 'components' are (1) the common
variance in the data and (2) the unique variance
associated with particular variables. Hence factor
analysis is a way of dividing up variation into its
common and unique parts which is directly analogous
to Converse's normal and deviating components. This
form of model came to be called two-factor analysis
(Rummel, 1970). Applying this logic to a series of
election results such as presidential percentages for
Democratic candidates over a set of areal units, we
would separate out each Democratic percentage into a
general element and a series of unique elements for
each election. Hence, the 1960 vote would reflect a
general Democratic level of vote (i.e. normal vote
component) and a deviation unique to 1960 and Kennedy
(i.e. short-term component).

This argument has transferred Converse's conceptualization to the field of areal data of actual
voting returns while losing none of his basic
meaning. Now we have identified the concept within a
factor analytic framework, and we can develop
reformulated conceptualization using our new more
sophisticated statistical tools. The major advantage
is that we do not have to restrict ourselves to one
single normal vote element as we move from two-
factor analysis to multiple-factor analysis.

Consider the 1852 election. What 'normal vote'
would we expect for a set of groups or areas at that
time? This question is difficult to answer, since
we are close to a realignment situation. Is the

normal vote the typical Democratic voting preceding
the 1852 election or can we see, through the advantages of hindsight, that it really relates to
subsequent patterns of Democratic voting. With
mulitple-factor analysis we do not have to make any
a priori decision on where 1852 fits, since we can
derive two general factors or normal votes to go with
the unique 1852 element. Hence, we may be able to
interpret the 1852 pattern of results as consisting
of two general patterns plus whatever was unique in
1852. The two patterns might represent first the
stability in voting represented by those voters
maintaining old habits and second the pattern of
those voters breaking with the past and looking
forward to a new alignment. It is of course highly
reasonable to expect old styles of voting to continue
many years after a realignment and new habits of
voting to diffuse differentially and hence create a
situation where two 'normal' vote patterns could
coexist simultaneously. In this situation a multiple
factor analysis will be able to separate out these
two general elements alongside the unique element.
Furthermore, over a long period of elections, we know
that there are several realignments leading to
several 'normal votes' and this is easy for the
multiple-factor model to handle as simply more than
two general factors.

The technical details of the factor-analytic
methodology employed in this monograph are described
in the appendix following chapter five. In this
discussion, we provide a nontechnical description
which is intended to make our subsequent results
accessible to a wide range of readers not familiar
with the intricacies of multivariate statistics.

The simplest way of viewing an exercise in factor
analysis is as a sophisticated reorganization of the
variation in the original data. If the data is
viewed as a 'data box' or matrix with variables
(elections) arrayed against cases (states), then a
factor analysis proceeds by the generation of a
series of additional matrices upon which an interpretation is based. The sequence of matrices employed
in the T-mode analysis for the third chapter is shown
in Figure 1.1, and we will describe each matrix and
its generation in turn.

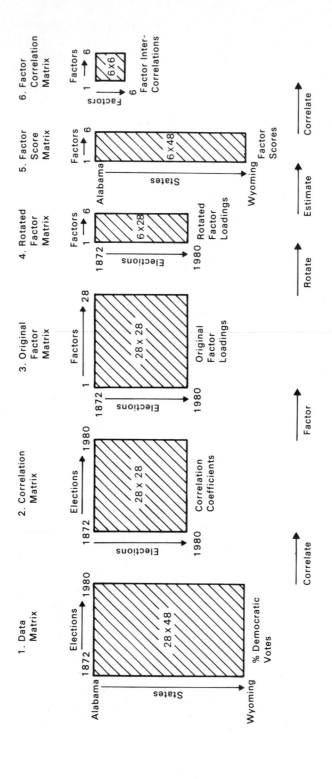

Figure 1.1   The Factor Analysis Procedure

1.   The Data Matrix.   This is the initial input of
the analysis.   In our example, the 48 contiguous
states are arrayed against the 28 elections from 1872
to 1980 inclusive.   The individual pieces of information in the cells of this matrix are the percentage
vote for the Democratic candidate at a particular
election in a specific state.   These 1344 (48 x 28)
pieces of information display the variation which is
to be analysed.   The variation of each original
variable is weighted equally and is standardized to
one unit of variance.

2.   The Correlation Matrix.   This is generated by
correlating each pair of columns in the data matrix.
The result is a 28 x 28 array of correlation
coefficients, each measuring the degree of similarity
between a particular pair of elections.   The diagonal
of 'self-correlations' (from top left hand to bottom
right hand corners) are estimated during the
factoring procedure and are called communalities (see
appendix).

3.   The Original Factor Matrix.   When the
correlation matrix is factor-analysed, the original
variables (elections) are transformed into a new set
of compound variables called factors.   Since every
original variable is standardized to one unit of
variation, it follows that the total variation in the
data is equal to the number of variables; in this
case 28.   The factor analysis reorders this variation
on the basis of common patterns between the
elections.   The most common pattern is represented by
the first factor whose variation will be some level
greater than one (this is given by the eigenvalue:
see appendix).   The second most common pattern of
elections will be represented by the second factor
and so on until 28 factors may have been generated.
The important difference between these factors and
the original variables is that, unlike the latters'
equality of variation, the former will include a few
patterns of common variation encompassing most of the
variation in the data followed by a sequence of
progressively more and more trivial patterns of
variation.   It is at this stage that the decision is
made as to how many factors will be utilized.   In the
analysis for chapter three, six factors were deemed

relevant   to our purposes (the criteria for this
assessment are discussed in the appendix).   The
actual items in the cells of this matrix are
'loadings' or correlations between the factors and
the original variables (elections).   However,
loadings are not usually interpreted until the next
matrix is derived.

   4.   The Rotated Factor Matrix.   The original
factors are transformed to ease interpretation.   The
purpose is to ensure that each factor corresponds to
a group of elections.   Only those factors chosen from
the previous stage are rotated to find clusters of
like-elections.   The cells of this matrix hold the
rotated loadings or correlations relating each
factor to each election.   This is the most important
part of the output and forms the basis of our
interpretations.   Each factor is interpreted by
scanning down its column of loadings to see with
which elections it is correlated.   In our analyses we
use an oblique rotation procedure which means that
the resulting factors are not independent of one
another.   This produces two sets of loadings, called
pattern loadings and structure loadings.   Only the
former are used for our verbal interpretation
although the latter are employed in the procedure for
estimating the factor scores in the next matrix.

   5.   The Estimated Factor Score Matrix.   The
loadings relate the factors to the variables
(elections) whereas the scores relate the factors to
the cases (states).   These estimations can be made
using several alternative methods which are discussed
in the appendix.   In our analyses we simply use an
average of values contained in the data matrix for
those elections most associated with a particular
factor.   If a factor satisfies our requirements for
association with three elections, then a state's
score for that factor is the average vote for the
Democrats in the state for those three elections
(suitably standardized).   This method is justified in
the appendix.   The end result is that for each factor
we have a score for every state.   Hence, the factor
scores can be mapped to show the geographical pattern
represented by a factor.   This will aid in interpretation of the factors as we shall see.

6. The Factor Correlation Matrix. We briefly
mentioned above that we generally employ an oblique
rotation procedure. This produces factors which are
themselves correlated with one another. We have
argued that realignments should not ordinarily
produce total changes from past voting patterns, but
would often incorporate parts of previous alignments.
Hence, we should not search for completely
independent voting patterns as our factors. The
oblique solutions enable us to trace the relationships between the factors we derive. Of course if
independent factors do exist then, they will be
reflected by zero or near zero correlations in this
matrix.

These are the six major elements of our factor
analyses procedures. In the discussion of subsequent
chapters attention will be focused upon the final
three matrices. The results will be illustrated
diagrammatically to show the temporal and spatial
patterns of the factors. For each rotated factor,
the loadings will be graphed over time to display the
'profile' of the pattern being described. If a
factor is measuring a normal vote pattern, we might
expect the loadings to remain high over a consecutive
sequence of at least four elections. Similarly the
scores will be mapped to show the geographical
pattern of a particular factor and, in particular, to
illustrate sectional tendencies. Finally, the
correlations between the factors will be displayed as
'linkage' diagrams using the temporal sequence of the
loadings profiles to suggest an approximate causal
structure.

Before we meet some factor analysis results in the
next chapter, two final points need to be emphasized.
First, the techniques we use treat every observation
equally. Hence, no account is taken of the vast
differences in electorate between, say, California
and Wyoming. We do not weight populous states more
than less populous states, but treat them, as the
Constitution treats them, as indestructible partners
of the federation. Of course California is more
important than Wyoming in terms of Electoral College
votes and, hence, figures in every candidate's
campaign strategy to a greater degree than smaller

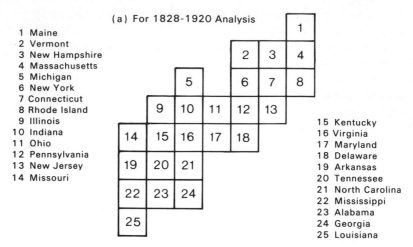

(a) For 1828-1920 Analysis

1 Maine
2 Vermont
3 New Hampshire
4 Massachusetts
5 Michigan
6 New York
7 Connecticut
8 Rhode Island
9 Illinois
10 Indiana
11 Ohio
12 Pennsylvania
13 New Jersey
14 Missouri

15 Kentucky
16 Virginia
17 Maryland
18 Delaware
19 Arkansas
20 Tennessee
21 North Carolina
22 Mississippi
23 Alabama
24 Georgia
25 Louisiana

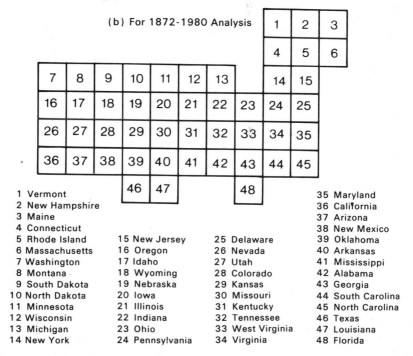

(b) For 1872-1980 Analysis

1 Vermont
2 New Hampshire
3 Maine
4 Connecticut
5 Rhode Island
6 Massachusetts
7 Washington
8 Montana
9 South Dakota
10 North Dakota
11 Minnesota
12 Wisconsin
13 Michigan
14 New York

15 New Jersey
16 Oregon
17 Idaho
18 Wyoming
19 Nebraska
20 Iowa
21 Illinois
22 Indiana
23 Ohio
24 Pennsylvania

25 Delaware
26 Nevada
27 Utah
28 Colorado
29 Kansas
30 Missouri
31 Kentucky
32 Tennessee
33 West Virginia
34 Virginia

35 Maryland
36 California
37 Arizona
38 New Mexico
39 Oklahoma
40 Arkansas
41 Mississippi
42 Alabama
43 Georgia
44 South Carolina
45 North Carolina
46 Texas
47 Louisiana
48 Florida

Figure 1.2   Cartograms

states (see for instance Tatalovich, 1979). Nevertheless, an election for the Presidency of the United
States does consist of separate contests for the
Electoral College votes of each state. It is the
results of these separate contests in terms of
Democratic vote percentages which constitute our data
so that the states are the basic units of analysis as
argued above. Given this position, we have chosen to
map our findings on cartograms where each state is
portrayed as equal in area. In our discussions we
will need to refer to states and their factor scores
and these are best illustrated where the states are
represented by the same areas. In this way the small
(in areal terms) states of New England and the Middle
Atlantic can be depicted on an equal footing with the
larger-area states of the West. Figure 1.2 shows the
cartograms used in chapters two and three for our
25-state and 48-state analyses respectively.
Although these diagrams may take some getting used to
initially, they are consistent with the treatment of
the states in the analysis and, hence, portray the
factor patterns more accurately.

The second point about our analysis is that since
it is based upon a correlation matrix, the Democratic
voting percentages for each year are considered for
each state in terms of deviations from the overall
average for that year. This means that comparisons
between years using correlations do not take into
account changes in the overall levels of voting
between the two elections. If, from one election to
another, the Democrats lost <u>exactly</u> 10% of their
support in <u>every</u> state, then the correlation between
the two elections would be perfect at +1.0. Although
in terms of electoral outcome the second election
might be a disaster, the <u>pattern</u> of support remains
the same and this is what the correlation coefficient
measures. Our analyses relate, not to changes in the
level of support, therefore, but to changes in the
pattern of support. We are thus dealing with the
winning alliances of states, both actual and
potential, which the Democrats have put together over
the years.

This point is best illustrated by reference to the
debate in the literature over whether 1928 or 1932

constituted the critical election which ushered in
the fifth party system (see, for instance, Lichtman,
1976). In 1928 the pattern of party support shifted,
but the Democrats still lost easily. In 1932 the
1928 pattern was maintained, but the level of support
for the Democrats was raised to give them a victory.
In this case we would argue that in 1932 the
Democrats reaped the rewards of a potential winning
coalition first developed in 1928. Hence, 1928 led
the way with a new pattern of support and so in our
analysis becomes the more interesting election. To
summarise, our analyses deal with patterns of support
reflecting different state or sectional alliances and
not the levels of support themselves. The latter is
discussed in the text as part of the commentary on
the factor analysis results.

Interpretation: Section and Party
For all of its matrix manipulations and multivariate
statistical heritage, factor analysis is in reality
only a relatively sophisticated measurement tool. It
calibrates new measures by compounding common
variance patterns from among a set of original
measures. In this study, we are searching for
patterns of normal voting by compounding common
elements of sets of election results. Like any other
measurement tool, factor analysis cannot be an end in
itself. It must have a role to play within a wider
theoretical framework which incorporates the concepts
being measured. We have already traced the major
outlines of our framework in the discussion of
electoral geography and the state above. In this
final part of chapter one, we specify the context of
our research more precisely.
    The calibration of normal vote patterns will depend
upon the major finding of all geography of voting
studies; namely, the long-term continuity of
geographical patterns of support. As Turner (1932,
p. 301) remarks, concerning his election maps of the
United States, for instance: "For the most part,
there is a tendency for similar regions to reappear
through long periods." Similarly Key makes the same
point regarding voting patterns over a century in the
states of Indiana (Key and Munger, 1959, p. 283) and
Tennessee (Key, 1964, pp. 240-243). Such continuity

across several generations of voters living in these
areas clearly indicates the salience of long-term
forces in American elections. These are what we hope
to measure in our factor analyses of party vote
percentages. In this manner, the calibration of the
normal vote links together the two key elements of
this study: section and party.

The two terms section and party both indicate a
division of the country: sections describe
geographical divisions of the state's territory and
parties mobilise electoral divisions in the state's
polity. The interactions of these two classes of
divisions are basic to an understanding of the
American state, and it is the purpose of this
monograph to open up for discussion once again this
theme which has been sorely neglected by recent
researchers.

The modern literature on American presidential
elections has differentiated these elections into
five party systems as we have seen. From our more
materialist perspective, we argue that the evidence
employed in that literature is too narrow, rarely
extending beyond election results and brief mention
of contributory social and economic forces. Given
our 'section and party' viewpoint, a rather different
periodization may be derived. In terms of the
interaction between section and party, three major
eras of presidential politics emerge. From the
adoption of the Constitution to the Civil War, we
have a politics of sectional compromise. This
includes both the first party system which eradicated
parties and the second party system which created
nonsectional parties. From the Civil War through to
Roosevelt's four terms we identify the politics of
sectional dominance where sectional patterns of
support are highly predictable and the North becomes
consolidated as the economic and political core of
the nation. This includes the third, fourth and
beginning of the fifth party systems. Since
Roosevelt, party patterns of support have been much
less predictable. This has been most spectacular in
terms of the disappearance of the Democratic 'solid'
South. Third parties were successful in this section
in 1948 and 1968 while Republicans were successful in

1964, 1972 and 1980.   This is the era of the 'decline
of party' when every election seems to be a critical
one--we shall term it the politics of sectional
volatility.   Northern dominance has receded, in 1980
the contest was between a Southerner and a Westerner,
but sectional patterns of voting remain.   It is
perhaps ironic that it is probably the Western states
that are now the most predictable, whereas in
previous eras they were the most unstable element.

This three-fold periodization of American politics
will be further described, justified and illustrated
in the remainder of the text.   In general terms,
these different types of politics relate to the
different uses made of sections and of sectional
conflicts by the parties.   In this interpretation we
closely follow the argument of Schattsneider (1959,
p. 68) that:

"He who determines what politics is about runs the
country, because definition of alternatives is the
choice of conflicts, and the choice of conflicts
allocates power."

From this, Schattsneider is able to conclude that
"The crucial problem in politics is the management of
conflict" (p. 71).   In the politics of sectional
compromise, it was sectional conflict itself that the
parties managed to avoid, whereas in the politics of
sectional dominance, this same conflict was mobilised
and exploited by the parties.

Parties have a vital role in this management of
conflict because they are the institutions which do
the managing.   Hence, we interpret parties, not in
ideal-liberal terms as 'pure' democratic institutions
that respond to popular demand, but as manipulators
of the electorate.   Parties are very powerful
institutions in terms of their control of election
options.   Returning to Sartori's (1969, p. 90)
analogy with the economic market of buyers and
sellers, he continues by asserting that "In practice,
moreover, the political entrepreneur exerts a greater
persuasive influence on the voter than does the
economic entrepreneur on the buyer."   This is because

"One can, however, vote only for and against a
particular party's candidates, one cannot vote for
or against a party system" (Jahnige, 1971, p. 473).

This in-built stability gives established political
parties overwhelming advantages in national politics
and accounts for there having been but one successful
'third' party (the Republicans of the 1850's) in two
hundred years of presidential elections.

The formal organization of political power in the
United States has long followed a pattern of duopolistic competition (Downs, 1957). This has
simplified the management task of manipulating
conflicts in order to achieve control of the state
through winning the highest executive office. For as
Schattschneider (1959, p. 59) observed:

"The parties organize the electorate by reducing
their alternatives to the extreme limit of
simplification. This is the great act of organization. Since there are only two parties and both
of them are very old, the veterans of a century of
conflict, it is not difficult for people to find
their places in the system."

This 'great act of organization' is reflected in the
party vote percentages and the state alliances which
produce the sectional patterns we describe below.
The normal vote itself is thus in a sense a
calibration of the people whose minds are made up for
them by the parties. As we measure and map the
normal vote patterns below, we must remember that
they paradoxically represent both great democratic
exercises in collective choice and the management of
the electorate by a self-sustaining political
duopoly.

CHAPTER 2

The Rise of Sectional
Politics in the East

The first popular election of an American President
occurred in 1828 with Andrew Jackson's defeat of the
incumbent John Quincy Adams. Jackson's candidature
can be interpreted as the first of the Democratic
Party which has a continuous history of fighting
presidential campaigns since 1828. James Earl Carter
was the Democratic Party's thirty-ninth candidate in
1980. It is this continuous sequence of party
electoral data which underlies our analyses in this
and subsequent chapters so that the starting point of
our quantitative contributions is perforce 1828. A
major purpose of the present chapter, however, is to
provide a back-cloth upon which to view presidential
elections and this inevitably means that we will
delve into matters prior to 1828. In fact, the
chapter is divided into four parts and only the final
part presents quantitative analyses from 1828 onward.
   The first part of the chapter concerns the nature
of the federal Constitution and its operation in its
early years. This is necessary first because it
provides the legal framework within which all
presidential elections through 1980 have been
conducted, and second because it provides insights
into the political culture in which the Founding
Fathers set up the first federal state. We will not
be concerned with all details of the debate
surrounding the adoption of the Constitution, but we
will draw attention to the salient elements of that
debate as it relates to our two themes of section

and party. This then leads on to the two subsequent
parts of the chapter which deal with the early
evolution of political parties and the development of
sectional economic conflicts within the new federal
state.

In his Farewell Address to the nation in 1796,
George Washington warned his compatriots that the
'will of party'can replace the 'will of the Nation'
and linked this danger to problems of economic
sectionalism within the new state (Hofstadter, 1969,
97). The second generation of American leaders
following Andrew Jackson but centred upon Martin Van
Buren created a partisan party system. The third
generation precipitated a sectional Civil War while
keeping to the notion of a party system. It is this
triumph, first of party and then of section against
Washington's advice, which we are able to analyse in
the fourth part of this chapter as we consider the
electoral response to party, section and presidential
candidates in the period starting in 1828.

THE PRESIDENCY IN 'A CONSTITUTION AGAINST PARTIES'
Given strong modern attestations of the importance of
parties to democratic government, it is a surprise
that the U. S. Constitution makes no mention of their
existence. Within the context of the political
culture of the time, however, the absence of parties
from the provisions of the Constitution is entirely
understandable. In fact the Founding Fathers used
the terms 'party' and 'faction' interchangeably;
as Hofstadter (1969, p. 9) points out: "If we
inquire into the place of parties in Anglo-American
thought during the eighteenth century, the root idea
we find is that parties are evil." This perception
was grounded in knowledge of the corrupt British
Parliament of the period. Hence, it is hardly
surprising that far from accepting parties, one of
the basic objectives of the Founders was to prevent
the development of disruptive factions. The
resulting framework has been termed, by Hofstadter
(1969, Chpater 2), "A Constitution Against Parties."

Despite this prevailing view among the delegates to
the Philadelphia Convention in 1787, several writers
have subsequently traced the origins of the American
party system to the Constitution (e.g. Key, 1964;

Chambers, 1967; Pennock, 1979). As Elazar (1972)
argues, the Constitution created the need for "a new
politics" to make it operational, and part of the new
politics was political parties. McCormick (1967),
for example, after pointing out that there were no
national political parties to emerge under the
Articles of Confederation, goes on to assert that

> "the critical new factor was the creation of a
> national political arena as the result of the
> adoption of the federal Constitution. Politics
> assumed an entirely new dimension--a national
> dimension....In particular, the constitutional
> arrangements for electing a President encouraged
> cooperation among political leaders throughout the
> nation in behalf of particular candidates....I
> would contend that it was the contest for the
> Presidency that was to exert the determining
> influence on the structure of the American party
> system."(McCormick, 1967, p. 94)

Let us, therefore, examine arrangements made for
Presidential selection as a prelude to our discussion
of party evolution.

Presidential Selection

Distrust of parties is deeply embedded in the fabric
of the federal Constitution, particularly in its
provisions for the election of the President.
Among those present at the Philadelphia Convention of
1787 were many delegates with objections to a
centralized national government with a strong chief
executive. In this they doubtless represented the
views of constituents to whom "nothing seemed more
reasonable than the belief that 'centralization was
to be dreaded and that the rights of states were to be
cherished and preserved'" (Beard and Beard, 1944).
A reason for this was that among the causes precip-
itating the War of Independence had been the
restrictions which the British Crown and Parliament
had placed on Colonial legislatures. To many,
distant government was despotic government. Even
Jefferson declared that his basic loyalty was to his
home state of Virginia, not to the nation. Some
participants, however, saw the lack of a strong chief

executive along with other limitations on central authority such as dependence upon the voluntary contributions of states for revenue, a classic "free rider" problem, as a chief and debilitating weakness under the Articles of Confederation. These differences of view generated substantial debate before the Convention decided to break sharply with the earlier pattern and to forge a symbol of national unity in one President rather than acknowledge diversity via a multiple executive representing states or perhaps sections. Supporting this decision was the thought that a single national constituency would include such a wide diversity of interests that broad domestic divisions would not make it possible to form cohesive factions. It was also felt that a selection premium would be placed upon candidates such as Washington with a reputation of distinguished service to the Nation (Ceaser, 1979, pp. 41-87). The President was envisaged as a statesman, not as a politician.

The Founders were well aware that the mechanism specified for choosing the President would become as important as the powers explicitly granted to the office. The central problem **was,** in Eidelberg's (1968, p. 169) words, "to guard the Republic against the extremes of oligarchy and democracy. But here the question arises: what was to prevent the Presidency from succumbing to one or the other of these extremes? The answer to this question lies hidden in what I regard as the most brilliantly conceived aspect of the Constitution, namely the presidential electoral system."

Several alternative mechanisms were considered before one was finally adopted. On at least three occasions a majority of state delegations to the Philadelphia Convention voted to have Congress choose the chief executive. Fears were raised, however, that the executive would not be sufficiently independent of that body and so intrigue, corruption and an exchange of favors between the executive and legislative branches would be promoted. Delegates who wanted a strong national leader, in particular, advanced these fears. Other proposals that the President be chosen by state legislatures, state

legislatures, state governors, or both were also
examined. These in turn were rejected because the
President would be overly indebted to localized
interests, and there was the possibility that each
state might support only its own favorite son
candidate, precluding strong support for a national
statesman.

While sometimes depicted as one of the more
conservative delegates, Morris of Pennsylvania argued
that the President "should be the guardian of the
people, even of the lower classes against Legislative
tyranny, against the Great and Wealthy who, in the
course of things,will necessarily compose the
Legislative body;" accordingly, he proposed that the
President should be directly elected "by the free-
holders of the country" (Eidelberg, 1968, pp. 173,
175). This is a suggestion which even today seems
attractive to those who prefer direct democracy
(e.g. Sayre and Parris, 1976; Blair, 1979). At the
time, direct popular election of the President
perhaps was viewed as too radical, despite Morris'
argument that contests in a single national constituency would produce moderate candidates because of
the diversity of localized interests embraced. His
proposal was rejected with only his home state of
Pennsylvania in favour. Rivalry between large and
small states was also at issue, since one of the
stated objections was that direct election would
give too great a weight to larger, more urban states.
Some also held that popular electors would be too
ill informed to be given the responsibility of
choosing the President; rather, as Hamilton argued
in The Federalist (1937, p. 441):

  "A small number of persons, selected by their
  fellow citizens from the general mass, will be the
  most likely to possess the information and
  discernment requisite to such complicated
  investigations."

A range of concerns thus entered the deliberations:
the political independence of the Presidency from
Congress and the governments of the states; regional
rivalries; the relative interests of large and small

states; and the role to be given popular opinion.
faced with an impasse, the Convention nominated a
"Committee of Eleven" with one member from each state
delegation to seek a compromise position. What was
written into the Constitution, excepting one change,
was this committee's proposed framework. The change
was a shift of the power for resolving an electoral
tie from the Senate to the House.

   According to the Electoral College system embodied
in Article II, Section 1 of the Constitution, each
state receives electors equal in number to its
representation in the House and Senate combined.
Article I apportions these on the basis of population
and the states as units, respectively. This was a
compromise between the interests of large and small
states. To minimize collusion in the selection
process, "no Senator or Representative, or Person
holding an Office of Trust or Profit under the United
States shall be appointed an elector." Furthermore,
electors are not to meet collectively in a single
location, but rather in each of the states and in
secrecy, thus further diminishing chances of cabal
and corruption in the selection process. Results
of each state's Electoral College voting are
transmitted to the United States Senate to be counted
in front of the House and Senate in Joint session.

   Since 1787 there has been one formal amendment to
the Electoral College framework. This was adopted
because of the tie between Jefferson and Burr during
the 1800 election. As originally stipulated, each
elector would cast two votes, including at least one
for a resident of a state other than the elector's
own to avoid a nonmajority due to multiple favorite
son candidates. In 1800, as in 1796, Federalist and
Antifederalist Congressional caucuses each chose
candidates for the Presidency and Vice Presidency.
In 1796, second vote defections from the Federalist
Adams-Pinckney ticket avoided a tie and gave the
Vice Presidency to Jefferson (Stanwood, 1928, p. 51).
But in 1800, all seventy-three Republican electors
cast one vote for Jefferson, who they assumed to be
the presidential candidate, and one vote for Burr as
their vice presidential candidate. Under the
original provisions of the Constitution, this was
interpreted as a tie in the contest for President

which threw the outcome into the House of Represen-
atives. A deadlock was precipitated by lame duck
Federalists who preferred Burr, as more moderate,
over Jefferson. Tensions were high. Republican
governors of Virginia and Pennsylvania were reported
ready to call out their state militia. Thirty-six
ballots were taken before all except four Federalist
delegations abstained to yield an outcome of ten
states for Jefferson, four New England states for
Burr, and two states with blank ballots. To prevent
the reoccurrence of such a situation, the Twelfth
Amendment, which stipulates that one of each
elector's ballots is for President and the other for
Vice President, was ratified in 1804. This is the
closest that the document has ever come to directly
acknowledging political parties. Later amendments
have influenced the scope of the popular franchise in
federal elections (including the 14th ratified in
1868, the 19th in 1920, and 24th in 1964), but the
basic framework of the Electoral College system has
not been substantially altered since this early
modification in 1804 (Congressional Quarterly, 1975,
p. 202).

  A framework less conducive to the emergence of
national parties than that established by the
Constitution can scarcely be imagined. A small
number of electors casting ballots in scattered
locations and in secrecy would seem to offer tight
protection against the emergence of national parties
as structured organizations with strongly committed
long-term popular followings. This was, of course,
exactly as was intended. Hamilton in The Federalist
No. 68 (1937, p. 442) justifies the Electoral College
on just these grounds:

  "as the electors chosen in each state, are to
  assemble and vote in the state in which they are
  chosen, this detached and divided situation
  will expose them much less to heats and ferments,
  which might be communicated from them to the
  people, than if they were all to be convened at one
  time, in one place."

Similarly Madison in <u>The Federalist</u> No. 10 (1937,
p. 58) had earlier argued that if a faction is a
majority, it "must be rendered; by their number and
local situation, unable to concert and carry into
effect schemes of oppression." This could only be
achieved, it was argued, by relying upon the
increasing size and heterogeneity of the new federal
state as harnessed in the Electoral College: "The
influence of factious leaders may kindle a flame
within their particular States, but will be unable to
speed a general conflagration through the other
states" (<u>The Federalist,</u> 1937, p. 61).

Clearly the architects of the provisions for
electing the President thought that they were
protecting the Republic from factions and parties
rather than, as subsequently occurred, providing a
national arena in which they would grow. In hindsight
we can see that sectional interests were reflected
from the very beginnings of presidential politics
through the practice of a 'balanced' Presidential/
Vice Presidential ticket of a Virginian (Washington)
and a New Englander (Adams) (Goodman, 1967, p. 68).
Instead of heterogeneity and size preventing parties,
it led to a necessity for their organization, since
"The larger and more diverse an electoral unit was in
population and social structure, and the greater the
number of social groups it contained, the harder it
was for a few to control things through informal
arrangements" (Goodman, 1967 p. 7). Hence, organizational needs soon resulted in the emergence of
political parties, first in Congress and around
Hamilton and Jefferson in Washington's cabinet and
then in presidential politics although the effect at
the grass roots level was retarded by obvious
preference for the former Revolutionary War hero
until the beginning of the nineteenth century.
Organized party politics emerged because after George
Washington the country had run out of generally
acceptable statesmen for nomination to the office of
President. This forced a retreat from the original
principles to the practical operation of the
Constitution centring upon conflicting partisan
leaderships. Ironically, Hamilton and Madison, the
two <u>Federalist</u> writers quoted above, lined up on

opposing sides as Federalist and Republican
respectively in what has come to be known as America's
first party system (Goodman, 1967). Hence, even at
the outset, there were forces which made the emergence
of parties at the very least a plausible eventuality.
Before examining the parties that emerged, however,
it is relevant to our argument to return to the debate
over the Constitution as reflected in the process of
ratification.

The Geography of Ratification

After the Constitutional Convention in Philadelphia
of 1787 delegates returned to their home states with
the task of ratifying what had been agreed. Study
of this process from a geographical perspective is
facilitated by having as our prime source the seminal
work of Turner's first Ph.D. student at the
University of Wisconsin, Orin Grant Libby (1894).
His work can be ranked alongside that of the French
geographer Andre Siegfried as a classic example of
research in electoral geography (Taylor and Johnston,
1979, Chapter 1). Within the field of political
history this "widely acclaimed and still used
investigation" (Silbey, Bogue and Flanigan, 1978,
p. 9) represents a pinnacle in the Turnerian
tradition. Perhaps more to the point, Libby was an
important source for Charles Beard's (1913) economic
interpretation of the Constitution which has become
highly controversial with critics using its short-
comings to attack materialist approaches to his
subject matter (Lynd, 1970, 47). Since many of our
arguments below will be materialist in nature, it is
important to clarify our position at this early
stage. In this subsection we return to the original
findings of Libby to refute Beard and to relate these
ideas to both the evolution of parties and to the
development of economic sectional interests.

Libby's achievement in producing his "Map
Illustrating the Geographical Distribution of the
Vote of the Thirteen States upon the Adoption of the
Constitution of the United States 1787-1788" is as
remarkable as the details on the document are
impressive. Production of the map involved scruti-
nising records of the debates in each of the thirteen
state conventions called to ratify the Constitution.

With state documents and other contemporary records
such as newspaper accounts and the correspondence of
participants, he undertook the massive task of
determining the identity of each delegate to the
state conventions, the town, county or perish
represented, and the direction of the vote cast.
Hardly simplifying this task, no composite and
authoritative source on the geographical delimit-
ations of smaller political units existed so that he
was forced "to make use of as early a map as was
available for each state, and then by study and by
comparison of maps, town and county histories,
statutes relating to boundaries, etc., to reconstruct
the conditions of 1787 or 1788 (Libby, 1894, p. 95).
In three instances, and possibly a fourth, Libby
found that a delegate had voted against the sentiments of his constituents. In other cases, towns
or counties were not represented at a state
convention, but it was possible to ascertain local
feelings from other records. By and large, however,
most areas were represented and "as a rule,
delegates acted on the Constitution with the
prejudices and interests of their constituents
keenly before their minds" (Libby, 1894, p. 5; see
also Chapter 4 "Instructions to Delegates,"
pp. 70-90). From his discussion of the events in
individual states, it is clear that delegates were
generally pledged to a position as a result of
constituency balloting on the question of adoption
itself or on the question of delegate selection, and
often on both.

A controversy remains, however, over how extensive
were the franchise and popular participation in the
ratification process. Libby is rather unspecific on
this, since his attention was concentrated on the
state ratification conventions. Beard, who
acknowledges a considerable debt to Libby's earlier
work, emphasizes the fact that the Constitution was
not ratified by a direct popular vote but rather by
indirect representation through state conventions
and that property qualifications reduced popular
participation in the delegate selection process in
degrees varying from state to state (Beard, 1914,
Chapter 9). Even in New York, where the principle

of universal manhood suffrage was applied, Beard
suggested that popular turnout was relatively low;
overall, he estimated that "not more than one-fourth
of the adult white males took part in the election of
delegates to the state conventions" (Beard, 1914,
p. 250). Several recent writers have questioned
Beard's evidence, however, (Brown, 1960, Dahl, 1966).
Political scientist Robert Dahl, for example, alleges
that the "view which held that property qualifications
greatly limited the suffrage in most states until a
decade or two after 1800 apparently has to be revised
in the light of more recent evidence" (Dahl, 1966,
p. 43).

Although the expression of popular sentiment on the
Constitution at the time of ratification was
indirect, it is highly plausible to regard the votes
cast for delegates and the balloting of these
delegates at the state conventions as constituting
the first critical election in the nation's history.
The map which Libby prepared from his research is,
therefore, of considerable interest for what it
reveals about the ecological pattern of political
cleavage across the infant nation's territory
(Figure 2.1). His original writing describes this
pattern on a state by state basis and can be referred
to for small scale details; for our purposes, it is
sufficient to examine the general patterns shown.

Perhaps the first thing which meets the eye is that
there is considerably finer variation in New England
than elsewhere. This can be explained by the fact
that townships were then as now the principal units
of local government. Areas of Federalist support
extended in an almost unbroken continuity along the
coast from Maine to Connecticut, except in Rhode
Island where opposition was strong enough to fore-
stall ratification until 1790. This prevented the
state from participating in the first presidential
election of 1789. Antifederalist feeling was
concentrated in "the part most remote from commercial
centres, with interests consequently predominantly
agricultural. It included fractious Rhode Island,
the Shays regions of Massachusetts and the centre
of a similar movement in New Hampshire" (Libby,
1894, p. 46).

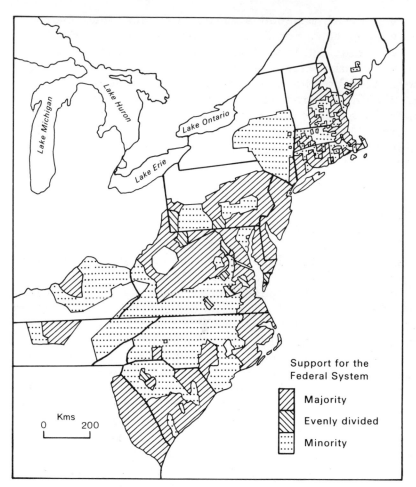

Figure 2.1   The Geography of Ratification

The interior of New York, with the exception of
Albany and Hudson which were both settlements of
substantial magnitude at the time, was solidly
against adoption of the Federal Constitution. This
was in part due to strong opposition by aristocratic,
and often Dutch, large landholders in the Hudson
Valley (Libby, 1894, pp. 25-26. Despite this, the
Constitution was carried in the state by the large
concentration of population in New York City and its
environs and by the manoeuvreings of Hamilton who was
able to achieve the enfrancisement of former
Loyalists for the ratification vote.

"To sum up, the Constitution was carried in the
original thirteen states by the influence of those
classes along the great highways of commerce, the
sea-coast, the Connecticut River, the Shenandoah
Valley and the Ohio River; and in proportion as the
material interests along these arteries of intercourse were advanced and strengthened, the
Constitution was most readily received and most
heavily supported. In other words, the areas of
intercourse and wealth carried the Constitution"
(Libby, 1894, p. 49).

It is Beard's interpretation of Libby's conclusion
that has led to some confusion. Beard's economic
interpretation of American history involved what
Lynd (1970, p. 50) refers to as "an essentially
unchanging conflict throughout American history
between capitalists and farmers." Beard uses Libby's
work to illustrate the operation of this conflict for
the ratification process as a capitalist victory.
Unfortunately careful evaluation of this source does
not support Beard's argument. Beard has particular
trouble in his treatment of Southern support for the
Constitution and more generally "altogether fails to
explain...how the Constitution could have been
ratified by a society in which more than nine out of
every ten adult white males were farmers" (Lynd,
1970, p. 53). This problem is overcome when we
interpret the cleavage underlying ratification not in
terms of landed interests versus manufacturing and
mercantilist factions, but rather as in Main's (1961,
p. 271) words "primarily a contest between the
commercial and noncommercial elements in the
population." Of course, commercial interests did not
stop at the boundaries of the towns, but included
many rural landowners, especially the rich planters
of the South. It is in the less accessible areas,
mainly inland and away from urban centres where
commercialisation had not yet reached, that opposition to ratification was concentrated. This is the
basic lesson we can draw from Libby's painstaking
research of nearly a century ago.
     Hence, we can adhere to a materialist interpre-
tation of the Constitution without supporting Beard's
simplistic version of the conflict. Those areas that

Both New Jersey and Delaware unanimo
the Constitution at their state conven
reasons may be held accountable for thi
small states and the protection of the i
small states inherent in Constitutional p
for state unit representation in the Sena
Electoral College were highly appealing.
factor was their proximity to Philadelphia
United States Constitutional Convention had
and whose newspapers strongly supported ratif.
Perhaps as important was the fact that these s
as well as Connecticut which also was strongly
ratification, were dependent on the ports of New
and Philadelphia for their foreign commerce. New
York and Pennsylvania levied stiff imposts on trad
with neighboring states. That the new Constitution
would eliminate the imposition of tariffs in interstate trade was thus an important incentive to
approval by surrounding states.

Much of the populated territory of Pennsylvania
showed strong support for ratification. There were,
however, areas of resistance, especially inland
where a small farming Presbyterian Scotch-Irish
minority objected to centralized government. Except
for Pittsburgh, a federalist stronghold in an antifederalist hinterland, support for the new form of
government declined toward the west in Pennsylvania
in 1788. Later, the western region of Pennsylvania
was also the centre of the Whiskey Rebellion of 1794
prompted by a federal excise tax on liquor which
imposed an economic hardhsip on small farmers (Abler,
Adams and Gould, 1969, p. 171).

In the South, the level of approval was often high
along the Atlantic Coast. Away from the coast
support tended to diminish, although as earlier found
in New York and Pennsylvania, the larger settlements
of the interior were more Federalist than their
surroundings. Exceptions to this pattern of interio
opposition appeared in Georgia which strongly
favoured adoption in hopes of receiving federal aid
against the Spanish and Indian threat from Florida
and in Kentucky along the Ohio River where the
opening of the Old Northwest to settlement was a
strong inducement. In Libby's words:

were developing as part of the capitalist world-
economy (Wallerstein, 1974) had property owners whose
interests lay in a relatively strong federal state to
protect their wider economic interests.   In the
frontier regions of the West, however, full incorporation into the world-economy had not yet occurred so
that support for extending centralized powers via the
Constitution only appeared in the pockets of
commercialization, such as Pittsburgh, or where there
were external dangers, such as Spanish and Indian
threats in interior Georgia.   It is in the 'true'
frontier where self-sufficiency was a necessity that
we find the major zones of antifederalism in 1787-
1788.

   This materialist interpretation is important for
our treatment of sections in subsequent discussion.
Libby's identification of a noncommercial West is
very different from the western sections that emerge
at a later date and which reflect economic specialization intimately linked into the world-economy.
Hence, Turner's explicit correlation of Libby's antifederalist areas with the areas supporting the
Populists a century later (Lynd, 19 70, p. 49) is
badly in error.   Turner's argument has been
subsequently used by Beard (Lynd, 19 70, p. 49), but
whereas antifederalist areas were still beyond the
reach and, hence, the impact of the world-economy,
the Populist revolt is intimately linked with the
world-economy and its recession in the late nineteenth century.   In our discussion of the three
sections, North, South and West, below, the West we
will be dealing with consists of states incorporated
into the Union and voting in presidential elections--
but a commercialised, and specialized West, not the
frontier, self-sufficient West of the federal
territories before admittance to the Union.   The
first of the western sections we will be concerned
with will be the Ohio Valley, the 'Old Northwest'
before the Civil War, but this region was only to
develop later in the first half of the nineteenth
century and so does not yet figure in our examination
of sectional presidential politics and the emergence
of parties around 1800.   At this early stage, the
sections of our discussion are to be found along the

eastern seaboard as combinations of the original
thirteen states of the Union.

PARTY: THE EVOLUTION OF THE UNWRITTEN AMENDMENT
The evolution of a party system in the United States
established a political institution as important as
any of those set up by the actual provisions of the
Constitution. This importance is attested to by its
common description as the 'unwritten amendment' to
the Constitution (Munro, 1930). This 'amendment' can
be said to have been 'carried' in all states by 1840;
since then presidential elections have been typically
popular two-party affairs. The United States, hence,
evolved what Key (1964, p. 224) refers to as "a
major innovation in the art of government" a generation or more before equivalent institutional
arrangements were developed in Europe. The obvious
question to arise is how did a Republic organized
under an 'anti-party' Constitution come to produce
the political innovation of a party system or, in
other words, how did the 'unwritten ammendment' come
to be generally accepted. Given the attitudes of the
Founders described previously, it is clear that the
evolution of a party system would not be a smooth,
uninterrupted process. In fact we will identify two
stages: first, a party system in which each side
attempted to eliminate the other; second, a party
system in which opposition became accepted as an
enduring part of the polity.

The First Party System and the Elimination of the
Opposition Party
The first party system did not reflect the initial
commercial versus noncommercial cleavage over
ratification of the Constitution illustrated by Libby
(1894). After the commercial interests of both the
North and the South had joined together to win
independence in 1776 and to create a Federal Constitution in 1787, they subsequently divided over the
way in which their new Republic would use its new
found powers. In Lynd's (1970, p. 60) words, they
"drifted, almost immediately, into sectional cold
war." Nevertheless, harbingers of North-South
sectional differences can be traced even to the
ratification conventions. For instance, Libby

(1896, pp. 36-37) noted that during the Virginia
Convention to consider the Constitution one delegate,
George Mason, expressed concern that

"the five southern states (whose produce and
circumstances are totally different from those of
the eight northern and eastern states) will be
ruined for such rigid and premature regulations may
be made as will enable merchants of the northern
and eastern states, not only to demand an exor-
bitant freight, but to monopolize the purchase of
commodities at their own price for many years, to
the great injury of the land interest."

This was prophetic indeed, but the cleavage which
Mason foresaw was not to come to full fruition for
more than half a century; the party systems that
evolved in the meantime had much to do with post-
poning armed sectional conflict.

Voting along sectional lines developed very quickly
in the new Congress that met in 1789 (Lynd, 1970,
pp. 54-55). This reflected the fact that:

"The philosophy of the Antifederalist, North and
South, in 1787 had special charmes for Southerners
in 1790 because the issue of Federal interference
with slavery had already appeared" (Lynd, 1970,
pp. 55-56).

This produced the coalitions which became the first
parties. The most common view of the process whereby
factional differences evolved into party competition
is that these spread outwards from the federal center
of government to the country as a whole. McCormick
(1970, p. 94), for example has written that.

"It would seem that down to 1796, at least, we are
confronted with a fairly clear case of parties
whose origins were of the 'interior' type, or
'internally created' parties to use Maurice
Duverger's typology. That is parties were formed
within the Congress and then were extended to the
electorate."

Chambers (1966, p. 81) illustrates one train of
thought that emerges from identifying 'interior' type
parties:

"The first American parties, or national parties,
emerged out of conflicts only in the 1790's. In
terms of economic groups what distinguished
Federalists from Republicans were cleavages between
mercantile, investing and manufacturing interests
and certain segments of agriculture, on the one
side and most planting and agrarian interests on
the other....Conflict grew out of contentions
between leading personalities, such as the
Federalists Alexander Hamilton and John Adams on
the one hand, and Republicans James Madison and
Thomas Jefferson on the other, contentions that
were sometimes as petty as they were colorful."

This emphasis upon personalities which comes from
arguments over 'interior' type parties tends to
trivialise the conflicts and to play down the
material interests underlying the debates. It
strains belief to think that personal differences
between Jefferson and Hamilton somehow led merchants
to have different interests from farmers or that
these differences were as yet unperceived
beyond Congress. Clearly the cleavages emerging in
Congress in the 1790's were undoubtedly of longstanding existence and these men were simply
spokesmen and organizers, though historically
important ones. There were already sectionally based
material interests so that what was emerging in the
1790's was a party system reflecting, albeit dimly,
the economic sectional differences of the time. This
was confirmed after 1820 with the demise of the
Federalists who declined to become only locally
important in some Northern states, particularly in
New England.
    The crucial election of the first party system was
that of 1800. Both parties nominated geographically-
balanced tickets, Adams of Massachusetts and Pinckney
of South Carolina for the Federalists and Jefferson
of Virginia and Burr of New York for the Republicans.
As mentioned earlier, the drama of the election of
1800 was heightened by the Electoral College tie

between Jefferson and Burr which precipitated passage
of the Twelfth Amendment. The election was also
dramatic in another and most important respect as
well, for it

> "completed the first democratic transfer of power
> in the nation's history, indeed in the history of
> modern politics. By the constitutional process of
> a free election, the opposition party led by
> Jefferson, the Republican, displaced the ruling
> party, the Federalist, which had dominated the
> government from its conception twelve years
> before....The election of 1800 was, therefore,
> critical in the most basic sense: it secured all
> the elections to come" (Peterson, 1973, p. 1).

For a time afterwards the Federalist party held on in
its northern strongholds. But, it did not again
substantially challenge Democratic-Republicans at the
presidential level, as McCormick (1967, p. 95)
points out

> "the parties became excessively unbalanced and took
> on a sectional alignment to the point where one
> sectionally oriented party, feeling that it could
> not compete, would no longer play the game
> according to the recognized rules."

During the War of 1812, for example, mercantile and
Federalist dissatisfaction prompted the nearly
secessionist Hartford Convention of 1814 which
complained that "the commercial states were in mortal
danger of being dominated and ruined by a combination
of southern planters and western farmers" (Beard and
Beard, 1937, p. 427).

The demise of the Federalists as they declined in
popularity and retreated to northern outposts was
entirely consistent with the anti-party philosophy of
the Founding Fathers who created both the Constitution
and this first party system. In fact, it shows the
strength of the forces promoting party development
that these anti-party politicians conducted the
highly contentious presidential election of 1800. As
Goodman (1967, p. 64) puts it:

"Paradoxically, though centralization promoted
national integration, it also led to the polari-
zation of the nation into parties by generating
conflicts which required new institutions for
their management and resolution."

Nevertheless, it should not be expected that these
political leaders would accept the electoral
competition in which they found themselves taking
part. They continued to mistake "parties for
factions, assuming that those with whom they differed
were disloyal to the nation and its ideals" (Goodman,
1967, p. 57). Quite simply "The Federalists and
Republicans did not think of each other as
alternating parties in a two party system"
(Hofstadter, 1969, p. 8). Parties may have been
necessary evils in 1800, but the goal of each was to
eliminate the other by incorporating the moderates
and isolating the extremists of the other party.
The success of the Republicans in 1800 spelt the
death knell of the Federalists culminating in the
'Era of Good Feeling' during which party competition
at a federal level ceased and presidential selection
amounted to a Congressional fief. By 1824 the first
party system was dead. The presidential contest of
that year took place between four sectionally-based
Republican factions. The occasion had become ripe
for the development of a new party system. This time
it incorporated acceptance of the role of an
opposition party as a legitimate alternative
government.

The Second Party System and the Acceptance of the
Opposition Party
McCormick (1967, pp. 96-97) has argued that
competition for the Presidency was the major
stimulous for the evolution of parties in America.
Hence, the subdued contest for the Presidency after
1800 caused the disintegration of the first party
system "because the chief purpose for which it had
been formed had lost its urgency." The revival of
competition for the Presidency in 1824 was the
springboard to the formation of the second party
system.

In 1824 the four sectional candidates each failed
to obtain a majority of Electoral College votes so
that the decision again was passed to the House of
Representatives which chose John Quincy Adams over
his main rival Andrew Jackson. Jackson was to obtain
his revenge four years later when the system for
popularly electing college delegates became used in
all states except South Carolina. In the meantime,
Jackson picked up the support of the New York
politician Martin Van Buren. Although this period is
commonly known as the Jacksonian era, in terms of
party political development, it is Van Buren who
dominates the proceedings from Jackson's sectional
victory of 1828 to Van Buren's own defeat in 1840
which "brought the second American party system at
last to fruition" (McCormick, 1967, p. 102).

Van Buren has an important place in the history of
American parties: "Martin Van Buren may be justly
called the founder of the idea of permanent party
competition in America and of the consensual theory
of the role of parties" (Ceaser, 1979, pp. 27-28).
In comparison with his predecessors, "Van Buren
was a heretic on one vital count: he accepted, he
even welcomed the idea of a permanent opposition.
And this in turn marked the longest single stride
towards the idea of a party system" (Hofstadter,
1969, p. 226). Whereas President Adams was still
thinking of eliminating opposing parties and seeking
harmony, Van Buren was hoping to replace the sectional
factions which fought the 1824 election with just two
great parties transcending sectional interests
(Hofstadter, 1969, p. 227). Hence, instead of
confusing parties with factions, Van Buren saw
parties as a way of overcoming factions. He sought
party loyalty as an alternative to sectional loyalty.

Van Buren's theory of party competition was
essentially one of organized control of popular
democracy: "Van Buren proposed the establishment of
permanent competition between two parties that were
safe and moderate in their principles and that
together would normally control the path of access to
the Presidency." (Ceaser, 1979, p. 30). The
importance Van Buren attached to overcoming sectional
rivalry can be seen from a letter he wrote in 1827 in

opposition to President Adam's views concerning
political 'harmony.'

> "If (party feelings) are suppressed, geographical
> divisions founded on local interests or, what is
> worse, prejudices between free and slaveholding
> states will inevitably take their place. Party
> attachment in former times furnished a complete
> antidote for sectional prejudices by producing
> counteracting feelings" (Ceaser, 1979, p. 138).

In fact Jackson's victory the following year was very
much a sectional affair as Adams, the former
Federalist, only succeeded in winning the New England
states. In 1832 this sectional bias persisted
although Jackson improved his support in New England.
In 1836 Van Buren, Jackson's Vice President from
1832 onward, faced a challenge from three sectional
candidates put forward by opposition groups. This
enabled the new Democratic Party to campaign on an
emplicitly partisan platform expounding Van Buren's
views on party competition. The officially appointed
campaign committee of the 1836 Democratic Convention
put out a lengthy document on the subject which
included the following statement:

> 'Hence, it is that in different parts of the country
> we see mischievous and misguided men attempting to
> weaken the bond of the union....(Sectionalism) is
> ever a ready and fruitful subject to create these
> jealousies and dissensions....It cannot be
> concealed from you that many of our opponents, both
> in the North and the South, under different names
> and denominations, are playing into each State's
> hands, by creating geographical parties, kindling
> sectional animosities, stirring up local jealousies
> and arousing all the angry passions" (Ceaser, 1979,
> p. 139).

In effect, this was prompting an election over party
versus section and the former won. Thus it was that
"The least studied of all our presidential elections,
the election of 1836, was of crucial importance in
determining the ultimate outlines of the Second Party

System" (McCormick, 1967, p. 99). "After 1836, the idea of partisan nominations was never again seriously challenged; it became part of the living Constitution" (Ceaser, 1979, p. 127).

But what sort of party system did this process towards legitimizing oppositions produce? Not surprisingly, it came up with two opposition parties (Lebowitz, 1968) with the Democrats built upon an anti-Adams coalition and the Whigs upon an anti-Jackson and anti-VanBuren coalition. This was an era of opposition party victories. Throughout the heyday of the second party system, the 'out' party won _every_ single presidential election, and the parties were in alternating possession of the Presidency at four year intervals. Indeed, no incumbent was able to win reelection between Jackson and Lincoln. It was in fact a "wondrous creation" (McCormick, 1967, p. 112) that Van Buren had catalyzed with oppositional coalitions finally adding up to a nonsectional party system within a highly sectionalized country.

SECTION: POLITICAL INTEGRATION VERSUS ECONOMIC SPECIALIZATION

At the time of the first census in 1790 the population of the United States was just under four million. The heaviest concentrations of population were along the Atlantic Coast, for although the Treaty of Paris with Britain in 1783 had given the United States territory westward to the Mississippi River (Pounds, 1972, pp. 74-75), much of this area remained undeveloped wilderness. From New England to Georgia, the six persons per square mile isopleth ran north-south along the crest of the Appalachians and the geographical center of population was about twenty miles east of Baltimore in the Chesapeake Bay (U.S. Statistical Abstract, 1976, p. 9).

This relatively narrow strip of settlement along the Atlantic coastal plain was by no means homogeneous. It is generally agreed that the thirteen former British colonies which became the new nation embraced three very distinctive regions or sections termed North, Middle and South (Whittlesey, 1957) with the former two commonly referred to as New England and Middle Atlantic respectively. This tripartite division was reflected in rural settlement

patterns (Trewartha, 1953), levels of urbanization
(Ward, 1971), cultural and religious mixes (Kelley,
1979), political traditions (Elazar, 1972) and
economic structure (Lee and Passell, 1979). All of
these elements are interrelated and we will briefly
attempt to bring them together by discussing them in
terms of their different roles within the world-
economy where the new Republic had to compete both
economically and politically.

Early Sections in the World-Economy

The world-economy of the late eighteenth century was
based largely upon trade in agricultural and other
primary goods under British hegemony. Two major
trade patterns had emerged, one centring upon India
in the East and the other upon the North Atlantic in
the West. In the latter, the British North American
colonies and subsequently the new United States were
an integral part. The new nation did not participate
as a single conglomeration of economic interests,
however, since each section evolved different
relationships within the world-economy (Chase-Dunn,
1980). In New England we find a classic case of
what Wallerstein (1974) refers to as a semi-
peripheral status: exploited by the international
core, but in its turn, exploiting a local periphery.
While receiving manufactured goods from Britain,
these were paid for by resources generated through
the triangular trade in rum, slaves and sugar in
which New England merchants played a full part (Ward,
1971, p. 23). Hence, the new Republic's most
northern section had a diverse economy based upon
shipbuilding, fisheries, commerce, and lumbering,
plus some light manufacturing and agriculture.

   The major centres of commerce were to the south in
the Middle Atlantic section, however. Philadelphia
had been the second largest city of the British
Empire before 1776; but by 1790 it was overtaken by
New York which has maintained its primacy into the
present day. Gordon (1978) has argued that North
American urban development based upon commerce was
inhibited under British rule as both economic and
political functions were usurped by London. Hence,
overall urban population actually was declining in
the colonies before the Revolution. With

independence Philadelphia and particularly New York
were able to forge new roles for themselves as the
prime commercial centres of the new state. As
Rubinson (1978) points out, in many ways New York
became the commercial capital of the American South
which failed to develop its own major urban centres.
This was important in maintaining a common trading
interest between the plantation South and the urban
Middle Atlantic which in turn formed a trans-
sectional basis for the ruling coalition which
emerged in the republic prior to the Civil War
(Rubinson, 1978).

In the South, the climate permitted varieties of
speciality crops which were in great demand in Europe
and becoming ever more so. Tidewater plantations in
Maryland and Virginia along the reaches of the
Chesapeake Bay specialized in tobacco which was
consigned directly from local wharves to European
ports. The only major southern urban settlements at
this time were Baltimore in the upper south exporting
food grains and Charleston in the lower south
monopolizing export trade in rice and indigo. Hence,
the southern section consisted of a typical
peripheral region within the world-economy supplying
agricultural produce for more advanced regions in the
core and semi-periphery. Major commercial trans-
actions were largly regulated in extra-regional
locations, notably in New York and, of course,
London.

The new republic, therefore, was linked into the
world-economy in three different ways by its sections
and encompassed within its territory booming
commercial centres in the Middle Atlantic separating
semi-peripheral New England from the peripheral
South. In a very few years a further complication
arose as the American West changed from being an
external arena to the world economy and instead became
commercially integrated as a further distinctive
agricultural zone in the world-economy of the first
half of the nineteenth century. These disparate
roles produced very different sectional economic
interests which centred upon competition for
attention by the federal government with its
monopoly of foreign, fiscal and trading policy. The
final outcome of this competition was the isolation

of the South and its defeat in the Civil War. To
contemporaries, this outcome was not seen as
inevitable, as it has sometimes been regarded by
historians in hindsight. Hence, in this part of the
chapter, we will trace the fluctuating alliances of
the sections through to the Civil War.

A major factor influencing sectional alliances
within the new Republic was the continuous stream of
innovations in communications and transportation
technology which was continually bringing the
sections closer together and changing the pattern of
interactions between them. In transport, turnpike
roads, steamboats, canals, and railways, plus related
communications developments, notably postal mail,
newspapers, and telegraph linkages, all contributed
to a 'shrinking' of the national space. While these
changes were binding the national territory together,
they also set in motion two contradictory tendencies.
On the one hand, transport and communication
revolutions integrated the national space into a
single social community. This integration is most
explicitly illustrated by the development of the
second party system with its anti-sectional bias
described above. On the other hand, cheaper and
regular transport links encouraged economic specialization, accentuating the original economic
differences between the sections. Thus while Van
Buren was effecting his political integration through
the creation of opposition political parties,
economic trends were widening the gulf between the
sections. This latter process prompted the divisions
culminating in the Civil War. Here can be
encountered the spatial interaction basis of the
party versus section theme already introduced.

Integration: Mass Mobilization of the Electorate
In our earlier discussion of the second party system
we emphasized its basic contribution in the
acceptance of the opposition party in American
politics. Its other major characteristic which is of
equal importance was that it mobilized mass participation in elections (Chambers, 1967, p. 11). In
this development it was following a democratizing
trend which was sweeping the young Republic. By the
early 1820's, for example, all but four of the

thirteen original states had discontinued the
property requirement for voting (Beard and Beard,
1944, p. 213). Furthermore, states admitted to the
Union after 1789 either adopted universal white
manhood suffrage or at most placed slight qualifications on the right to vote as a part of their state
constitutional framework. Nationally, selection of
delegates to the Electoral College changed equally
dramatically so that by 1828 all states except
Delaware and South Carolina chose presidential
electors by popular ballot. It was in this arena--
popular election for president via the Electoral
College--that a mass mobilization of voters throughout the whole nation occurred.

The dimensions of this achievement of the second
party system can be indicated through a few basic
statistics. The ethos of Jacksonian egalitarian
politics is reflected in the fact that the election
of 1828 attracted the participation of over one
million voters representing more than half of the
electorate; by 1840 nearly two and a half million
voters turned out, comprising over eighty percent of
the potential electorate. It is worth briefly
looking at these two elections and their campaigns,
since they represent the origin and the culmination
of the second party system's remarkable achievement
in mass mobilization.

After Jackson had been defeated for the Presidency
in the House of Representatives in 1824, a Jackson
coalition emerged, including Van Buren, to ensure a
reversal of the result in 1828. Lebowitz (1968,
p. 67) describes how:

"Newspapers were established around the country to
spread the party line. Correspondence and vigilances
committees emerged to guide and coordinate local
activities. Legislative bills were tailored to
increase support from doubtful regions. And the
people were provided with songs, slogans, and
talismans to reinforce their faith....The Jackson
machine had elected a President."

This was what we would today consider a blatant case
of 'selling' a presidential candidate, and in

Ceaser's (1979, p. 167) words "the parties became
tremendous advertising agents." Lowi (1968, p. 243)
goes as far as to assert that the campaign was
significant in spanning the country with no common
programme: "Thenceforth, parties were not 'built
out from the centre of government' like earlier
formations, but 'built up' as a Federal structure of
existing national factions and state components"
(Lowi, 1967, p. 243). The 1828 Democrats thus
illustrated how to mobilize and to manage mass
participation in electoral politics.

After their loss of 1836, the Whigs turned the
tables on the Democratic party machine and "demonstrated in the log cabin and cider barrel campaign
of 1840 that it could more than compete with its
rival in playing on the democratic theme" (Ceaser,
1979, p. 166). "Issues were consciously
de-emphasized" (Chambers, 1967, p. 12) as
politicians became the heroes of popular culture with
nicknames such as "Old Hickory" and "Old Tippecanoe,"
the victors of the 1828 and 1840 elections
respectively. The 'show-biz' characteristic of
American elections, for which they still remain
distinctive in the western world, originated at this
time. According to Chambers (1967, pp. 11-12)

"In an era when men often lived far from one
another and even town dwellers were often starved
for entertainment and excitement, the party battle
took on the form of a game and a major source of
entertainment. It thus filled a need that has
been served in our own time by...theatre, moving
pictures, sports contests, radio and television....
Thousands did march, flaunt transparencies of party
heroes, cheer at mass rallies in town squares or
rural groves, and go to the polls to vote."

Ceaser (1979, pp. 164-165) pinpoints this period,
specifically after the 1840 campaign but before the
1844 campaign, as when the word 'politician' itself
took on derogatory implications.

The techniques of election management and popular
mobilization pioneered under the second party system
would not have been possible without concurrent

developments in communication. Mass political
mobilization did not occur in a vacuum; improved
means of transport and communications were its
preconditions (Chambers, 1967, p. 12 and McCormick,
1967, p. 113). Key (1964, p. 476) describes the
process as follows:

"The revolution in communications technology has
profoundly altered the character of campaigning and
perhaps changed, too the fundamental bases of
political power....In Andrew Jackson's day the
facilities for reaching the mass of the people were
meager indeed. In the campaign of 1828 Jackson's
chief means for circulating his views was the
United States Telegraph, a partisan newspaper with
a circulation of 40,000 weekly. Its successor, the
Washington Globe, by 1834 had a daily circulation
of 12,000. Democratic doctrine proclaimed in the
leading articles of this paper were reprinted by
local newspapers over the country, but only after
the Washington newspaper had been conveyed to their
offices by the primitive transport of the day."

The link between information diffusion in the
pretelegraphic period and transport systems has been
carefully analysed by Allen Pred (1977, Chapter 2).
Unfortunately for our purposes, Pred concentrates
upon commercial information flows and does not
consider the partisan characteristics of the press at
this time. Hence, he does not consider information
dissemination from Washington as a node, but we can
see from his analyses of New York, in particular, how
major changes in information flows between newspapers
occurred from 1817 to 1841. At the first date the
dissemination of newspaper information involved a
substantial time lag and inland centres received news
from New York in weeks rather than days. But by
1841 Chicago, New Orleans, and Jacksonville
representing Northwestern, Southeastern, and South-
western corners of the contemporary commercial United
States only had to wait approximately ten days to
receive New York information (Pred, 1977, Figures
23b and 23c, pp. 48-49). Hence, although Key
dismisses the communications recources of the time as
'meager' in comparison to modern communication

facilities, they, nevertheless, enabled a national
mass politics to evolve. This was further facilitated as other means of information flow also
expanded enormously. As well as annual newspaper
circulation multipling sixfold to nearly 150,000
between 1810 and 1840, miles of postal routes leapt
more than fourfold from 36,000 in 1810 to nearly
160,000 in 1840 (Pred, 1977, pp. 40 and 59). Add to
this the thousands of partisan pamphlets produced,
and we have a picture of an evolving community, in
the basic sense of that word, inventing the mass
party political game.

It was, however, a highly fragile community managed
by conservative politicians. Ceaser (1979, p. 36)
explicitly sums up the situation:

> "Martin Van Buren purposely established parties to
> control or manage change....Parties would be
> moderating agencies....It would be correct to say
> that the doctrine of party competition was designed
> by Van Buren to introduce a bias against change."

This is a very explicit illustration of
Schattsneider's interpretation of parties, introduced
in Chapter one, as managers of public opinion. The
resulting political integration was fundamentally
superimposed because "Each party had been put
together piecemeal from a bewildering variety of
local cleavages and ethnocultural hostilities"
(Burnham, 1967, p. 294). The geographical pattern of
this artificial system now seems 'surprising'
(Brock, 1973, p. 54); as Sundquist (1973, p. 43)
points out

> "One has only to look at the adjacent Yankee states
> of New Hampshire and Vermont, which were settled by
> people of the same stock, were comparable in
> economic structure, and shared a common intellec-
> tual and religious tradition. Yet, through some
> accident of development, New Hampshire became a
> Democratic state and Vermont a Whig state, not by
> narrow margins but by overwhelming ones."

Such mass management could not survive beyond the
1850's. What it avoided, indeed what it was intended
to defuse, was the other effect of transport and
communication innovations: the ongoing intensifi-
cation of economic specialization which was forcing
sections of the nation apart.

Specialization: Economic Competition for the West

The original three "Atlantic' sections of the
thirteen states were soon joined by western interests
in the federal political arena. As we have seen in
the geography of support for ratification of the
Constitution, the views of the noncommercialized
western frontier were overridden in a process Fifer
(1976) has called 'unity by inclusion.' This
disposition of the West continued to produce
discontent. In Boorstin's (1965, p. 419) words:

> "...the new central government in America would
> exercise power over land and life in a new American
> empire in which new colonies were euphemistically
> called the 'public lands' or the 'national domain'
> or the 'public domain.' The empire was remarkably
> similar in political structure to that which had
> driven the earlier American Colonies to revolt.
> The new national government, for example, at first
> dared to legislate for and to tax this new
> empire....If the British had once used Americans as
> pawns in a world-wide battle for empire, so now the
> new American government in Washington used
> Westerners as makeweights between sections of the
> heavily settled East."

But, as settlement across the Appalachians increased
and as new states were carved out of formerly
federally-administered territories, the West itself
emerged as a section to be reckoned with in federal
politics. The democratizing process described
earlier was largely instigated and often spread from
origins in the West where social differences in the
population were typically much less than in seaboard
states. The victory of Westerner Andrew Jackson of
Tennessee only served to emphasize the emergence of
this section to rival the original ones. Before
1824 Eastern sections had provided all previous

Presidents. In fact although some differences
continued to exist between the commercial interests
in the Middle Atlantic and the new manufacturing
interests in New England, the emergence of the
Western section--the 'Old North-West of the Ohio
Valley'--largely coincided with the coalescence of
the two northern seaboard sections into a single
North-East interest, incorporating New England and
the Middle Atlantic regions. Hence, a threefold
sectional structure remained, but it was geographically transformed into one of South, North-West and
North-East. The situation to emerge by the 1820's
has been summarized dramatically by Billington
(1960, p. 329):

   "The settlement of the trans-Appalachian frontier
   brought the United States face to face with a
   terrifying problem: how could an industrial
   Northeast, a cotton growing South and a small
   farming West live side by side in peace?"

The ultimate answer, of course, was that they
eventually could not, but the interesting point is
why the conflict was not precipitated until the
1860's. Part of the reason can be found in Van
Buren's party system as we have seen, but there were
also the economic ties which initially, at least did
not tend to irrevocably pull the North-West towards
the North-East. This enabled Southern hopes for an
agrarian-based South and Northwest coalition against
the more populous Northeast to remain realistic well
into the nineteenth century.
   In the national political arena in Washington
competition between the three sections centred upon
three areas of federal responsibility: public lands,
international tariffs and internal improvement
policy. From the very start of the Republic when the
Atlantic states agreed to give up their claims to
Western territories, the federal government had had
to deal with the problem of disposing of public lands.
This included conditions of sale which in turn
related to the type of farming to be practiced and
brought up the slavery issue. Hence, land policy
became closely related to conflict over extending the

institution of slavery into the new territories
culminating in the Missouri Compromise of 1820 on the
balanced admittance of 'slave' and 'free' states.
In this conflict the Northwest tended to side with the
Northeast against the South, although they in turn
were divided by the role of land sales as a source of
federal revenues. Both eastern sections, the Northeast and the South, favoured dear land while the
Northwest wanted cheap land to attract people and
investment.

On trade tariffs sectional rivalries were somewhat
more complicated. Billington (1960) has shown how
Protection Bills in Congress from 1824 through to
1846 elicited sectional responses with the South
favouring free trade to maintain its role as a raw
material (cotton) provider to Britain. On this issue
the Northeast was divided. Commercial interests in
New York which depended upon foreign trade continued
to support low tariffs (Rubinson, 1978) while
manufacturing interests, especially in New England,
favoured protection from the more advanced industrial
producers of Britain. Tariff attitudes in the Northwest varied from one of common cause with allied
Southern agrarian interests to one of growing support
for the Northeast as the West became more and more
closely tied to the Northeast region as a trading
partner.

This brings us to the third area of federal
policies over which the sections competed with one
another for influence. Revenues from higher tariffs
and the sale of public lands would normally more
than cover government expenses. One use for surplus
was to promote transport improvements, either
directly by the federal government or by giving
improvement grants to the states. The most famous
example was the National Road linking Cumberland,
Maryland, with Wheeling, West Virginia, which
completed an overland route to the Ohio Valley under
federal financing. Governments at state and city
levels and private companies added other roads to the
interior, such as the Mohawk Turnpike from Albany to
Buffalo, the Pennsylvania Road from Philadelphia to
Pittsburgh and the Great Valley Road—Wilderness and
Nashville Roads system from Virginia into Kentucky

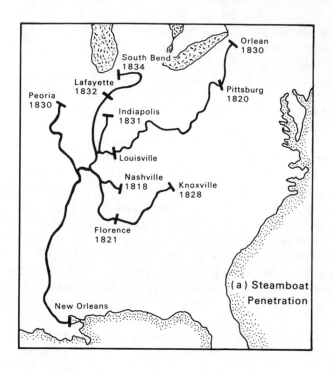

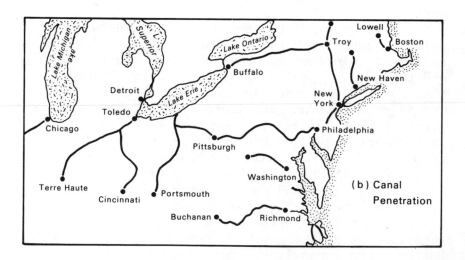

Figure 2.2   Sectional Competition for the Northwest

and Tennessee. It has been estimated that the
Pennsylvania and National Turnpikes carried 40,000
tons of freight per year and cut shipping costs from
the Ohio Valley to the Atlantic coast by half (Lee
and Passell, 1979). Nevertheless, these attempts to
link East and West economically were overshadowed by
developments in water transport which before the
advent of the railways was far cheaper and quicker
than overland traffic.

It is in the realm of water transport that the
competition between Northeast and South was first
fully engaged "to tap the surplus-producing areas
developing in the trans-Appalachian country as the
self-sufficient economy of the frontier gave way to
crop specialization during the 1820's" (Billington,
1960, p. 329). The initial advantage went to the
South as the development of the steamboat enabled
this section to exploit natural waterways linking the
Ohio Valley with New Orleans. This transport innovation overcame two problems: first, steamboats
provided enough power to return up the fast flowing
rivers; and second, they were designed with a small
enough draft to navigate the shallows. The first
steamboat New Orleans was launched in Pittsburgh at
the head of the Ohio River in 1811, and by 1819
thirty-one steamboats were trading on the Mississippi
and Ohio waterways and by 1840 the number reached
one hundred eighty-seven. Figure 2.2(a) shows the
extension of the trading area of these waterways as
steamboats penetrated further and further into the
Northwest hinterland. By the early 1830's upstate
New York and Pennsylvania, Illinois, Indiana and
Tennessee were directly connected to New Orleans by
steamboat.

The Northeastern response was to create its own
artificial waterways in the canal system. The most
important was the Erie Canal linking the Hudson River
with Lake Erie and giving New York direct access to
the Northwest on the shores of Lake Erie. This
stimulated other eastern cities to promote canals
inland, such as the Pennsylvania Canal linking
Philadelphia with Pittsburgh on the Ohio. These are
shown in Figure 2.2(b) where we can see that a
further system of canals was designed to feed into

Lake Erie and, hence, to extend the transport
hinterland of New York. The two maps in Figure 2.2
very clearly express sectional rivalries concerning
Northwest trade with steamboats giving an initial
edge to the South to be followed by canals,
especially the Erie Canal, changing the balance back
in favor of the Northeast.

The transport competition between the sections was
conclusively settled with the coming of the railways.
The Northeast had the commercial institutions and
investment contacts with Britain to establish an
early lead in railway development. This is not to
say that Southern interests did not attempt to
harness the new innovation for their own ends. In
1835-1836 state legislatures in South Carolina and
Tennessee issued charters for the Louisville,
Cincinnatti and Charleston Railway which, according
to one South Carolina politician "would join the two
sections in perpetual economic union" (Billington,
1960, p. 339). However, the depression of the late
1830's led to a stopping of construction in 1839 and
ended the South's most ambitious attempt to tie
itself economically to the Northwest. In contrast,
railways linking the Northwest to the Northeast
multiplied. This reflected the economic comple-
mentarity which had built up between the regions,
making northern railways safer and better invest-
ments. By comparing consumption and production of
grains by sections, Billington (1960, p. 399) has
shown that the Northwest as a surplus region and the
Northeast as a deficit region formed natural partners
to the detriment of the South. This situation was
accentuated by foreign trade patterns which emerged
after the repeal of the British Corn Laws in 1846.
Prior to this, most of the American farm surplus was
sold to the West Indies and Latin America so that New
Orleans enjoyed the locational advantage. After 1846
"the center of the export trade shifted to the
Atlantic ports closest to Britain's consumer" as
exports of grain to Europe increased by 170 percent
in a single decade (Billington, 1960, p. 400).

The final result of this process of transport
innovation and changing market circumstances was to
economically bind the Northeast to the Northwest.

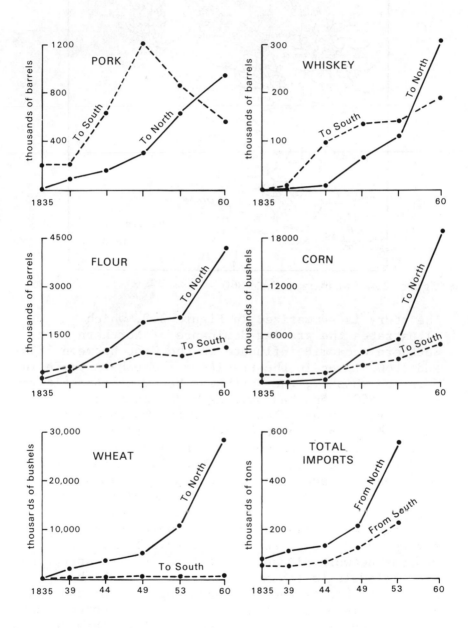

Figure 2.3   Trading Links of the North-West, 1835–1860

Figure 2.4   Railways in 1860

The story is summarized in Figure 2.3, which
illustrates the growing dominance of Northern over
Southern economic influence in the West between 1835
and 1860.   Even in the traditional southern trade in
pork and whiskey, the North was becoming competitive
by the 1850's and had overtaken the South by 1860.
In flour, corn and wheat trade, the North was to
dominate as early as the 1840's.   Similarly in terms
of imports, Northern sources consolidated their
traditional lead and by 1860 totally dominated the
Northwest's trade.   The map of railway lines in
operation by 1860 illustrates the complete transport
integration of the Northeast with the Northwest
(Figure 2.4).   Although railways were to be found
throughout the settled areas by this time, the
densest network already identified an area spreading
from Illinois to the Atlantic, a region which was
shortly to become the Manufacturing Belt of the USA.
By 1860 this area is discernable as the economic core
of the Republic.   Sectional conflict was thus reduced
to a contest of North versus South, core versus
periphery.   The stage was set for the demise of the
second party system and the outbreak of the Civil War.

In the federal political arena alliances quickly
reflected these new economic circumstances. The
positions of the three sections can be summarized as
follows (Billington, 1960, p. 353):

	Public Land	Tariffs	Improvement
West	low price	protective	federally built
South	high price	low tariff	no support
Northeast	high price	high tarrif	federally built

From hindsight, we can see the weak position of the
South whose interests only coincided with the Northeast over public land. In fact this was the most
important federal issue for the Northwest and it was
federal land policy after 1845 which brought the
Northeast and the Northwest together in a political
alliance cementing their economic integration.
    The best interpretation with which to conclude this
early sectional history is to be found in Lynd's
(1970) updating of Beard's original materialist
ideas. The War of Independence and the Constitution
brought together sectional interests in a common
national cause to create a new state. Once this was
achieved sectional conflict, although cleverly
managed politically, became endemic as different
interests competed to decide what sort of society
the new nation would become;

  "A showdown could be postponed, however, because
  each sectional society expected to augment its
  power from new states to be formed in the West.
  What Turner's frontier thesis explains is why
  Beard's second American revolution (the Civil War)
  was so late in coming." (Lynd, 1970, p. 60)

Consequently, sectionalism was not fully reflected in
political party terms until the rise of the
Republicans and the emergence of the third party
system. It is the hesitant rise of sectional
politics east of the Mississippi which we analyse
quantitatively below.

TWO NORMAL VOTE PATTERNS: 1828-1920
The analysis at this stage deals with twenty-five
states east of the Mississippi which were popularly

electing Presidential College delegates by 1836.
These states were identified in Figure 1.2. This
eastern part of the United States formed the
essential geographical scope of presidential politics
before the Civil War, but obviously as more states
were admitted to the union, analysis needs to take
cognisance of the area west of the Mississippi. Such
analyses are the matter of the next chapters. Here
we extend our analysis beyond the Civil War as far as
1920 for comparative purposes. We are interested in
the change from nonsectional to sectional normal
voting and this can only be seen over a fairly long
time horizon. Initially, we intended to use only
nineteenth century elections and terminate this
analysis at 1896, but since we found some delay in
the establishment of the sectional normal vote after
the Civil War, it seemed necessary to extend our time
period in order for this sectional normal vote to be
adequately represented. Of course, the 1896 election
appeals as a means for defining our time period
because it is commonly designated as an important
critical election. In fact in this 'eastern'
analysis at the state level 1896 does not emerge as a
distinctive break-point. This will be discussed
further in the next chapter when the trans-
Mississippi west is incorporated into the analysis.
At that time this eastern 'finding' will be used for
comparison. In our discussion of the analysis below
we concentrate on the rise and fall of the nonsectional normal voting pattern designed by Van Buren
to be replaced by a normal sectional voting pattern.

The analysis carried out on 25 states over 23
elections was as described in Chapter one and
detailed in the Appendix: a common factor model with
oblique rotation of all 'interpretable' factors. In
this case five factors were extracted which between
them accounted for 91.5 percent of the original
variation in the data. The factor pattern loadings
after oblique rotation are presented as 'loading
profiles' in Figure 2.5. In this diagram factors are
presented, not in the order of their extraction (and,
therefore, importance), but in order of the time of
their emergence. Numerical values of the factor
pattern loadings along with details of their

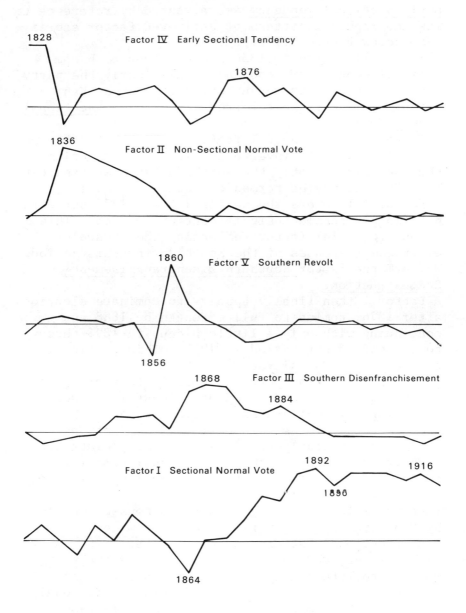

Figure 2.5   Factor Loading Profiles, 1828–1920

derivation are given in appendices.   From Figure 2.5
we can name the factors as follows:

Factor IV is clearly the Jackson factor loading
high in 1828 and 1832 only. We term this factor
Early Sectional Tendency as warranted by reference to
its geographical pattern of estimated factor scores
(See below Figure 2.7(a)).

Factor II starts in 1836 and declines to become
insignificant after 1856 and so is clearly the party
system of Democrats versus Whigs created by Van
Buren. This will be referred to as the Nonsectional
Normal Vote.

Factor V is an unusual factor picking out 1856 and
1860 although with inverse loadings. This reflects
the inclusion of only the Northern Democrat candidate
for 1860 and may be termed the Southern Revolt.

Factor III covers the period 1864 to 1876 but does
not finally become insignificant until 1888. This
is an artificial factor reflecting the unusual
electoral responses of the South during this period.
We term the factor Southern Disenfranchisement-
Reconstruction.

Factor I then finally appears to dominate elections
after 1876, coming to full strength by 1888 and
continuing with only a little hiccup in 1896 through
to the end of our period in 1920. This is clearly
the Sectional Normal Vote.

The relationships between these factors are given
by their correlations drawn as a 'causal' structure
in Figure 2.6 which uses the time sequence to define
the direction of the main correlation relations.
Notice how the early sectional tendency relates to
both its seccessor in the nonsectional normal vote
and the final pattern of the sectional normal vote.
This shows that the early Democratic electoral
response which was being marshalled nonsectionally
by Van Buren in fact more closely resembled the
final sectional pattern to emerge after 1876. As we
might expect, the southern revolt is inversely
related to both of these sectional factors since it
represents southern rejection of their traditional
ties with the Democrats. Finally this diagram
emphasizes the artificiality of the Southern
disenfranchisement-reconstruction factor since it

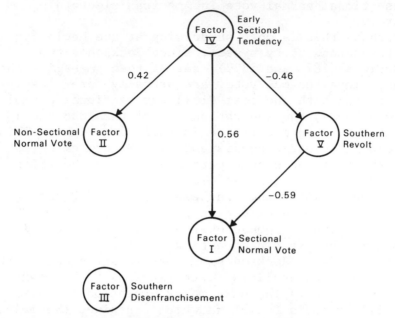

Figure 2.6   Factor Correlations, 1828–1920

does not significantly correlate with any of the
other factors produced in the analysis.

The general picture to emerge is that of an early
sectional pattern which developed around Jackson, was
marshalled by Van Buren into a nonsectional pattern
leading to a very confused pattern in 1856 followed
by a southern revolt in the Democratic Party and an
artificial pattern through Reconstruction before the
final emergence of the normal sectional pattern.
For a more detailed look at these findings and their
relations with our previous discussion as well as
other sources, we will consider each of the major
normal votes in turn.

The Rise and Fall of the Nonsectional Normal Vote
The distinctiveness of the nonsectional normal vote
is emphasized, not only by its contrast with the
sectional normal vote that followed it, but also by
its contrast with the temporary voting patterns that
surround it.   Both the early sectional tendency and
the southern revolt are, as their labels suggest,
explicitly sectional in their patterns which
particularly highlights the perculiarity of the

nonsectional normal vote in American electoral
history.

Perhaps this is most surprising at the beginning
of the second party system, since Jackson's two
elections (1828 and 1832), rather than presaging the
nonsectional normal vote, are actually more closely
correlated with the post-Civil War sectional normal
vote: hence, the separation out of the 1828 and 1832
elections to form a factor in their own right. This
finding is clearly consistent with McCormick's (1967)
treatment of the second party system when he writes
that "sectional bias was clearly revealed in the
election of 1828" and "the election of 1832 had
remarkably little effect on party formation" (p. 98).
This sectional response over just two elections is
shown in the pattern of estimated scores in
Figure 2.7(a). Jackson's support is strongest in the
Deep South and declines northeastwards to be weakest
in New England. The only major exception to this
spatial trend is Louisiana which contained the major
port of New Orleans. It seems that at this time,
before the eclipse of New Orleans trade by northeastern ports (as shown in Figure 2.3), mercantilist
interests were strong enough for Louisiana to be less
impressed by Jackson's common credentials than other
southern and western states. Despite this anomaly,
however, the scores illustrate how Jackson built his
electoral success on a South-West alliance.

The lack of continuity in electoral patterns after
Jackson justifies our earlier emphasis upon Martin
Van Buren as the outstanding architect of the second
party system. The nonsectional normal vote begins
precisely when Van Buren becomes the Democratic
candidate. Again this is consistent with McCormick's
(1967, p. 99) interpretation that the 1836 election
"was of crucial importance in determining the
ultimate outlines of the second party system." He
identifies the paradox that "highly sectional
responses in a series of presidential elections
(1824, 1828, 1832) resulted in the formation of nonsectional parties." The cause of the paradox was
Van Buren's candidacy and campaign of 1836 which
eroded some of Jackson's southern and western
Democrat support and replaced it by Democratic gains

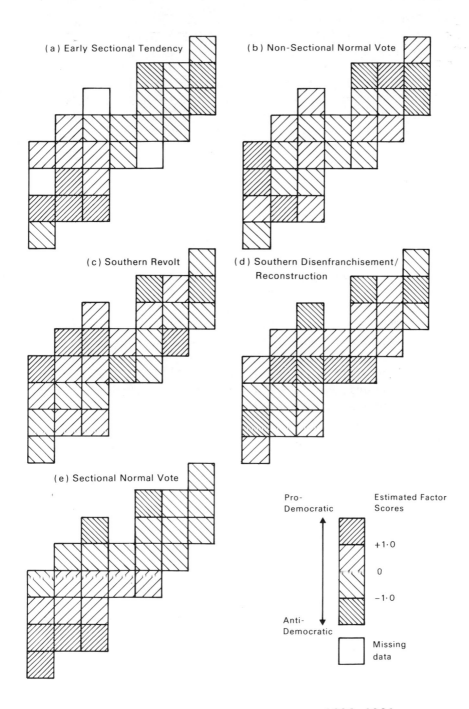

Figure 2.7 Estimated Factor Scores, 1828–1920

in Van Buren's own Northeast. The result is shown in
Figure 2.7(b) which graphically illustrates
McCormick's (1967, p. 109) observation that

> "The second party system was extraordinary in that
> the two parties were fairly evenly balanced in
> every region. Between 1836 and 1852, as in no
> other period in our history, each of the parties
> **was** truly national in its extent."

The mixture of support and rejection of Democratic
Party candidates in Figure 2.7(b) shows more intrasectional contrasts than the usual inter-sectional
competition. In particular, we can observe the
contrasts within New England where New Hampshire and
Vermont exhibit very different responses, something
previously noted by Sundquist (1973, p. 43).
However, the intermeshed pattern of pro-Democrat and
pro-Whig states in all sections is the most important
feature of Figure 2.7 (b). This is the spatial
manifestation of Van Buren's 'wondrous creation.'
    The nonsectional normal vote comes to an abrupt end
after 1852 with what Rose and Urwin (1975) refer to
as the eruption of regional voting. In this analysis
this change is represented by a bipolar factor
expressing opposite patterns of voting in 1856 and
1860. This reflects the breakup of the Whigs in the
1856 election to be followed by the fission of the
Democrats in 1860. But, in fact, traditional voting
loyalties seem to have been maintained within
sections while the parties themselves split along
sectional lines (Lipset, 1960, pp. 372-386). In 1856
a three-party contest pitted the Democrats against
the American Party and the Republicans in the North,
but only against the American Party in the South
where the recently formed Republican Party did not
offer electoral slates. The result was a southern
bias in the pattern of Democrat voting for the first
time since Jackson. In contrast in 1860 the
Democratic Party split as southern delegates refused
to accept Stephen Douglas and called their own
convention which nominated John C. Breckenridge.
This meant that the official Democratic candidate
Douglas, had a northern bias to his support.

For estimating the scores on this bipolar factor, we
have treated the 1860 performance of Douglas as the
'usual' pattern for this factor since it has the
highest absolute loading. The resulting scores are
shown in Figure 2.7(c) and the pattern can be seen to
be very complicated in a manner befitting the
electoral situation. In general, the 'pro-Democrat'
areas are in the central states of the old Northwest
since parts of the South are lost to the Democrats
and Republican strength in New England is already
apparent. (Remember that in interpreting this map
'pro-Democrat' only refers to 1860; for 1856 read
'anti-Democrat').

One way of interpreting this situation is to treat
the 1860 election as two second-party system contests
with one in each section. In this way the
Republicans are 'Northern Whigs' and the
Constitutional Unionists 'Southern Whigs' so that in
the North there was a 'Whig victory' and in the South
a 'Democrat victory.' Such an interpretation
emphasizes continuity in voting behavior at the
grass roots level, acknowledgment of which can take
the form of rather extreme statements such as
Lipset's (1960, pp. 375-376) asserting that "The
election of 1860, like every election since 1828 was
fought out between the supporters and opponents of
Andrew Jackson." Such arguments provide good
ammunition to justify our methodology which concentrates upon relations between party and state, rather
than upon individual voting behavior. The important
characteristic of 1856 and 1860 was not what was
happening to the voters, but what was happening to
the parties. Party managers were unable to maintain
Van Buren's anti-sectional party system so that
sectional issues could no longer be avoided The
1860 election is not important because "men continued
to vote along traditional party lines" (Lipset, 1960,
p. 378) but because the party lines themselves
changed. Furthermore, "It was not slavery that was
the main issue but the question of who would dominate
the Federal state" (Chase-Dunn, 1980, p. 223). The
election precipitated the Civil War whose aftermath
produced what we have previously termed the era of
sectional dominance. Let us see how that is
represented in our analysis.

The Establishment of the Sectional Normal Vote

Although Simpson (1978, p. 84) suggests that "The
sectional alignment of parties which helped produce
the Civil War was perpetuated, and indeed
strengthened, by the war's divisive effects" this is
not readily apparent in our analysis. The
establishment of the sectional normal vote was
delayed first by the war itself, then by military
occupation and then Reconstruction. This is directly
reflected in our Southern disenfranchisement
reconstruction factor.

This 'artificial' factor illustrates the pattern
of control of southern politics by northern
Republicans and their southern allies. The disenfranchisement of Confederate whites and the placing
of blacks on the electoral rolls after the passage of
the Thirteenth Amendment completely changed the
nature of southern politics for a few years after the
readmittance of southern states to the Union in
1868-1870.

It is this rather artificial pattern of support
which the factor picks out (Figure 2.7(d). While
Northern and especially New England support for the
Republicans is consolidated, the South presents a
quite varied situation depending upon the form of
Reconstruction, the numbers of blacks and their
electoral enrollment. For instance, Mississippi
particularly stands out upon our map as anti-
Democratic and this is consistent with its very high
black Republican support. During this period, the
state sent the only two black Senators to reach
Washington before Edward Brook from Massachusetts in
1966.

The temporal pattern of this factor (Figure 2.5) is
interesting since although the aftermath of the
election of 1876 brought the compromise of a northern
Republican-southern Democrat alliance to elect
Rutherford B. Hayes, the factor profile shows that
this pattern of voting did not finally disappear
until after 1888. This finding is entirely
consistent with Kousser's (1974, p. 11) argument
concerning the 'unsolid South' of this period:

"Twentieth century Southern politics did not spring
full-grown from the heads of those who negotiated

the Compromise of 1877. What followed after
Reconstruction was a period of transition,
uncertainty, fluctuation...."

In the South the Republican proportion of presidential voters stayed at about one quarter from 1872 to
1888 but then declined below one fifth and even below
15 percent by 1904 (Kousser, 1974, Table 1.1, p. 12)
so that he concludes:

"The statistics for the three decades (1872-1908)
demonstrate the length of time required for the
shift from the Reconstruction system of stiff party
competition...to the twentieth century system of
the solid, apathetic South" (Kousser, 1974, p. 13).

Our analysis is thus consistent with Kousser's (1974)
interpretation in the way in which this factor does
not entirely disappear with the end of Reconstruction. This should not be overemphasized, however.
In Table 2.1 we have listed the former Confederate
states separately and shown their individual paths
back into the Union and then into the 'Solid South.'
Readmissions were complete by 1870 and conservative
white governments established in these eleven states
by 1877. This 'redemption' was reflected in federal
politics by the fact that all Electoral College votes
from southern states were given to Democratic
presidential candidates from 1880 onwards to the end
of our twenty-five state analysis. Although the
solid South of the early twentieth century was not
immediately established after the Civil War the South
had become a loyal one-party section for the
Democrats by 1880.
    Table 2.1 shows two anomolies in the 1868 election
when Democratic voters were able to support their
presidential candidate in Georgia and Louisiana.
This accounts for the slight pro-Democrat recording
of these two former Confederate states on the scores
in Figure 2.7(d). The most notable feature of this
diagram is, however, the way in which with the North,
particularly New England (except New Hampshire) and
Michigan, firmly in the Republican camp and with
Reconstruction in the South, the main Democratic
strongholds of this period are to be found in the

Table 2.1. Establishment of the 'Solid South'.

	Readmission to the Union	Establishment of White Conservative Government	Presidential Election Year When Democratic Proportion First Reached		
			50%	60%	70%
Alabama	1868	1874	1876	1884	1904
Arkansas	1868	1874	1876	1896	1896
Florida	1868	1877	1880	1892	1892
Georgia	1870[1]	1871	1872[2]	1876	1876
Louisiana	1868	1877	1880[3]	1880	1888
Mississippi	1870	1876	1876	1876	1888
North Carolina	1868	1870	1876	1932	1936
South Carolina	1868	1877	1880	1880	1884
Tennessee	1866	1869	1872	1932	----
Texas	1870	1874	1876	1876	1876
Virginia	1870	1870	1876	1880	1936

[1] Georgia admitted in 1868 but military rule reestablished until 1870.

[2] Georgia recorded 64% for Democratic candidate in 1868.

[3] Louisiana recorded 71% for Democratic candidate in 1868.

Source for the first two columns: Patrick (1967, p. 142).

border states with southern sympathies, notably
Delaware, Maryland and Kentucky. However, it must be
emphasised again that this is a somewhat artificial
factor, based as it is on northern control of the
South, and that it is not correlated with any other
factor.

The sectional normal vote finally emerges in 1880,
resulting from the failure of the Republicans to
prevent the South from falling into the Democrat
camp. In Figure 2.5 the sectional normal vote
becomes the most important pattern from 1880 onwards
and totally dominates from 1888 apart from a minor
hiccup in 1896.

The scores for this factor show the most extreme
sectional pattern that we have encountered. All the
South and border states (except Missouri) are more
Democrat than the nation as a whole while all the
North is more anti-Democrat. Hence, we have come
full cycle: a stable sectional political party
system which had threatened to appear from the
original fumblings towards party politics in
Jackson's election has finally surfaced. The party
political conflicts in the federal arena now
reflected the economic conflicts of the emerging
industrial state. In order to understand the
dynamics of this system, we need to widen the
geographical scope of our analysis and to include the
far western states, a task which we leave to the next
chapter. What we have described in this chapter is
how it took over a century for economic sectional
interests to break through into a stable normal vote.
The rise of sectional politics in the East was indeed
a very slow and tumultuous process.

CHAPTER 3
The Structure of
Sectional Politics

On September 15, 1858, two mail coaches left Tipton,
Missouri, and San Francisco, California, to
inaugurate the first weekly transcontinental mail
service. The route chosen was particularly
significant. From both Tipton and San Francisco, the
stage coaches first travelled southward to follow a
route of 2812 miles via southern California, Arizona,
New Mexico, Texas, and Arkansas. This 'oxbow' route,
as Northerners termed it, represented one of the last
examples of direct Southern influence on the shape of
the emerging space-economy of the United States in
the nineteenth century. It was made possible by an
annual subsidy of $600,000 provided by the Postmaster
General, Aaron V. Brown from Tennessee, in a
Democratic administration.

This was a minor episode in the westward extention
of communications, but it is important to our
discussion because it suggests that the 1850's,
rather than beginning a new era of American politics,
instead represented the closing period of a political
alignment which was to disappear with the Civil War.
This interpretation runs counter to the standard
classification of party politics which uses the 1856
election to start the third party system. Super-
ficially, this periodization is attractive. The 1856
election was the first election in which the main
opponents for the Presidency fought under Democrat
and Republican party labels in a contest whose

outcome was sectionalized for the first time since
1832. It is however, over simplified to suggest that
by 1856 "the sectional alignment was all but
complete" (Simpson, 1978, p. 78) as our analysis of
eastern electoral patterns in the last chapter
demonstrated. The entire balance of sectional
interests was irreparably altered by the Civil War so
that earlier events such as Aaron V. Brown's oxbow
route became the quaint and seemingly irrational
decisions of a bygone age. After the Civil War, the
North was firmly in control of the American space-
economy, and this created a brand new political ball
game. The first new politics of sectional compromise
set up by the Federal Constitution and described in
the last chapter gave way to a second new politics
of sectional dominance on a truly continental scale
in the wake of the Civil War. This second new
politics is the subject of this chapter.

The analyses begin with 1872 by which time all of
the former Confederate States had rejoined the Union.
The performance of Democratic candidates for the
Presidency again forms our data base as we attempt to
describe and interpret the sectional politics which
emerged after the Union victory in the Civil War.
As in the last chapter, however, we start with a
sketch of the economic and political background
against which the elections took place. This background is especially important during the era because
post-Civil War links between economics and politics
were quite explicit. According to Hofstadter (1948,
p. 211):

"There is no other period in the nation's
history when politics seems so completely
dwarfed by economic changes, none in which
the life of the country rests so completely in
the hands of the industrial entrepreneur."

Whereas the popular heroes of the early nineteenth
century were politicians, those of the late
nineteenth century were the famous and infamous new
rich captains of industry such as Andrew Carnegie,
John D. Rockefeller and George Pullman. Even within
social science there emerged a social Darwinism which
justified both massive inequalities and a lack of

government initiative and intervention as industrialists began to totally dominate the society. When George Hearst entered the Senate, it was already known as the 'Millionaire's Club' and he was able to declare, quite sincerely, that "the members of the Senate are the survivors of the fittest" (Hofstadler, 1948, p. 217). Politics and economics had become inseparable in a fast growing and, as some would judge, cruel industrial society.

In the first part of this chapter we selectively treat those aspects of economic change most relevant to our theme of section and party. This involves describing the evolution of modern American sections in terms of the settling of the West and the closing of the frontier, the rise of the urban-industrial core, and America's assumption of a new role in the world economy. The emphasis is upon the use of sectional divisions by the leaders of the economic core to maintain their dominance of the economy. The specific role of party and presidential politics in the arrangement is then presented in our main analysis. In the next chapter, aspects of this analysis are repeated separately for each section, North, South, and West, in an attempt to unravel the complexities of the relationship between section and party at a sub-national scale.

SECTION AND PARTY SINCE THE CIVIL WAR
If the Tipton to San Francisco mail coach service corresponded with the death throes of the first 'new politics,' "the joining of the Union and Central Pacific railroads in Utah on May 10, 1869, may be said to symbolize a truly nation-wide economy" (Perloff, et.al., 1960, p. 191) upon which the second new politics was based. Sectional competition involving the South as a formidable regional antagonist was replaced by the sectional dominance of the North in a process which is sometimes termed the "nationalization" of the economy.

While the economy was becoming more integrated, however, the new politics associated with the nationalization of the economy was itself highly sectionalized. Here we can identify an interesting paradox in American history. The pre-Civil War

situation consisted of economically competitive
regions but non-sectionalized politics. This became
transformed into a post-Civil War era of economically
integrated regions but a sectionalized politics.
While the economic changes reveal an expected
nationalization of structure, the complete opposite
is true of the political changes. Hence, the pattern
of American party political development runs counter
to Rokkan's (1970) ideas of a progressive reduction
in territorial politics in favor of a nationalized
functional politics. The explanation of this
discrepancy seems to lie in the size and heterogeneity of the United States compared with the
European states which Rokkan was modeling (Taylor and
Johnston, 1979, pp. 107-123). The continental scale
of American politics in the latter half of the nineteenth century meant that sectional politics were
not the local cultural response to centralization
which Rokkan describes for European states but rather
reflected broad economic interests within the
expanding national economy. Hence in America
territorial politics in terms of sections were also
functional politics in terms of economic interests.
A temporal correlation between economic regional
integration and political regional separation is,
therefore, not so unlikely a combination as an
initial consideration would suggest.

The Nationalization of the Economy
In the last chapter we described how transport
innovations, and railways in particular, had
economically integrated the 'Old North West' with the
Northeast to produce a single 'Northern' section by
the 1850's. This integration culminated in the
North's support for Lincoln in 1860 which precipitated the Civil War (Billington, 1960, pp. 614-615).
However, as this old West was being absorbed into a
new sectional alliance, a new West was developing
beyond the Mississippi. In 1850 California joined
the Union and plans for a transcontinental rail link
can be traced back even earlier to 1845, but the old
politics of sectional stalemate prevented a start on
the project for "so long as sectionalism plagued the
nation, no road could be built" (Billington, 1960,

p. 645). The federal government did order an army
survey in 1853, but this only accentuated sectional
rivalries by identifying four feasible routes, two in
the north and two in the south. The Civil War ended
this political deadlock (Whittlesey, 1957, p. 271).
In 1862 a route between San Francisco and Omaha which
had been earlier linked to Chicago was agreed upon
in Congress. Seven years later the start of a
nationally integrated economy was signaled with the
joining of rails at Promontory Point, Utah. "The
last spikes," according to Charles and Mary Beard
(1937, p. 136):

> "were connected by telegraph wires with leading
> cities in all sections of the country so that
> the final strokes of the hammer could convey
> to the uttermost points some of the thrilling
> pride that animated the conquerors of plain,
> desert, peak, torrent, and ravine. The work
> that Lincoln had sanctioned was now finished....
> Steam and steel were to master a continent."

By 1883 all four of the transcontinental routes
earlier identified by the army survey had become
existing railway links between the East and West,
but the primacy of the northern routes was indicative
of the new balance of power among the sections. The
economy was certainly becoming nationalized, but
equally surely the reorganization revolved around the
economic leadership of the North. In the second half
of the nineteenth century the USA was transformed
into a major industrial state and the process of
industrialization was concentrated in the North.
Urban growth associated with the new economic growth
produced an American Manufacturing Belt stretching
from the Atlantic to Lake Michigan. It was this
"continued industrialization (that) eventually
required the mobilization of resources on a
continental scale, thereby heightening territorial
specialization and regional inter-dependence across
the nation" (Perloff, et.al., 1960, p. 286). The
result was that

"By 1910 the force of urbanization was being felt
throughout the entire country. The New England,
Middle Atlantic and Great Lakes regions had
developed well-established urban hierarchies.
The rest of the regions...were developing a
different pattern of urban centres" (Perloff,
et.al., p. 17).

The highly integrated urban system of the
Manufacturing Belt was surrounded by a system of
peripheral centres in resource regions which emerged
as dependent upon the manufacturing core. Their role
was one of integrating their particular region's
resources to the needs of the core. New Orleans,
San Francisco, and Minneapolis became regional
centres before 1900 as major commercial gateways to
the Mississippi basin, central valley of California
and the northern plains respectively (Berry and
Horton, 1970, p. 27). In the early twentieth century
further gateway cities emerged for southern
California (Los Angles), the central plains (Kansas
City), Pacific northwest (Seattle), Texas (Dallas and
Houston), and the southwest (Phoenix). But (Berry
and Horton, 1970, p. 35)

"In each case, the basic conditions of regional
growth were set by the heartland. It served as
the lever for successive development of newer
peripheral regions by reaching out to them as
its input requirements (needs) expanded, thus
fostering economic specialization of regional
roles in the national economy....Flows of raw
materials inward, and of finished products
outward, articulated the whole."

This economic core-periphery structure actually
consisted of a three fold geographical pattern of
sections. The North constituted the core, but the
periphery was not united. Instead, it consisted of
very distinctive southern and western portions. Much
effort in the nationalization of the economy was
expended upon the economic development and peopling
of the West and the harnessing of its resources for
the North. In the meantime, the South's economic

development also fell even more strongly under
Northern dominance. After the Civil War this
formerly competitive section sank to "a tributary
non-material economy dominated by absentee owners"
(Perloff, et.al., 1960, p. 177) and became locked
into the national economy as the most backward
section. Hence, despite the massive westward shift
of population from 1870 to 1910, the South's share
of total primary sector employment in the USA still
increased (Perloff, et.al., 1960, p. 136). The
result was a division of the periphery into dynamic
West and backward South. This would form the basis
of a 'divide and rule' political strategy by northern
interests from the Civil War onwards.

The situation which characterized the post Civil
War period up to 1910 suggests a classic case of what
is commonly termed 'internal colonialism.' Not all
authorities draw this conclusion, however. Perloff,
et.al., (1960, p. 192) argue explicitly against this
'political' interpretation that the North imposed
its will on rural America. They maintain that the
process was not one of 'sectional imperialism' but
merely an expression of economic organization that
became necessary as the country became continental in
scale. Of course there were many alternative forms
of potential economic organization and before 1860
southern interests certainly envisaged a very
different spatial order than the one that emerged
after 1870. The spatial organization that did emerge
was precipitated by a sectional war victory and it is
very much an understatement to claim merely that
"sectional interests were a waning influence,
complicating administration and policy" (Perloff,
et.al., 1960, p. 192). The question is whose policy
was complicated for whose interest. The truth is,
of course, that the South lost the war and paid the
penalty, both by being made economically dependent on
the North and by missing out on the Western bonanza.

At the end of the nineteenth century modern urban-
industrial America had been achieved in the form of a
distinctive three-section core-periphery spatial
structure. This structure proved to be relatively
stable over the next half century. Hence, Perloff,
et.al., writing in 1960 (p. 222) could assert that

"By 1910 the dominant regional pattern with which we
are today familiar had already taken shape." The
South remained the backward section, the West dynamic
and the North continued to dominate the economy. In
1957, for instance, the Manufacturing Belt contained
nearly the same proportion (46%) of the U. S.
population as it had in 1900 (Perloff, et.al., 1960,
p. 49). Nevertheless, changes were occurring and
Perloff, et.al. (1960, p. 22) were careful enough to
point out that "the apparent fixity of the twentieth
century regional structure can be overstated." We
now know that they were writing in a period when the
patterns they so carefully documented were undergoing
the beginnings of a major transformation, for
according to Berry and Horton (1970, p. 35) since
1950 the:

"Advantages for economic growth have been found
around the 'outer rim' of the country...as
advances in technology have reduced the time and
costs involved in previous heartland-hinterland
relationships....Hence the explosive metropolitan
growth of South, Southwest and West."

Although we may not entirely accept the technology
emphasis of Berry and Horton's statement (See Gordon,
1978), there has occurred since the mid-twentieth
century what Berry (1970, p. 21) has termed "the
emerging inversion of American geography." As the
old Northern core stagnates or even decays, the far
West and South have become the growth regions of the
national economy. This has become popularly known as
'the rise of the Sun Belt' (Sale, 1976).
    The third quarter of the twentieth century
witnessed an increasingly strong challenge to the
economic hegemony of the Northern core, even from the
vantage point of the region's long dominant special-
ization--manufacturing. Between 1960 and 1975 nearly
1.5 million new manufacturing jobs were added to the
nation's economy as a whole. But, during the same
period, New England and the Middle Atlantic sub-
divisions experienced an absolute loss of nearly 800
thousand manufacturing jobs and the North Central
Division (roughly correspondent to the trans-Ohio old

Northwest) saw its industrial employment expand at a
rate less than half that of the national norm.
Commenting upon these trends, Sternlieb and Hughes
(1978, pp. 7-8) recently argued that:

"A very powerful momentum has built up over the
past fifteen years, sweeping employment and
population growth away from the older metropolitan centers of the Northeast and North Central
states to the newer growth poles of the South
and West. The 'rise of the sunbelt' and the
'decline of the Northeast' are not inventions
of the popular media, but are ominous long-
term realities."

The transcontinental scope of the American economy,
a scope whose beginnings were symbolized more than a
century ago with the driving of a golden rail spike
at Promontory Point, Utah, has had a lasting, yet
dynamic, impact upon the backdrop of American
politics. Whereas politics for many Americans may
yet remain "essentially a local experience" (Kelley,
1979, p. 48), their responses to local conditions
have embedded within them responses to changing
regional, national and even international economic
complementarities and cleavages. In the next section
we examine the electoral patterns thus produced by
more than a century of political cross-currents upon
the voting map of the nation.

The Regionalization of the Polity
Perhaps the most distinctive feature of American
politics since the Civil War has been its regional
nature. As Brunn (1974, pp. 259-260) notes:

"Even a casual examination of the political scene
in the United States suggests that indeed not all
states or sections share similar views about
political issues and the role of government
and the individual in the political processes.
What is behind such sentiments is the recognition
of distinct political regions that can be
identified, measured and analysed."

The first American politics stifled such regionalism,
especially during the period of the nonsectional
normal vote, but the sectionalist forces released by
the Civil War persisted into the second American
politics. It is this post-Civil War political
regionalism and its role in the national politics
that concerns us here.

The major recent attempt to derive American
political regions through a long-term historical
approach is that of Elazar (1972) which was introduced into geography by Brunn (1974). Elazar (1972,
pp. 84-85) identifies three overarching factors in
the political development of individual American
states--political culture, sectionalism, and
frontier--which "embrace and shape the primary social,
economic, and psychological thrusts that influence
American politics." Although Elazar emphasises
political culture in the work cited by Brunn, the
three factors are viewed as interrelated elements of
a composite process producing unique orientations to
political action in different portions of the
country, for like all culture, political culture "is
rooted in the cumulative historical experiences of
particular groups of people" (Elazar, 1972, p. 89).
The linkages between political culture, sectionalism
and frontier are even more carefully drawn by Elazar
in a study of the midwest in which he pays direct
tribute to Turner who

> "saw the twin forces of sectionalism and the
> frontier as the most important sources of
> political, economic, and social development,
> as well as political conflict, in the American
> scheme of things....His search for a socio-
> logical basis for geographically measurable
> political differences in the United States remains
> the starting point for all considerations of the
> place of sectionalism and regionalism in American
> life, particularly in line with the new awareness
> of the influence of geographic differences on
> American society which has developed in recent
> years" (Elazar, 1970, p. 102).

Carrying on in the Turnerian tradition, though with
a new style and object of investigation, Elazar thus
adds the additional theme of cultural differentiation
to Turner's principle themes of section and frontier.
He is able, therefore, to interprete the 'geology'
of American politics as a "product of the interaction
between the frontier process and 'raw' geography"
(Elazar, 1970, p. 102) and to see that:

> "The national political culture is a synthesis of
> three major political subcultures that jointly
> inhabit the country, existing side by side,
> or even overlapping. All three are of nationwide
> proportions, having spread in the course of
> time from coast to coast. At the same time each
> subculture is strongly tied to specific sections
> of the country, reflecting streams and currents
> of migration that have carried people of
> different origins and backgrounds across the
> continent in more or less orderly patterns"
> (Elazar, 1972, p. 93).

The three subcultures have their origins in the
initial three Atlantic seaboard sections identified
at the beginning of the last chapter. In New
England there arose a Yankee culture, termed
'moralistic' by Elazar, which emphasizes community
over individual in the search for public good in
service of the public interest. The Middle Atlantic
section spawned an 'individualistic' culture
emphasising private concerns in a 'businesslike'
conception of politics. Finally, in the Old South
grew up a 'traditional' political culture rooted in a
precommercial attitude that accepts the 'right' of a
social elite to govern.

All three political cultures spread across the
continent from their Atlantic origins, sometimes
altered or augmented by the political views of later
immigrants. The moralistic culture, for example, was
built upon in the northern Midwest by fundamental
Protestant immigrants from northern Europe. The
final result is a mixed pattern of political cultures
across the country, but with a noticeable latitudinal
bias corresponding to the locations of the original

sections (Elazar, 1972, Figures 11, 12 and 13 and
Brunn, 1974, Figure 9-7).

If we accept Elazar's political cultures as a basis
of our political regionalization, we immediately come
across the problem that he does not specifically
identify a particular western culture. In this sense
Elazar departs from Turner's emphasis upon the
western frontier with its distinctive set of
political ideas and relations. Instead, major
features of western politics are interpreted by
Elazar as reflections of the three Atlantic cultures.
Hence, the West's predication for third party revolts
is said to be derived from a blend of the moralistic
culture's attitude toward political parties as
subordinate to principles and the individualistic
culture's emphasis upon private initiative and
reward. More recently, the political rise of the
sun belt has led to emphasis being placed upon
western conservatism as a derivation from Southern
traditionalistic culture. Nevertheless, when Elazar
comes to discuss sections, he returns to a North-
South-West trilogy which we have previously
identified (Elazar, 1972, Figure 14):

> "The nation's sectional alignments are rooted in
> the three great historical, cultural and economic
> spheres into which the country is divided: the
> greater North-East, the greater South and the
> greater West" (Elazar, 1972, p. 122).

Elazar illustrates his three 'spheres' literally as
semicircles drawn on a map of the United States. As
circles, they overlap producing three 'border zones'
through Indiana, Ohio and West Virginia between
Northeast and South, through Illinois and Wisconsin
between Northeast and West, and finally through
Missouri, Arkansas, Oklahoma, and Texas between South
and West. All this seems reasonable as a sketch map
of the situation, but it is hard to accept Elazar's
(1972, p. 122) claim of "nearly perfect accuracy" for
his arbitrary geometric boundaries. We will provide
an alternative methodology for more precisely
describing and measuring the extent of these three
major sections.

Most of the factor analyses carried out in this study employ a T-mode approach so that elections are classified as 'normal votes' and their patterns established over the states. For a regionalization we transpose the procedure into an S-mode approach so that it is the states that are classified with respect to elections: the correlation matrix analysed here is between states, not between elections. Hence, states with similar profiles of support for Democratic candidates over time will tend to be highly correlated and to load on the same factor. In this case we are searching for a region-alization rather than a set of normal votes so that we employ the common factor model with orthogonal rather than oblique rotation (see Appendix A). The output, however, is essentially of the same form irrespective of the factor model used.

Application of the common factor model to the 48 x 48 interstate correlation matrix for elections from 1872 to 1980 produces three dominant factors which between them explain 92.5% of the common variation. This is a very high proportion for so few factors. The original factors have been rotated to simple structure using the Varimax criterion to produce a distinct regionalization. The resulting loadings are shown in Table 3.1, where they are arranged by ranking the states in terms of the factor each loads highest upon. This makes it easy to identify the groups of states associated with each factor. We can see that northern states group on Factor I, southern states on Factor II and most western states on Factor III. Integrating this analysis with our previous discussion of economic sectionalism, we can designate our electoral regions as Northern Core, Southern Periphery and Western Periphery, respectively. The terminology implies that the groups represent more than mere geographical clusters and this neatly accomodates the only spatial discontinuities in our classification which are the allocation of Washington and California to Factor I. Although geographically speaking, they are western states, they have long been more urban than their neighbors and have always been much less of an economic periphery than other western states. Their

Table 3.1   Factor Loadings for S-Mode Analysis:
            1872–1980.

	FACTOR I	FACTOR II	FACTOR III
Connecticut	.95	.03	.10
New Jersey	.93	.19	.15
New York	.92	.04	.20
Pennsylvania	.92	−.08	.26
Maine	.86	−.14	.14
Illinois	.86	.05	.38
Vermont	.84	−.18	.21
West Virginia	.84	.22	.23
New Hampshire	.83	.30	.02
Wisconsin	.83	.00	.36
Michigan	.83	−.12	.43
Massachusetts	.82	−.33	.15
Maryland	.79	.51	.12
Ohio	.78	.22	.43
Rhode Island	.78	−.22	.11
Delaware	.78	.35	.13
Iowa	.77	.05	.48
California	.76	.11	.51
Minnesota	.75	−.22	.51
Washington	.71	.01	.64
Indiana	.61	.59	.37
Missouri	.60	.43	.45
Virginia	.02	.94	.05
Alabama	−.16	.91	.12
Florida	.02	.90	.05
Texas	.08	.89	.25
Tennessee	.27	.88	.18
Louisiana	−.23	.87	.07
North Carolina	.17	.86	.22
Georgia	.02	.86	.12
Arkansas	.12	.83	.37
Mississippi	−.39	.81	.03
South Carolina	−.33	.80	.02
Oklahoma	.34	.76	.49
Arizona	.37	.73	.62
Kentucky	.57	.64	.17
New Mexico	.57	.61	.60

Table 3.1, continued.

	FACTOR I	FACTOR II	FACTOR III
Idaho	.16	.28	.94
Colorado	.05	.16	.94
Nevada	.17	.27	.93
Kansas	.18	.16	.90
Wyoming	.37	.19	.86
Nebraska	.18	.35	.84
South Dakota	.46	−.08	.81
North Dakota	.48	.05	.80
Montana	.38	.27	.78
Utah	.24	.46	.75
Oregon	.60	.03	.71
Sum of squared loadings	17.13	12.30	11.64

incorporation as outliers of the northern core does not seem unreasonable. This leaves the western group much more concerned with primary economic production as its peripheral role would indicate and, hence, this is further consistent with our factor labeling.

This inductive classification into three sections will be used in two ways in our subsequent discussion. In this chapter we will extend our consideration of the functional aspect of the classi- fication from the economic issues already dealt with to the political uses of the country's divisions. In the following chapter the regionalization will be used as the basis for an analyses of Presidential election patterns in each of the sections individ- ually.

Before we apply this discrete regionalization, however, it is worth considering the mixing and merging of the three factors in many of the states. Although the classes are derived by allocating each state to the factor upon which it loads highest, several states load relatively highly on more than one factor. This aspect of the factor analysis out- put allows us to identify overlapping patterns in our

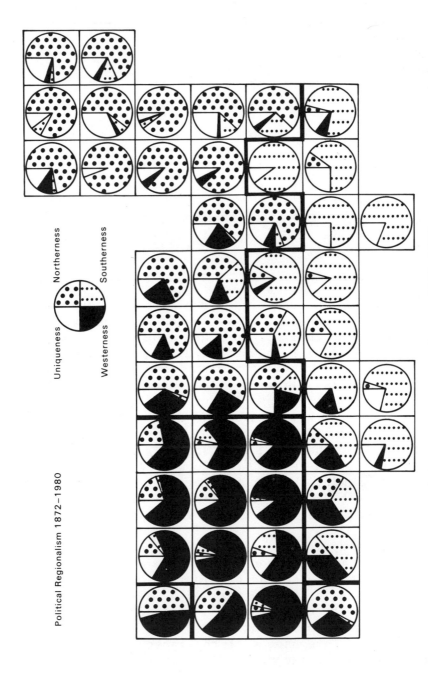

Figure 3.1   The Regionalization of the Polity, 1872-1980

regionalization and we need to discuss this
interesting feature of the analysis.

On Figure 3.1 the total variation in the electoral
response of each state is represented by a circle.
These circles are divided into sections in terms of
the proportion of a state's electoral response which
can be accounted for by each regional factor. These
proportions are easily derived as the squares of the
loadings from Table 3.1 (see Appendix A). The
squares of the loadings on the first factor indicate
the 'northerness' of a state's voting habits and the
'southerness' or 'westerness' can be measured
similarly using second and third factor loadings.
The unshaded portion of each circle indicates the
proportion of electoral variation in a state which is
unaccounted for by the three factors; this unshaded
portion thus represents a state's unshared, or
unique, electoral variation. Regional boundaries
based upon our groups of states in Table 3.1 are also
depicted to relate the overlapping pattern to our
regionalization. These sections are similar to
Elazar's 'greater spheres' but with some important
differences which become even more apparent as we
look at the overlaps.

Factor I defines our northern core and generally
measures northerness in the electoral habits of
states. This factor dominates New England and Middle
Atlantic states and declines in importance westwards
until it reaches a boundary along the middle of the
northern and central plains. In fact, this boundary
neatly separates those eastern plains states which
entered the Union before the Civil War from those
which entered at a later time. The pre-Civil War
states were part of the geographical coalition that
formed the victorious Northern section. Northerness
continues as a significant though not dominant
component into the northern tier of western states
and this seems to reflect the Yankee migration and
spread of the moralistic culture into the Northwest
as described by Elazar (1972). In the two Pacific
states of Washington and California which we have
previously noted as the two most urban of western
states, their northerness is greater than their
westerness which classifies them as outliers of the
northern core.

Along the border with the South, the electoral
response change is much more abrupt, although
northerness does penetrate into Kentucky in the
border South and into New Mexico and Arizona in the
Southwest. In general, therefore, the northerness
factor is the most widespread, producing both the
largest section in number of states, twenty-two, and
the greatest penetration into other sections.

In contrast the Southern periphery factor is far
more concentrated. It dominates the voting pattern
in all the old Confederate States which are ranked
one to eleven on Factor II in Table 3.1 column 2. Of
the border states only Kentucky is allocated to the
South, although Maryland and Missouri have
significant southerness in their voting responses;
also Indiana and, to a lesser extent, Delaware are
partially southern though primarily northern. The
interesting feature of this regionalization is that
the South extends along the Mexican border through
New Mexico to Arizona. This is consistent with
Elazar's description of the spread of Southern
traditionalistic culture through to Arizona. In fact
Arizona was the only western territory to declare
itself part of the Confederacy, leading to the only
significant military action in the West during the
Civil War. The only other western state to show any
southerness in its electoral response is Utah.
Significantly California has very little of its
variation related to the southern electoral response.
This places just fifteen states in our South section
and with southerness being relatively rare in the
remainder of the Union.

Our Western periphery section is the smallest,
consisting of only eleven states. However, the
pattern of westerness extends beyond the sectional
boundaries far more than southerness. Thus both
Washington and California, not surprisingly, have
important western components in their electoral
responses. These non-dominant, but significant
western components, spread over both the boundary
with the northern core and the boundary with the
southern periphery. To the south, Arizona, New
Mexico, Oklahoma, and Arkansas all have important
western components in their electoral habits. In the

northern core an appreciable degree of westerness
can be traced into all of the states of the 'Old
Northwest' from Iowa through to Ohio. Hence, this
analysis is able to distinguish these two pre-Civil
War sections--Northwest and Northeast--in terms of
their post-Civil War degrees of westerness. This
suggests the impressive sensitivity of the technique
which we have employed and justifies our brief
discussion of the overlapping patterns of electoral
habits.

One final point concerning the sectional overlapping needs to be made. On a few occasions
negative loadings occur which can lead to a
misreading of Figure 3.1. For example, Mississippi
has a noticeable northerness component in its
electoral response which may seem somewhat
surprising. In fact a check with Table 3.1 confirms
that Mississippi loads negatively on Factor I so that
in this case the variance explained by this factor
should be interpreted as anti-northerness. The
variance explained by Factor I in Louisiana,
Alabama, and South Carolina as well as Mississippi is
of this same nature. Similarly, the small amounts
of variance accounted for by Factor II in
Massachusetts, Rhode Island, Vermont, Maine,
Michigan, Minnesota, and South Dakota are all based
on negative loadings and, hence, reflect anti-
southerness in electoral habits. Interestingly,
there are no anti-westerness elements in either the
northern core or the southern periphery. Although
these negative patterns seem reasonable in their
interpretation, their importance should not be over-
estimated. Even in Mississippi, only fifteen percent
of the electoral variance is accounted for in this
manner and in the northern state with the highest
anti-southern component, Massachusetts, it accounts
for only eleven percent of that state's variance.
Thus, the main findings of the analysis are three
independent factors which are greatly dominated by
positive loadings defining the northern core,
southern periphery and western periphery. There is
indeed, as Turner once observed, "a geography of
political habit" in the United States which is of
lasting persistence.

The Political Use of Sections

In the discussion so far we have described the
sections that emerged after the Civil War and have
shown how these three regions can be derived
inductively from state voting habits. Hence, there
is a near symmetry between the material base of the
Union and political response in terms of voting for
President. This should not be seen as a necessary or
simply deterministic relationship, however. We
showed in Chapter Two how before the Civil War
sectional economic conflict was actually stifled by a
nonsectional voting pattern. Nevertheless, since the
Civil War, the political patterns do seem to mirror
economic spatial structures and it is this
particular situation which concerns us here.

The three section pattern of core and two peripheries is just one of an infinitely large number of
possible ways in which the United States could be
spatially organized. The emergence of this spatial
structure is a reflection of economic conflicts
mobilized by the political parties into the political
arena. Schattschneider's (1960) view of parties as
managers of conflict was introduced in Chapter One
and we can now relate his ideas to our electoral
regions defined above. His basic thesis is that:

"what happens in politics depends on the way in
which people are divided into factions, parties,
groups, classes, etc. The outcome of the game
of politics depends on which of a multitude of
possible conflicts gains the dominant position"
(Schattschneider, 1960, p. 62, italics in
original).

Hence, it follows that

"Every shift of the line of cleavage affects the
nature of the conflict, produces a new set of
winners and losers and a new kind of result...
every change in the direction and location of
the line of cleavage produces a new majority and
a new allocation of power" (Schattschneider, 1960,
p. 63).

Politics, therefore, consists of the effort to use
latent conflicts by either suppressing or exploiting
them. The breakdown of the second party system
occurred when the parties failed to suppress
sectional conflict and the Republican party emerged
to exploit just that conflict. After the Civil War,
the new majority was to be found in the enlarged
northern section and the new allocation of power was
to be found in the industrial interests of the new
economic core. Similarily, Schattschneider draws the
following conclusion:

"All forms of political organization have a bias
in favor of the exploitation of some kinds of
conflict and the suppression of others because
organization is the mobilization of bias. Some
issues are organized into politics while others
are organized out" (Schattschneider, 1960, p. 70;
italics in original).

The three-section spatial organization can,
therefore, be interpreted as a particular mobilisation of bias. Thus sectionalism is a political
device for submerging rival competing conflicts.
This is exemplified by the way in which the periphery
became divided between South and West to prevent an
alliance against the core. Hence, despite their
similar peripheral economic positions of dependency
in the emerging industrial economy, the northern core
largely succeeded in keeping the periphery divided
and its own power intact. A classic case is provided
by the demise of the agrarian revolts of the late
nineteenth century:

"the use of sharply sectional alignment to destroy
the radical agrarian movement in the 1890's
illustrate the uses to which the sectional
strategy can be put. The revival of sectional
antagonism was used to drive a wedge between the
western and southern branches of the Populist
movement" (Schattschneider, 1960, p. 73).

The resulting "extreme sectionalism" of the first
quarter of the twentieth century was almost the exact

opposite of Van Buren's second party system. In the
last chapter we described the objective of that
system to be a suppression of sectionalism. In
contrast, the new system:

> "was structured not around competition between
> parties, but around the elimination of such
> competition both on the national level and in a
> large majority of the states. The alignment
> pattern was broadly composed of three sub-systems:
> a solidly Democratic South, an almost equally solid
> Republican bastion in the greater Northeast, and a
> quasi-colonial West" (Burnham, 1967, p. 300).

This is, of course, essentially the regionalization
we have identified for the whole period from 1872 to
1980. The fourth party system (1896-1928) represents
the heyday of the influence of that sectional
arrangement in facilitating northern core political
control through the Republican party. Nevertheless,
the same basic pattern of sectional politics was
evident before the fourth party system and has
persisted in various forms right down to the present
day.
  Sectionalism is by no means the only cleavage
exploited in American politics, but it has been
strengthened by its relations with other cultural and
economic cleavages to be used as a basic device in
presidential electoral strategy. As we have
emphasized previously, presidential elections are
about winning states in the Electoral College so that
de jure spatial organization makes de facto sectional
spatial organization a vital consideration. While
previous Republican party managers may have perfected
the sectional strategy three quarters of a century
ago, their modern counterparts are still thinking in
these terms, although the proposed sectional
alliances are somewhat inverted. Hence, Republican
promoter Keven P. Phillips advocates an 'emerging
Republican majority' based upon a sectional alliance
of projected conservative bastions in the West and
Border States along with the 'contingent bastion'
of the South against the Northeastern liberal
establishment (Phillips, 1970, p. 472). Party

strategy may change over time, but the allure of
endeavoring to mobilise some cleavages and to
subordinate others through sectionalism continues.
The resulting shifts in sectional support patterns
are the subject of the analyses which follow.

The Frontier Thesis and the World-Economy

Before we come to consider our quantitative
analyses, there is a final theme underlying the
sectional responses in presidential elections that
requires consideration. In the last chapter we
showed how the early sections developed distinct and
separate relations with the rest of the world-economy
which inevitably led to antagonistic economic
interests and to Civil War. It is now necessary to
continue this story beyond the Civil War through to
the mid-twentieth century when the United States
became a champion of free trade and the leader of a
liberal world economic order.

This mid-twentieth century stance of the United
States is very much at variance with the policy of
the Northern-dominated Federal government during
and after the Civil War. In fact one of the first
acts of the War Congress in 1861 was to institute a
highly protectionist trade policy. This can be
interpreted as a standard semi-peripheral trade
response towards a dominant core state. In this
case, the Republican Party was protecting northern
manufactures from more advanced and efficient manufactures in England. While the policy suited
Northern sectional interests at that time, it was not
so advantageous for the agricultural interests of the
West. The settlement of new lands and the growth of
the railways generated increasing quantities of meat
and grains which flooded on to the market in the
final third of the nineteenth century. There were
two major outlets for this production: the rapidly
expanding urban population of the Northeast and the
European market, particularly Britain. But over the
period, supply was outstripping demand in both
domestic and world markets so that prosperity was
eluding the American West. This was reflected
politically in the third party revolts culminating in
the Populist movement of the 1890's. More important
ultimately, however, was the development of

sectionalism within the major parties as both
Democratic and Republican establishments were
challenged by their 'western wings.'

It was during the economic depression and
political upheavals of the 1890's that Frederick J.
Turner evolved his frontier thesis. It was super-
ficially a pessimistic analysis: the 1890 census had
confirmed the end of free agricultural land so that
the era of the internal frontier had come to an end.
This passing of the frontier was not merely of
historical interest to his contemporaries since
Turner associated the frontier with promoting the
best features of democratic America by serving as a
'safety valve' to maintain social harmony. Turner's
ideas had a direct impact on at least two subsequent
Presidents, Theodore Roosevelt and Woodrow Wilson
(Williams, 1966). Modern historians, however, have
tended to neglect the frontier thesis because of
their narrow interpretation of its content. The
emphasis has been upon a static view of the frontier
concerning such questions as the relations between
frontier society and democracy. Such discussion
seems to have little relevance to twentieth century
urban America (Williams, 1969, pp. xii-xiii). The
practical importance of Turner's ideas, however, was
their spatial dynamic nature--quite simply, the
frontier was the leading zone of expansion.

In a dynamic interpretation of the frontier, there
is no reason to stop at the Pacific Coast. Turner's
thesis should be seen as part of a political literature that condoned American expansionist policy in
the 1890's. At about the same time as Turner's ideas
were receiving widespread currency, Admiral Mahan
was developing geo-political models for America's
future role in the world and Brooks Adams was
explicitly promoting American imperialism. All three
authors adhered to an "expand or stagnate approach to
the American economy" (Williams, 1966, p. 364). In
this context Turner's thesis becomes "the expansionist theory of prosperity and history: expansion
had made Americans democratic and prosperous. The
implication was clear: no more frontiers, no more
wealth and welfare" (Williams, 1966, p. 365). The
"magic escape route" from this depressing scenario

was simple--commercial expansion--and the solution
was becoming more and more relevant to both eastern
and western economic interests:

"The expansion of the frontier by trade into South
America and the Pacific in the 1880's and early
1890's was increasingly associated with the idea
of an ever increasing commercial frontier which
would alleviate discontent at home" (Jones, 1972,
p. 223).

Hence, the western settlement frontier was to be
replaced by a Chinese trading frontier!

The above interpretation of the Turner thesis is
based upon the work of William Appleman Williams
(1966, 1969) whose major contribution has been
to show that the outburst of American imperialism in
the late 1890's was not a brief aberation, but
represents a continuation of a consistent theme of
expansion running throughout American history (Jones,
1972, p. 211). In previous eras large tracts of land
had been bought to prevent the closing of the
frontier and in the 1840's the United States had gone
to war to maintain her territorial expansion. In the
period after the Civil War, western expansionism was
directly linked to finding markets for its surplus
agricultural products. One local observer conceded
that "the western mind is essentially imperial in its
tendencies" (Williams, 1969, p. 370). However,
western interests were not the dominant force in the
federal government so that policies of foreign
expansion were to come to fruition only after more
and more northern industrial interests came to see
the need for expansion to sell their increasing
manufacturing surpluses. America was emerging from
its semi-periphery role in the world economy and
becoming part of the industrial core; in other words,
it was directly raising a challenge to worldwide
British hegemony. This can be first seen in the
1888-1892 Republican administration in which
President Harrison and his Secretary of State Blaine
emphasised market expansion through a trade
reciprocity program over simple protectionism
(Williams, 1969, p. 321). Long term western demands

were becoming consistent with emerging northern
interests so that

> "the expansionist outlook that was entertained and
> acted upon by metropolitan American leaders during
> and after the 1890's was actually a crystallization
> in industrial form of an outlook that had been
> developed in agricultural terms by the agrarian
> majority of the country between 1860 and 1893"
> (Williams, 1969, pp. xvi-xvii).

The United States, therefore, entered the twentieth
century as a major political power in the world
economy based upon its industrial strength
concentrated in the Northern section.
   This new global role of the United States was based
upon a somewhat ambivalent foundation, neatly
summarised by Calleo and Rowland (1973, p. 47):

> "While this imperialism broke with American
> tradition in one sense, it seemed its logical
> completion in another. While the imperialists
> turned from traditional isolationism, they were
> also merely extending overseas the traditional
> American faith in territorial expansion as the
> key to domestic harmony."

In the twentieth century, America has oscillated
between an interventionist and an isolationist
foreign policy. This was presaged by the
imperialist/anti-imperialist debate during the
Spanish War of the 1890's but, as McCormick (1967)
points out, the distinction was more one of tactics
than of goals. Throughout the twentieth century
American foreign policy has aimed at obtaining
American economic leadership of the world economy
although there have been differences of view as to
how that goal can be best achieved.
   Traditional suspicion of formal political
involvement has been strong, especially in the
American West, but this does not mean western
interests have been any less dependent upon the world
economy. The ideal form of economic leadership is
market-based with the most efficient producer (i.e.
America) dominating the world economic order with no

need for any direct external political intervention.
This liberal dream of the isolationists was altered
by the rise of Soviet Russia as a world power since
1945. The resulting reaction has been a mixture of
liberal economics based upon the General Agreement on
Tariffs and Trade (GATT) for the 'free' world and the
geopolitics of containment around the 'communist'
world (Calleo and Rowland, 1973). In terms of
parties and sections, foreign policy has become a
bipartisan and national issue, an instrument for
producing both a decline in party politics and an
impetus to national integration based upon sectional
consensus.

It may be possible, however, to exaggerate the
electoral importance of foreign policy. During his
loosing campaign of 1960 when Nixon endeavored to
defend his Republican predecessor's record in the
foreign policy area against his opponent's "missile
gap" gambit, for example, Nixon was counseled by the
then Governor of Illinois that "You can say all you
want about foreign affairs, but what is really
important is the price of hogs in Chicago and St.
Louis" (Hess, 1972, p. 3). This counsel, of course,
was consistent with a conventional notion that
partisan politics stops at the water's edge.
Nevertheless, according to one observer, international issues played a dominant role in five of the
presidential campaigns conducted between 1952 and
1976 (Hess, 1980, pp. 96-111). The exceptions were
in 1960 when the question of a Catholic in the White
House was prominent and in 1976 when the burden of
Watergate proved too great for the Republican
candidate.

The nonpartisan characteristic of foreign affairs
can also be over stressed, for two reasons. First
what differences as do emerge in Presidential
campaigns of a foreign policy character are capable
of mobolising ethnic cleavages within the electorate.
During both World Wars, for example, Irish Americans
and German Americans frequently found the platform of
one party more appealing than that of the other.
Second, foreign policy initiatives involving international trade may impact different regions
differently and thus come to play a role in electoral

outcomes.   A good example is provided by Carter's
efforts to forge a trade agreement with China on the
eve of popular balloting in 1980.   His trade embargo
of the Soviet Union in the wake of that nation's
incursion into Afghanistan was feared by his advisors
to potentially cost him votes in the American grain
belt; an agricultural trade agreement with China,
therefore, was seen as an antidote in keeping with
the theme of liberal economic expansionism.

THE RISE AND FALL OF THE SECTIONAL NORMAL VOTE
In the last chapter, the rise of the sectional normal
vote was described for comparative purposes with
emphasis upon the preceding nonsectional normal vote.
The sectional normal vote was not then considered in
detail because that analysis was based upon only
twenty-five eastern states and any full discussion of
sectional politics after the Civil War must consider
the added western dimension.   In the analysis
reported below all forty-eight contiguous United
States are utilized for all elections since 1872.
This is the same data employed for the regionalization exercise above which consisted of an S-mode
analysis.   Here we revert to the T-mode so that the
elections become the variables and the states the
objects, as we search for cross-temporal patterns in
the voting profiles of the states.

We have employed a common factor model with oblique
rotation as described in Appendix A and as employed
before in Chapter 2.   The missing data problem was
more important for this data set, since only thirty-
seven states participated in the 1872 election.   The
eleven missing states were reduced to just four by
1892 and by the 1912 election all forty-eight
contiguous states had joined the union.   Hence, the
missing data procedure described in Appendix A was
adopted.

The analysis produced six interpretable factors
which between them explained 92.6% of the total
variation.   The factor pattern loadings after oblique
rotation are illustrated as loading profiles in
Figure 3.2 and specified in the appendix.   As in
Chapter 2 the profile diagram orders the factors, not
in terms of their extraction from the correlation
matrix, but in the order of their time of emergence.

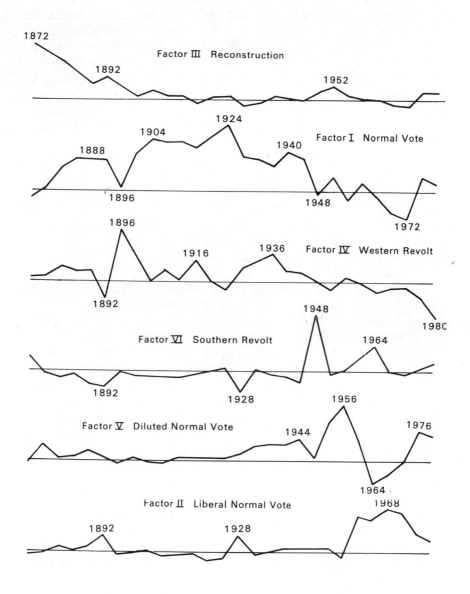

Figure 3.2   Factor Loading Profiles, 1872–1980

From this figure we can name the factors as
follows:

Factor III is clearly a Reconstruction factor which
is similar to the Factor III identified as the
Southern Disenfranchisement-Reconstruction factor in
the analysis of Chapter 2. It seems clear that we
are picking up the tail end of a factor that can be
traced back to the Civil War itself. The addition of
the western states to the analysis thus does not seem
to have affected this factor since it largely
measures a particularly unusual North-South balance
in Democratic support immediately after the Civil
War.

Factor I emerges out of the Reconstruction period
to dominate in all but two years from 1884 to 1944.
This is clearly the most important factor which
obviously qualifies it as identifying a stable normal
vote pattern. We shall see, of course, that it is a
highly sectionalised pattern and so this is the
Sectional Normal Vote that has been so familiar in
American politics.

Factor IV is a minor factor which picks up Western
Revolt when the western states deserted the
Republicans. This is particularly the case in 1896
when Bryan created a southern western Democratic
alliance and it also emerges weakly for Wilson in
1916 as well as for Roosevelt in 1932 and particularly 1936. These are clearly good years for the
Democrats when they obtained western support to add
to their southern periphery. This factor reappears
in 1980 when, in complete contrast to the earlier
pattern, Carter's vote loads negatively, indicating
a new western revolt, this time against the
Democrats.

Factor VI is another minor factor picturing a
Southern Revolt as the South deserted the Democratic
Party in 1948 and to a lesser degree in 1964.
Perhaps surprisingly, the more recent erosion of
Democratic support in the South is not recorded on
the factor.

Factor V represents a rather shadowy reflection of
the sectional normal vote building up gradually
through the Roosevelt elections but only dominating
in the 1950's with the Stevenson-Eisenhower contests

and then again in the first of the Carter elections.
We refer to this as the Diluted Sectional Vote.

Factor II represents a new pattern that emerged in
1960 and continued until Carter reintroduced the
Southern sectional element to the Democrat vote in
1976. This vote pattern seemed to be establishing
itself as a new normal vote before 1976 and we shall
refer to it as the Liberal Normal Vote.

The relationships between these factors is given by
their correlation matrix which is drawn as a 'causal
structure' in Figure 3.3. As in Chapter 2, this
diagram specifies the direction of the correlation
relations using the time sequencing of the factors
(Figure 3.2). Notice how the Sectional Normal Vote
(Factor I) literally stands at the center of the
casual structure. Unlike its equivalent factor in
Chapter 2, the Reconstruction pattern (Factor III)
here is positively correlated with Factor I.
Similarly the Diluted Sectional Vote (Factor V) is
positively related to the Sectional Normal Vote.
Both revolt factors are correlated to the Sectional
Normal Vote, the Southern Revolt (Factor VI)
negatively and the Western Revolt (Factor IV)
positively. Finally, the latter revolt factor is
negatively related to the Liberal Normal Vote
(Factor II) which reflects the conservative alliance
of West and South in the 1960-1972 period. Hence,
the picture our analysis provides is one of a
Reconstruction pattern before the Democratic capture
of the South leading onto the major sectional
normal vote when the South was consolidated behind
the Democrats. From this position of sectional
alliances, there have been brief revolts of West
against Republicans and South against Democrats, the
latter preceding the Diluted Sectional Pattern and
the former being reversed into the Liberal Normal
Vote. The failure of either of these two patterns to
be maintained is the basis for our identification of
a new era of American politics from the breakup of
the sectional normal vote in 1948. The latest two
elections are particularly unusual in that they
indicate throwbacks, 1976 briefly to the 1950's and
1980 to an inverse of 1896! They exemplify the
current volatility of the American electorate which

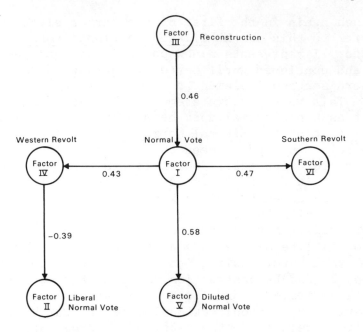

Figure 3.3   Factor Correlations, 1872–1980

is the hallmark of the third 'new politics'
identified at the end of Chapter 1. We develop
this point along with those previously discussed
when we deal with the factors individually in more
detail below.

Although the sequence and timing of the results of
this analysis of elections differs somewhat from the
standard classification into party systems described
in Chapter 1, we will be able to link with that
familiar arrangement on several occasions in our
discussion of the individual factors below.   Before
we do so, however, it is of particular interest to
relate our sequencing with that of Ginsberg (1972)
who has classified party platforms for elections
from 1844 to 1968 in terms of major issues.   Although
he is at pains to show that his results closely
resemble the party system framework, a close look at
his tables indicates a particularly close affinity
with our results.   In terms of the salience of
issues, for example, "there tend to be three clusters
of dominant issues--internal sovereignty, from 1852
to 1868; capitalism from 1872 to 1940; and

international cooperation from 1944 to 1964"
(Ginsberg, 1972, p. 609). This produces a long
period to the 1940's when issues remained based upon
capitalism. Clearly this long sequence is consistent
with our Sectional Normal Vote except for its earlier
start. The consistency between party platforms and
patterns of voting is truly remarkable and supports
our alternative sequencing of elections in contrast
to that of the common party system typology.

Reconstruction Factor
The three Reconstruction Acts of 1867 were passed
over President Johnson's veto by a radical Republican
majority in Congress. These acts provided for
military government in ten of the former eleven
Confederate states. The exception was Tennessee
which had been readmitted to the Union after it
ratified the Fourteenth Amendment, giving blacks
equal protection under the law. These military
governments ordered state conventions to be selected
by electorates including enfranchised blacks, but
excluding the participation of former Confederate
supporters. These conventions produced the state
Reconstruction Acts under which six states were
readmitted to the Union in 1868 and the remaining
four in 1870 (Table 2.1). Hence, by the 1872
presidential election all eleven former Confederate
states cast Electoral College votes once again. This
provides a rationale for utilizing elections
since 1872 in the analyses of this chapter.
   The terms of the new state constitutions meant that
"control of the South passed into the hands of new
coalitions of voters, characterised by their
opponents as 'scalawags' (Southerners who cooperated
with the new regines); 'carpetbaggers' (Northerners
who descended on the South to line their own
pockets); and blacks" (Simpson, 1978, p. 92). In this
manner Republicans were able to temporarily maintain
their control of federal politics using their new
southern supporters. The situation was short-lived,
however. By 1876 'Redeemer' movements had been
successful in several southern states and this led to
disputes concerning Electoral College votes from the
south in the election of Rutherford Hayes. The
result was a deal between southern Democrats and

northern Republicans in which the latter's southern
supporters were effectively ditched to secure Hayes
the election.   In 1876 Republicans still controlled
South Carolina, Louisiana, and Florida, but after
the presidential election compromise of 1877, white
redemption was able to triumph over radical
reconstruction throughout the region.

Factor III of our analysis may be viewed as
capturing the decline of the Reconstruction voting
pattern.   Notice that its profile in Figure 3.2 does
not show any abrupt change about the 1876 or 1880
elections, but suggests a gradual decline as the
sectional normal vote comes to dominate federal
politics in the 1880's.   The Reconstruction pattern
does not finally disappear until the 1890's when the
Populist movement gave a new basis for an anti-
conservative-Democrat alliance in 1892, only to be
absorbed nationally by the Democratic Party in 1896.
Thereafter opposition to the Democratic Party in the
South largely disappeared along with black and much
poor white suffrage.   Hence, like our analysis in
Chapter 2, this factor is consistent with Kousser's
1971 discussion of the establishment of the 'solid
South.'

The gradual changeover from the Reconstruction
pattern to the sectional normal vote is also
consistent with Kleppner's (1979) recent statistical
treatment of the third party system.   He divides this
electoral system into two phases before and after
1872-1873 with the period which we are dealing with
here termed the 'stable phase.'   In this period there
are no major realignments, but there is a distinct
secular trend--"The Democrats tended to gain strength
over time in those parts of the country in which they
had initially been weak" (Kleppner, 1979, p. 25).
Hence, while the Democrats were consolidating their
position in the South, they were also becoming more
competitive in the North and West.   The end result of
such a process could only mean Democratic success at
the federal level, a success so near in 1876 and
finally achieved in 1884 at the commencement of the
sectional normal vote in Figure 3.2.

The pattern that dominated the election of 1872,
but then declined as described by Kleppner is shown

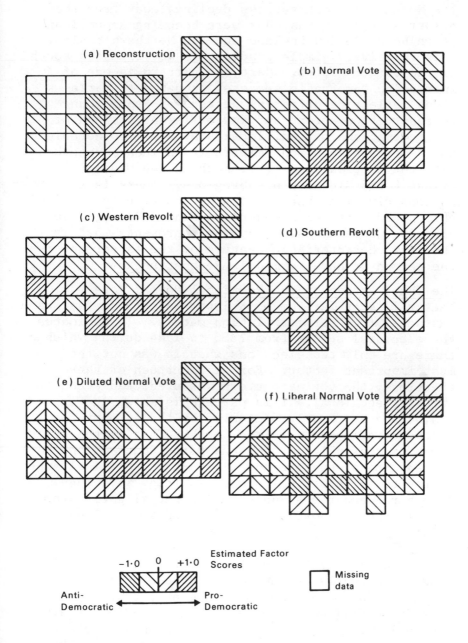

Figure 3.4 Estimated Factor Scores, 1872–1980

by the estimated factor scores in Figure 3.4 (a). In
the North, Democrat success declines away from the
border states towards what were becoming Republican
strongholds in New England and the Northern Plains.
This relatively simple gradient is not repeated south
of the border states. Here the pattern is one of
increasing Democratic success, though with variations reflecting different degrees of Republican
reconstruction effort and the different timings of
the redemptions of individual states. Also notable
is the extent to which Democratic influence extends
into the Northeastern core, both in the Middle
Atlantic and Midwestern subregions. There is an
obvious division, but it does not completely
correspond with the Mason-Dixon line. Hence, this
blurring of sectional cleavages represents what is
the most characteristic feature of the factor and is
the reason we have termed it <u>Reconstruction</u>.

<u>The Three Phases of the Sectional Normal Vote</u>
Factor I is by far the most important of the factors
extracted from our correlation matrix. It dominates
the electoral series from 1880 to 1944 during which
there are only two elections when it was not the
most important factor. For all fourteen of these
elections, the voting pattern was predictable and
strongly sectional. This pattern is shown in Figure
3.4(b) and is clearly dominated by the strength of
the Democratic Party in the South. This is the solid
South, par excellence, the one party South which
seemed such a separate and distinctive political sub-
system to all political observers (e.g. Key, 1949).
Elsewhere Democrat support varies but slightly from
lows in the far north, especially in New England.
    This familiar pattern was not consistently high
throughout the 1884-1944 period, however. Three
phases can be identified (Figure 3.2). An initial
phase is abruptly halted by the 1896 election after
which the factor becomes more dominant through to
1924 to be followed by a period when loadings again
show a lower level to 1944. These phases relate to
the previous identifications of party systems, the
early phase coinciding with the final stages of the
third party system, the high loadings phase with the

fourth party system and the final phase with the beginnings of the fifth party system as described in Chapter One. We will treat each phase in turn.

   The three elections preceding 1896 form a small subset during which the Democrats finally secured the fruits of a secular voting trend in their favor as described under the Reconstruction factor. With Grover Cleveland, they won two of the three elections, as they were able to build a successful electoral alliance upon a southern base plus competitive northern and western intrusions. This success floundered in the depression of the 1890's with President Cleveland repudiated by his own party in 1896 when the Democrats adopted William Jennings Bryan as their candidate. This election is clearly important as it abruptly ended the brief Democrat hegemony and led to the Republicans becoming the normal 'in-party.'

   From 1900 to 1924 the high plateaux of loadings represents Republican dominance as the Democrats were largely contained in their southern stronghold. The highest loadings exactly match the three disaster years for the Democrats of 1904, 1920, and 1924. This is the period of non-competition par excellence. The voting is highly sectional and comes to resemble three separate subsystems--a conservative Democratic South, a conservative Republican North and a progressive Republican West. The only Democratic victor of this period was Woodrow Wilson who succeeded in 1912 because the Republicans split and Theodore Roosevelt stood as a Progressive. Wilson's subsequent success in 1916 coincides with the low point in the profile loadings of this period and also reflects, though to a lesser degree, the Western Revolt factor discussed below.

   The third phase of the sectional normal vote begins in 1928 and continues until 1944. This is a second lower phase which again reflects a brief Democratic hegemony. Although the Republicans won the 1928 contest, that year did represent a recovery for Democrats especially in the North. This is a critical election according to Key (1955), an 'Al Smith revolution' which preceded Franklin D. Roosevelt's successes from 1932 onwards. The final

four sectional normal vote contests all represent
Democrat successes under Roosevelt's leadership, but
notice how Democratic success in this period is also
based upon the Western Revolt factor which actually
loads highest in 1936.

Since our sectional normal vote pattern covers
elections which critical election theory allocates to
three different party systems, we should consider how
our analysis matches existing theory at this stage.
First, as far as 1896 is concerned, our analysis
suggests a breakup of the sectional normal vote and
its replacement by what we have termed the Western
Revolt pattern. Since this is a separate factor, we
will discuss it in some detail under the next
heading. The break between the fourth and fifth
party systems is less dramatic but is nevertheless,
discernable from our analysis as we have seen.
Whether this highlights a critical election or a
series of critical elections seems doubtful, however.
Lichtman (1976) has carried out a careful correlation
analysis at the county level for the period and
concludes that:

"No election between 1916 and 1940 qualifies as a
critical election, and taken together these
presidential elections form a more intricate
pattern than is predicted by critical election
theory" (Lichtman, 1976, p. 320).

Instead of just comparing consecutive pairs of
elections, Lichtman considers the whole correlation
matrix and finds no two-fold division about 1928/1932
using an elementary linkage analysis. At the state
level we can extend his correlation comparisions
where we find that the two elections most related to
1928 are 1888 and 1944 (both r = +0.82). Clearly
1928 does not represent any new pattern, but merely
the return of Democratic competitiveness in the north
as occurred in the early (e.g. 1888) and the later
sectional normal vote (e.g. 1944) phases. Hence, we
can concur with Lichtman (1976, p. 341) when he
concludes that "The clash between Al Smith and
Herbert Hoover does not resemble a presidential
contest in which a basic realignment of the

electorate was taking place." Lichtman (1976)
suggests that perhaps 1928 should be classified as a
deviating election (p. 330), but later argues that it
"represents a return to more usual patterns of
political allegiance that had been disrupted in 1920
and 1924" (p. 330). Lichtman (1976) concludes that
the voting pattern is too intricate for critical
election theory to describe; we would argue that it
is not the complexity of election responses that is
the problem, but the particular form of the theory.
At the level of the state, the pattern is relatively
simple: 1928 does bring a change, not a major
realignment, but a change in the balance of the
sectional normal vote into what we have termed its
third phase.

To summarise, the sectional normal vote straddles
three generally acknowledged party systems which
coincide, not with major realignments, but with
changes in sectional balances between the parties.
The first and third phases represent Democratic
hegemony as they became competitive outside the
South while the second phase represents sectional
voting at its extreme and coincides with Republican
control of federal politics "by the insulation of
industrial elites from the threat of effective,
popularly-based 'counter-revolution'" (Burnham,
1967, p. 284). The third phase coincides with a
resurgence of Democratic hegemony owing to the
stresses of the Great Depression.

Revolts of the Peripheries

In the last chapter our factor analysis did not
identify 1896 as a particularly significant election.
In the earlier factor loading profiles, 1896 is
represented as a minor hiccup in the Sectional Normal
Vote (Figure 2.5). As we noted, the importance of
1896 cannot be assessed from an analysis of just
eastern states. We can see the validity of this
argument in the way 1896 is portrayed by our
continental-wide analysis. The 1896 contest
represents a complete break in the sectional normal
vote pattern in which it is replaced by a new factor
which we have termed Western Revolt. The pattern of
factor scores is shown in Figure 3.4(c). The voting
alignment is no less sectional than the pattern it

interrupted, but it does involve an alternative
sectional alliance. Quite simply we have a dichotomy
of the core versus both peripheries. Republicans are
contained in their northern strongholds and
especially in New England, while the Democrats weld
an agrarian coalition incorporating support in the
southern and western peripheries. This is clearly a
potentially dangerous threat to the Republican Party
and its industrial backers. In 1896 William Jennings
Bryan increased the Democratic vote won by Cleveland
in 1892 by over a million, but he still narrowly lost
to William McKinley because of an unusually high
voter turnout. The alliance was shortlived, however,
for by 1900 the sectional normal vote reappeared
even though the candidates remained unchanged. As we
have previously indicated, this is a vital period in
American politics and we will consider the circumstances surrounding these elections in some detail.

In 1892 the Democratic Party was successful in
electing Grover Cleveland to a second, though nonconse-
cutive, term. At the same election, however, General
Weaver, the Populist candidate, polled a million
votes and won four western states at the expense of
the Republicans (Taylor and Johnston, 1979, pp. 142-
144). Cleveland's administration was soon in
difficulties precipitated by an economic depression,
and the President's laissez-faire, pro-business
attitudes soon elicited the formation of a coalition
of radical opponents. In the 1894 midterm
Congressional elections, the Democratic Party
suffered its heaviest-ever defeat. This presaged
what was to become a Republican dominance of
Congressional politics across the next generation
(Hollingsworth, 1963, p. 17). The major electoral
conflict centered around the President's repeal of
the Sherman Silver Purchase Act returning the United
States to a purely gold-based currency. This
produced the new, often intraparty, sectional
alliances which were to appear in the next
presidential election of 1896; according to
Hollingsworth (1963, p. 28):

"In both houses the Democrats had divided upon
sectional lines. Most of the agrarian South and

West had allied in opposition...members from the
industrial North and East, with rare exceptions
sided with the President....The basis for new party
alignment was slowly evolving."

Hollingsworth (1963, p. 29) goes on to argue that
"William Jennings Bryan and the free silver heresy of
1896 did not contribute as much as is generally
assumed to party division," but there is no doubt
that the rejection of Cleveland and the nomination of
Bryan by the Democrats crystallized in organizational
form the incipient peripheral alliance of previous
years. This alliance was most explicitly expressed
by the adoption of Bryan to be also the People's or
Populist Party candidate. The joint nomination
produced a major reaction from northern sectional
interests, who branded Bryan with terms of disap-
probation ranging from socialist to the devil
himself. Newspapers reacted with "the most widespread shift of party allegiance in the history of
presidential elections" (Hollingsworth, 1963, p. 61).
Bryan, 'the people's candidate,' took to the campaign
trail in the first of the continental-wide whistle-
stop tours as "The convenience of the modern railway
now made it possible for him to use his voice to make
a personal appeal to the people throughout the
country" (Hollingsworth, 1963, p. 85). His secretary
estimated that he spoke 60,000 to 100,000 words in
making up to thirty-six speeches per day during the
campaign (Hollingsworth, 1963, p. 86). Sundquist
(1973, p. 143) added this up to represent a personal
campaign trail of 18,000 miles addressing between
three and five million people. In fact it was more
of a crusade than a campaign.
   Although Bryan finally lost, he did produce a new
distinctive national voting pattern and is usually
viewed as herald of the arrival of the fourth party
system. For instance, Sundquist (1973, p. 143)
argues that "the election of 1896 was a realigning
one, not simply a deviating election. A major shift
in party allegiance remained." Similarly Kleppner
(1979, p. 19) produces the following standard
argument:

"The fourth party system, from 1893 to about 1932,
emerged from the incapacity of the third system
to accomodate the emergent demands of the cash-
crop agrarians of the South and West coupled with
the onset of an urban-industrial depression in
early 1893."

Although the depression eased after McKinley's term
of office began, it is not at all clear why the
sectional alliance of 1896 disappeared so quickly.
From our analysis, 1896 is very definitely a
deviating election since it appears to be based on an
electoral pattern different from both previous and
subsequent elections. This simple fact has been
widely recognized, but its importance has not been
fully appreciated. For instance, Hollingsworth
(1963, p. 185) describes the 1900 election as a
return to past patterns:

"the Democrats had regained strength in most of
the nation's cities....Meanwhile the G. O. P.
regained strength in the traditionally Republican
areas of the Rocky Mountains, the Pacific Coast,
the wheat belt, and the rural areas of the East."

Even Sundquist (1973, pp. 151-153) describes a return
to pre-1896 presidential election patterns so that
"the new line of cleavage established in 1896 by no
means supplanted the old...the regional party system.
..rather than being weakened by the new upheaval, was
reinforced."
    There are clearly difficulties of interpretation
here. It is simply incorrect to assert, as Sundquist
(1973, p. 144) does, that "The 1896 election was the
first to be fought out along the new line of
cleavage." The election of 1896 must be classified
as a deviating election. The interesting election
then becomes that of 1900 which was truly remarkable
in reversing the 1896 upheaval and in actually
reinforcing the earlier sectional normal vote. In
the past most research has concentrated upon the
spectacular election of 1896. Our interpretation
points to 1900 as the key election--how did the
Republican Party manage to resist the Democrats in

the West while consolidating their own dominance in
the North? This major feat of electoral management
has been under researched due to an enormous emphasis
upon 1896 which continues in the literature. Let us,
therefore, attempt some sort of beginning to an
explanation of the startling reversal toward
sectional normal voting in 1900.

Discussion of the 1896 election has focused upon
the silver versus gold debate which clearly separated
the two candidates. This was the way in which the
sections' different interests in the world-economy
were articulated at this point in time. The silver
campaign actually amounted to an economic nationalism
whereby the "American goldbugs" were seen "as the
willing accomplices of British control of the world
marketplace" (Williams, 1969, p. 306). Thus "Silver
was vital because it would place the farmers of the
South and Northwest upon equal footing in the market
of the world" (Williams, 1969, p. 364). However, as
merely an expression of economic nationalism, the
silver issue could be successfully defeated with new
prosperity based upon other forms of economic
nationalism. Hence, McKinley emphasised reciprocity
to replace protection as the international stance of
the Republicans in the election of 1896. In office
this produced the imperialism of 1898 discussed above
and the Open Door Notes of 1899 which formed the
basis of American trading policy for the first half
of the twentieth century. This policy was enough to
divert Western interests away from Bryan's silver
policy, as the Republican administration no doubt
anticipated: "In approaching the problems of the
new political economy, McKinley laid great stress on
ending social unrest and on the relationship between
overseas economic expansion and domestic prosperity"
(Williams, 1966, p. 362).

And so it came about that 'social imperialism'
produced a reversal of the 1896 pattern:

"It was no accident that a jingoistic spirit became
particularly intense in the same regions in which
the demands for agrarian reforms had recently been
so pronounced and in which a discontented constituency, frustrated by Bryan's defeat, was vociferous.

Many agrarians discouraged in their struggle for
domestic reforms, embraced the opportunity to
carry their crusading ardor to the Cuban battlefield, when the conflict was viewed as a struggle
between tyranny and popular rule....Just as the
agrarians of the West and South were disposed to
see themselves as underdogs in their own country,
they viewed the Cubans as the oppressed victims
of Spanish tryanny" (Hollingsworth, 1963,
pp. 130-131).

Thus, it was easily enough for the West, the home of
the frontier-expansionist thesis, to be brought back
into the Republican fold and for the South to return
to its conservatism in continued support for the
Democrats. Bryan briefly campaigned on an anti-
imperialist platform in 1900. But he got little
response and so returned to the dead issue of silver
as the route to the world's markets. So, the
sectional normal vote was reinstated and, thence,
reinforced by a return to economic prosperity which
followed the election.

The Western Revolt factor did not entirely
disappear in 1900, however. Elements of a West-South
peripheral coalition reappeared briefly in 1916 and
again in the early Roosevelt years when the factor
again managed to overcome the sectional normal vote
in importance in 1936 (Figure 3.2). This reflects
nationally popular Democratic candidates who were
able to maintain the solid Southern Democratic base
and to gain support from the West. It is in the
presence of this factor for these years that we can
find the reasons for Lichtman's (1976) difficulties
in classifying these elections based upon simple
correlations:

"The presidential election of 1916 would present
a perplexing classification problem for any devotee
of critical election theory. Only the Democratic
vote of 1936 better forecasts Democratic voting in
1940 and only the Democratic vote of 1932 better
forecasts Democratic voting in 1936....Perhaps
critical election theory requires us to argue that
1916 actually began the New Deal era of American
politics" (Lichtman, 1976, p. 333).

The election years referred to by Lichtman all contain some element of Western protest in their voting patterns and this would seem to be why 1916 appears so like the Roosevelt elections.

This is an appropriate point to recall the methodological argument of Chapter One. A simple correlation analysis just allows one to make pair-wise comparisons and, in this case, to become somewhat perplexed. A factor analysis, on the other hand, extracts patterns of common variance from a matrix of correlations so that for each election different components of variance can be identified. In order to solve Lichtman's queries, we need to have identified two patterns underlying these elections, something which simply cannot be achieved in a simple correlation study. This is a neat example of the advantages of our factor analysis methodology.

Finally we must make a brief comment on 1980 as an "inverse" example of the western revolt factor. As noted in the preface, the attractiveness of Reagan for the western electorate produced a disaster for the Democrats in that region equivalent to their lean years at the height of the sectional normal vote. Unlike that period, however, and despite his southern credentials, Carter did not have a solid southern base of Democratic support. Hence the election is represented as a reversal of 1896—a Western and Southern revolt from the Democrats. This election belongs to a different election era, however, and will be discussed more fully below and particularly at a sub-national level in the next chapter.

The second peripheral revolt also illustrates the utility of our factor analysis approach. The sectional normal vote is abruptly brought to an end in 1948 by what we have termed the Southern Revolt factor. Most studies of American elections do not identify 1948 as especially significant. A major exception is the work of Ladd and Hadley (1978) who identify 1948 explicitly as the 'first rending' of the New Deal coalition producing "a major local transformation...from which there has been no recovery" (p. 135). This election is particularly important for our analysis in that it represents the

first and vital break in the continuous Southern
support for the Democratic Party following
Reconstruction.

Of course, the Dixiecrat revolt of 1948 is well-
known. Southern Democrats protested against civil
rights policy at the 1948 Democratic convention and
withdrew to nominate J. Strom Thrumond as a States
Rights candidate. In the ensuing election Harry
Truman was able to win without the traditional solid
South core of Democratic support. As we can see from
the loading profile (Figure 3.2) this effectly
terminated the sectional normal vote but failed to
become established as anything more than a 'revolt'
factor--the only other appreciable loading relates to
Barry Goldwater's Southern Republican successes in
his 1964 defeat.

The pattern of the factor scores for the Southern
Revolt are shown in Figure 3.4(d). Across sections a
rather heterogeneous set of outcomes in the sections
are illustrated. The South is particularly divided,
but elsewhere other divisions reflect Western and
Northern gains for the Democrats. However, as for
the Western Revolt, no permanent or long lasting
alliances appear to have been forged as a result.

Since this factor is particularly relevant to the
South, we will discuss the effects of 1948 and their
impact on the South in more detail in our separate
analysis of that section in the next chapter. What
is of interest from a national perspective, however,
is the general failure to identify 1948 as an
important election. Many observers have accepted
that the fifth party system, which was supposed to
start in 1928 or 1932, had become modified by the
1960's. But they have been too concerned with seeing
whether each succeeding election was critical
(Sunquist, 1973, ix), rather than looking to 1948 and
to the dramatic change in sectional alliances that it
involved. Burnham (1967, p. 303) comes close to our
position when he argues that "There is much reason
for subdividing the fifth party system into parts at
about the year 1950." Before 1950 he refers to as
the 'New Deal proper' which indicates that Burnham is
bracketing Truman with Roosevelt in terms of their
policies. The crucial difference is of course that

Roosevelt could keep the South in his electoral
coalition in a way that Truman could not. Quite
simply, 1948 represents the end of the sectional
normal vote and ushers in a new era of federal
politics. The main reason why this has not been
generally appreciated seems to be no more profound
than sectional intellectual myopia--non-southern
white investigators have not been capable of looking
beyond their parochial perspective and admitting that
Southern Revolt could have long-term federal
political implications. Our factor analysis has
rectified this shortsightedness.

The New Volatility
     It is perhaps ironic that the modern era of
politics, when every election is thoroughly scrutinized by a whole army of political scientists and
sociologists, should exhibit none of the regularity
of earlier periods. The result has been that the
search for order in modern elections has been
distinctive for its lack of success. Burnham (1967,
p. 304) has summed up the situation:

   "The period since 1950 may legitimately be
   described as one of great confusion in American
   party politics, a period in which the classic New
   Deal alignment seems to have evaporated without
   being replaced by an equally structured ordering
   of politics."

Hence, the continuing quadrennial search for a new
critical election in every presidential outcome since
Key introduced the concept in 1955.
     One of the major reactions by political scientists
to this situation has been quite subtle: If party-
voting will not behave in a predictable way, let us
declare a realignment without parties! This idea
draws its main inspiration from the work of Walter
Dean Burnham on party decomposition which started
with an article in 1969 simply entitled "The End of
American Politics." This has been followed up by
books such as Broder's (1979) The Party's Over and by
student readers such as Fishel's (1978) collection of
articles entitled Parties and Elections in an Anti-
Party Age in which he informs us "That we live in an

'anti-Party Age' is beyond doubt" (p. xi).   The
clearest statement of the thesis has come from
Burnham (1975, p. 308):

> "The American electorate is now deep into the most
> sweeping transformation it has experienced since
> the Civil War.   It is undergoing a critical
> realignment of radically different kind from any in
> American electoral history.   This critical
> realignment, instead of being channeled through
> political parties as in the past, is cutting
> across older partisan linkages between rulers and
> ruled.   The consequence is an astonishingly rapid
> dissolution of the political party as an effective
> intervenor between the voter and the objects of
> his vote at the polls."

A wide range of evidence has been used to support
the argument with the most widely cited being a
decline of registered party supporters and an
increase in the number of registered independents.
This is sometimes seen as a product of "the international emergence of the United States as an
imperium" (Burnham, 1967, p. 305) since the 1940's,
coinciding with the rise of nonpartisan foreign
affairs as major political issues (Ginsberg, 1972).
Clearly if elections become more about international
matters and contested on the basis of a bipartisan
foreign policy debate, the salience of party must
inevitably decline.   In presidential elections this
has been most obviously reflected in the growing
tendency towards ticket-splitting.   Minor office
candidates can no longer expect election on the
coattails of a party's Presidential candidate.
Hence, while several recent presidential elections
have involved landslide victories (e.g. 1964 and
1972), these have not been reflected in the
concurrent Congressional elections.   Clearly voters
have been saying that what is good for America in
terms of party is not necessarily good for their
local district or state.
    The decline of party thesis must be linked to the
impact that the Michigan school's American Voter has
had upon electoral studies.   As was briefly

described in chapter one, this report concentrated
upon the individual voter and found him or her to
have negligible knowledge or interest in politics.
It may well be, however, that this very influential
finding is peculiar to the period in which the study
was carried out. The 1950's were an unusual period
with Eisenhower being viewed as 'virtually
nonpartisan' (Margolis, 1977). This offered little
basis to choose between the parties in an era
dominated by Cold War politics; it is not surprising
that voters surveyed then should seem
'nonideological.' However, Pomper (1972) has been
able to show that since 1956 voters have increased
their awareness of differences between parties on
major issues so that "By 1968 each of the two parties
seemed to have a much clearer identity." In simple
terms, the Democrats were becoming identified as more
liberal and the Republicans as more conservative.
This perception was heightened by party switches such
as the liberal New York Republican John Lindsey to
the Democrats and the conservative Texas Democrat
John Connolly to the Republicans. Certainly within
the Republican Party there were forces operating to
create a new conservative alliance under the
Republican banner (Phillips, 1970). However, in
1972 the overwhelming Republican victory of Richard
Nixon seems to have obscured these trends (Margolis,
1977), and the candidature of Jimmy Carter in 1976
and 1980 has further prevented a simple conservative-
liberal party distinction from developing.

   Nevertheless, we suggest that it is far too early
to write off political parties to the degree that
Burnham's thesis implies. That the link between
party identification and voting is much more
complicated, especially in presidential elections,
cannot be doubted. It is equally true, however, that
parties do remain very important elements of the
American political universe. Presidential contests
are still events dominated by two candidates
representing and being nominated by the two major
parties. This has been highlighted by the complete
failure of John Anderson's candidature in 1980.
Despite both major parties seemingly nominating
vulnerable candidates, Anderson was able to make very

little headway in his campaign and was soundly beaten
in every state. The number of independent voters may
have risen, but American presidential elections are
still solidly two-party affairs.

From the perspective of our analyses, the decline
of party has not been accompanied by any dissolution
of sectional spatial structure. The simple sectional
normal vote may have disappeared, but it has not been
replaced by some sort of pseudo-random spatial
arrangement. American politics has remained
sectional although this has been expressed in new
ways. In 1964, for instance, the South as a section
supported Goldwater and in 1980 the West as a section
rejected Jimmy Carter. Certainly professional
political organisers continue to think in sectional
terms. Phillips (1970) has described a sectional
strategy for the Republicans which essentially allies
the West and South and Hamilton Jordan formulated a
successful alternative sectional strategy for Carter
in 1976 which was more concerned with forging a North-
South alliance (Wayne, 1980, pp. 164-165). Both of
these recent campaign plans continue a long history
of sectional thinking that has been traced in some
detail from 1932 by Raymond Tatalovich (1979).
Hence, the new Volatility of American politics
incorporates sectional responses; it does not
eradicate them. With this point in mind, we can now
return to our factor analysis and its treatment of
the post 1948 period.

The sectional normal vote has not been succeeded by
a single new arrangement that we could positively
identify as a new normal vote pattern. On the other
hand, the volatility of the current period is not
expressed as a series of single election factors
either. The eight elections since 1948 are largely
divided between two new factors (Figure 3.2), one of
which seems to reflect an attempt to rebuild the
sectional normal vote and another which seems to be
genuinely new. The Diluted Sectional Vote (Factor V)
covers the first two elections of the period plus the
1976 election. The pattern of factor scores is
shown in Figure 3.4(e) and it can be seen to be a
rather pale reflection of the earlier sectional
voting (Figure 3.4(b)). The South remains

pro-Democrat, but not as strongly as before, while
the West becomes equally strong for the Republicans.
The North seems to hold the balance between these two
sections. This sectional arrangement was developed
in the 1950's as the candidature of Eisenhower
generated a brief period of Republican success
harking back to the sectional alliances of the
Republican heyday at the height of the sectional
normal vote. In 1976 Carter, as a southern
Democratic candidate was able to regain the South so
that his successful candidacy loads highest on this
factor. However, this was only a temporary effect as
the 1980 results have shown.

The final factor in our analysis covers the period
1960 to 1972 and did seem to be turning into a new
normal vote. We are terming Factor II the Liberal
Normal Vote to indicate its success in sustaining a
single pattern over four consecutive elections
(Figure 3.2). It coincides with a move towards
liberalism within the Democratic Party in the 1960's
(Pepper, 1972) which resulted in the erosion of their
old southern base. The pattern of factor scores is
shown in Figure 3.4(f) and shows the Democrats to do
best in the North, worst in the South and with the
West lying somewhere in between. It is an impressive
factor since it encompasses two landslide victories
in opposite directions--1964 and 1972. Clearly a
pattern was emerging, but stable levels of voting had
not been achieved. Perhaps a better label would have
been 'volatile normal vote' which links in well with
Burnham's decline of party argument. Whatever
interpretation is preferred, the pattern was
terminated as the main factor by Carter in 1976, as
we have previously indicated.

The 1976 pattern of a diluted normal vote was
clearly exceptional. We can perhaps interpret the
1976 election as representing the death throes of
Democratic support in the South at presidential
elections. In 1980, against all early expectations,
even Carter lost the South except for his home state
of Georgia. The result was perhaps the epitomy of
the volatility of the current era of politics
producing a very new pattern of presidential voting.
However, something akin to Reagan's success was

predicted a decade ago by Phillips (1970) in his
conservative alliance of West and South. We may
expect future elections to reflect alternative
sectional alliances as the Democrats attempt to
rebuild a liberal normal vote allying North and West
(which they managed for Factor II) while the
Republicans attempt to consolidate the conservative
West-South alliance of Ronald Reagan. Notice that
this scenario moves the western section into the
centre of the federal political stage as the two
older eastern sections merely function as alternative
allies for the West. This emphasizes the
distinctiveness of the new federal politics and the
decline of the North as the dominant section. In
fact, 1980 represents the first presidential election
in which both major candidates came from the other
two sections. This left the North to be directly
represented only by the candidature of the unsuccessful independent John Anderson from Illinois. We
may even tentatively suggest that Anderson represents
the first signs of a 'northern revolt!' Such issues
and their relationship to the rise of the sun belt
and decline of the North are discussed more fully in
the next chapter.

CHAPTER 4
Voting Structures within the Sections

All of our analyses so far have been concerned with
how sectional cleavages interact to produce national
voting structures. Often, however, patterns
encountered at one scale of analysis are found to be
altered or absent at another (Alker, 1969; Schwirian,
1972; Johnston, 1978). This is probably true of the
American polity since it is, as Elazar (1972, p. 3)
observed, both "a system and a system of systems."
One manifestation is the process for selecting a
President, some of the characteristics of which were
discussed in the second chapter. From the beginning,
it was intended that presidential elections be
federal rather than national events. Since the
process has been formally altered by Constitutional
amendment only once, in 1804, it is still the case
that (Wayne, 1980):

> "The most significant strategic aspect of the rules
> of the game is the method of aggregating electoral
> votes...In building their electoral majorities,
> candidates begin from positions of strength, move
> to areas in which they have some support, and
> compete in most of the big states regardless of the
> odds."

The electoral gains to be had from capturing large
states has always been evident to presidential
candidates. There has been controversy, however,

over how these gains are best evaluated. Brams and
Davis (1974), for example, argued that the relative
impact of two states can be indexed by the quotient
of their Electoral College votes to the 3/2's power.
This exponential relationship has been challenged
(Colantoni, Levesque and Ordeshook, 1974), but Brams
(1978, p. 114) contends that presidential candidates'
distributions of campaign effort has closely matched
the 3/2's allocation rule during recent elections.

Controversy over the exact functional form of
Electoral College influence has partially overshadowed the relevance of other considerations. Two
of these are particularly pertinent. First,
electoral votes are captured on a "winner-take-all"
basis by state so that candidates are encouraged to
emphasise competitive over safe states in allocating
campaign resources (Wayne, 1980). Second, while
states are formally independent units under the
Electoral College system, popular voting patterns are
regionalized into the sectional voting structure
uncovered by the S-mode analysis of the last chapter.
As a consequence, campaign activities and campaign
promises aimed at one state within a section are
likely to generate support from other states of the
same section, but may also reduce support from states
within other sections. The existence of a sectional
voting structure has been pragmatically understood by
practicing politicians with the result that campaign
effort in recent presidential elections has typically
been allocated as follows (Tatalovich, 1979, p. 493):

"Both Democrats and Republicans give first and
second priority to, respectively, the Northeast and
the Midwest. Less important and with equal ranking
are the West and South for the Republicans, but the
South ranks third and the West fourth for the
Democrats."

The sections thus acknowledged by the participants
themselves correspond, with the joining of the Northeast and Midwest, to those formally uncovered within
the last chapter in general outline. Even within
sections, however, there may be variations in
electoral response, since, as Kleppner (1979, p. 28)

recently noted, it is a characteristic of the
American electorate that "The parts are not simple
microcosims of the whole; the sectional patterns are
not reflections of some larger national pattern." The
purpose of this chapter, therefore, is to examine the
character and extent of intrasectional electoral
variations as they contrast with one another and with
the national electoral structure identified in the
last chapter.

The sections employed in the subnational analyses
are those established through the S-mode factor
analysis discussed previously (Table 3.1 and Figure
3.1). The procedure once again involves T-mode
factor analysis with oblique rotation on Democratic
voting proportions, but applying it only to states
within each of the three sections in turn. In this
fashion each section is treated as a separate universe
for analytical purposes so that its specific voting
structure can be independently identified. Figure 4.1
shows the states included in each section.

The sectional analyses start with the election of
1896, rather than that of 1872. There are several
major reasons for this. First, this beginning point
corresponds with the South-West peripheral alliance
which briefly flashed into existence just before the
turn of the century only to be quickly supplanted by
the resurgence of the sectional normal vote in its
strongest national phase. Thus by starting the
subnational analysis in 1896, we are able to focus
upon what happens to the Southern and Western revolts
at a sectional scale and to examine the different
forms that the breakup of the sectional normal vote
develops in each of the sections. Second, by
restricting attention to the sections as they have
existed since the close of the Western frontier,
their electoral structures in the modern metropolitan
and industrial era are given emphasis in close
analogy with the "Funnel of Causality" concept
developed by the authors of The American Voter
(Campbell, et.al., 1960). Third, the data set parti-
tions used minimize the significance of several
technical problems which are encountered when factor
analysis is applied to data matrices with missing
observations or fewer cases than variables (see

(a) Southern Periphery

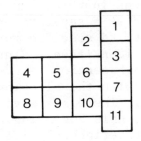

1 Kentucky
2 Virginia
3 Tennessee
4 North Carolina
5 Arizona
6 New Mexico
7 Oklahoma
8 Arkansas
9 Mississippi
10 Alabama
11 Georgia
12 South Carolina
13 Texas
14 Louisiana
15 Florida

(b) Western Periphery

1 North Dakota
2 Montana
3 South Dakota
4 Oregon
5 Idaho
6 Wyoming
7 Nebraska
8 Nevada
9 Utah
10 Colorado
11 Kansas

(c) Northern Core

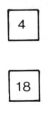

6 Wisconsin
7 Michigan
8 New York
9 Connecticut
10 Rhode Island
11 Massachusetts
12 Iowa
13 Illinois
14 Indiana
15 Ohio
16 Pennsylvania
17 New Jersey
18 California
19 Missouri
20 West Virginia
21 Maryland
22 Delaware

1 Vermont
2 New Hampshire
3 Maine
4 Washington
5 Minnesota

Figure 4.1   Cartograms for Analyses Within Sections

Appendix A).   The sectional results are examined in
this order: Southern Periphery, Western Periphery,
and Northern Core.

SOUTHERN PERIPHERY: FROM STABILITY TO VOLATILITY
Virtually all observers agree that the South is the
most distinctly characterisable of the major American
sections.   Its persistent symbol, as the geographer
John Fraser Hart (1976, p. 1) recently stated, has
been:

> "the statue of the Confederate soldier which stands
> in the county seat.   Hands resting on the barrel of
> his grounded rifle, knapsack and blanket roll on
> his back, he stares in stony silence to the north
> whence came the invading Yankee armies....Before
> the war the South was one of the dominant sections
> of the United States; afterward it languished into
> a stagnant backwater outside the mainstream of
> American national life."

It has been more than a century since General Lee
handed his sword to General Grant in surrender at
Appomattox on April 9, 1865.   As the first modern war
fought with the telegraph, railroad, machine gun,
submarine and areal photography, the human losses on
both sides were staggering: three hundred fifty
thousand Federal and a quarter of a million Confederate fatalities with more hundreds of thousands
wounded (Beard and Beard, 1944, p. 280).   Direct
economic losses were over three billions of 1860
dollars to each side (Lee and Passell, 1979, p. 224).
But, whereas little of the North's direct economic
loss was in destroyed physical capital, four-tenths
of the Southern loss can be so accounted.   This
slowed the region's recovery to the degree that
three-quarters of a century later President Franklin
Roosevelt pointed to the South as "the nation's one
economic problem" during the depths of the Great
Depression (Hart, 1976, p. 3).   Even today per capita
income in the old Confederacy is below that of the
nation as a whole, although the gap has recently been
narrowing at an accelerating rate.

Despite the section's uniqueness, cast in the mold
of the antebellum institution of slavery and honed by
a clash of arms, it is an excess to paint the South
with an undistinguishable grey. One internal
division apparent in both topography and culture
differentiates the coastal lowland where a plantation
economy once held sway from the upland South where
mountainmen, mining and moonshine have been a mixture
with a low flash point. This division is also
political (Turner, 1932; Wright, 1932, pp. 666-672).
In fact, one of the clearest examples of electoral
geography in the Siegfried style by an American
researcher is Ellsworth Huntington's (1963, p. 254)
essay on "The Relation of the Soil to Aristocracy and
Democracy" in which, examining voting patterns in
Alabama from the colonial era to the 1920's, he
concluded that "The character of the soil was the
foundation of the train of courses which made that
particular region politically conservative, whereas
the poverty of the soil elsewhere made the people
more radical." As Phillips (1970, p. 254) recently
noted:

> "the mountains (and some adjoining plateau and
> foothill areas) opposed secession, fought for the
> Union...and thereafter voted Republican. When the
> Civil War ended, the Southern highlands, like the
> rest of Dixie, voted as they had fought. With
> only minor changes, this pattern persisted from the
> end of Reconstruction to the Dixiecrat days after
> World War II."

V. O. Key also called attention to the correlation
between topography and partisanship. In his classic
study of Southern Politics (1949), for example, he
included a cartographic analysis of Tennessee showing
voting pattern in the state from the 1860's to the
1940's in which the uplands stand out as staunchly
Republican. At a state level of analysis, this
pattern tends to recede into the background except in
Kentucky, Tennessee, and, of course, West Virginia
which was classed as Northern by the S-mode analysis.
Since the Second World War other cultural,
economic, and partisan divisions have developed. The

South is still less urbanized than the nation, but
the region contains several of the country's fastest
growing metropolitan areas, such as Miami,
St. Petersberg, Atlanta, and Dallas-Fort Worth.
These cities symbolize the South's recent transformation from an agrarian to a modern metropolitan-
industrial economy.

Cotton is King no more. California now harvests
more cotton than Alabama, Georgia, and South
Carolina combined (Hart, 1976, p. 37). While the
crop is still prominent in the alluvial "Delta," and
in the Black Belt Prairie of Texas, other crops have
supplanted cotton in most of the agricultural South.
Enterprise, Alabama, boasts a monument to the boll
weevil which forced its citizens to switch to peanuts
early in the century. The most widespread
replacements for cotton, however, are grass and
trees: much former cotton land is either pasture for
a cattle industry in competition with the Midwest, or
forest for a wood products industry which threatens
New England.

The real story of the modern Southern Rennaissance,
however, is written along the Gulf Coast where oil,
gas, petrochemicals, tourism, retirement and land
development are booming industries. Houston, Texas,
offers an example. Its population has increased more
than tenfold since the turn of the century. A mayor
of Houston once remarked that "without air conditioning, Houston would not have been built—it
wouldn't exist." This is only part of the explanation. Air conditioning may make the city
habitable, but oil makes it wealthy. One third of
the oil refining capacity of the United States lies
along the Houston Ship Channel. Parallelling this
sixty mile channel are more than a thousand miles of
pipelines uniting the world's largest petrochemical
complex. With the recent movement of the Shell Oil
Comporation from New York to Houston, the city is
now headquarters for twenty-four of the nation's
twenty-five largest oil companies. That Confederate
soldier in the county seat now competes with such new
symbols as the Space Shuttle at Cape Kennedy and a
cartoon mouse at Disney World. Today, as Hart (1976,
p. iii) also observed, "there is not one South, but many."

The Solid South

In order to evaluate the impact of the Southern
Renaissance upon the voting behavior of the region,
it is necessary to examine the section's voting
structure from 1896 to 1980. Application of T-mode
factor analysis to state level Democratic returns for
the fifteen Southern states shows that three factors
are sufficient to describe the region's voting
structure during this era (Figure 4.2). It may be
recalled that when patterns were examined for the
United States as a whole for 1872 to 1980 in the last
chapter a total of six interpreted factors were
encountered, although one of these, the Reconstruction factor, faded from importance before 1896.
Thus, a different factor structure is obtained using
the same analytical criteria as those employed at the
national scale when the Southern region alone is the
subject of analysis (see Appendix A). This obviously
supports Kleppner's (1979) assertion that sectional
patterns are not merely reflections of national ones.

   Examination of the factor profiles shows that
Factor I, labelled the Solid South, is by far the
most important in terms of total variance accounted
for. Indeed, of the twenty-two elections which
occurred between 1896 and 1980, thirteen, or slightly
more than half, exhibit loadings of .80 or more on
this one factor. This demonstrates a truly
remarkable period of electoral stability in the
region spanning the time from the first Bryan
election to the last of the four Roosevelt
elections--from the Populist revolt to the New Deal.
During this time Democratic presidential candidates
could count upon the electoral support of the region,
for this was indeed the era of the one-party solid
South.

   The rise of the solid South following Reconstruction was briefly examined in the last chapter in
relation to the appearance of the sectional normal
vote at national scale. The solid South factor for
the section itself obviously aligns very closely with
that national pattern, suggesting an important
corollary to Kleppner's assertion: sectional voting
structures may sometimes reflect national ones,

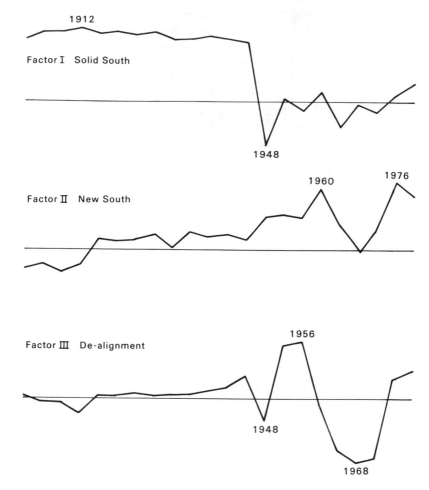

Figure 4.2   Factor Loading Profiles, Southern
              Periphery 1896–1980

although the actual causal direction may in fact be
the reverse of this.

   It is of interest to note that while the national
sectional normal vote varied somewhat in intensity
over time, leading to a distinction between its three
phases, this is hardly true of the solid South factor
which exhibits an essentially horizontal profile up
to its collapse in 1948.   This is partially
deceptive, however.   As we noted in the first
chapter, factor analysis is more keenly sensitive to
changes in the pattern than the level of the vote.

Thus, the fact that average Democratic proportions
jumped from a sixty to seventy percent range between
1896 and 1924, with a dip below this during the Al
Smith contest of 1928, to a seventy to eighty percent
range during the New Deal is somewhat obscured by the
technique employed. Nevertheless, the impact of this
shift on the Electoral College was scarcely important
as Roosevelt's runaway Southern majorities became
merely wasted votes at this level; the extra popular
votes yielded no extra electoral votes (Taylor and
Johnston, 1979, p. 398).

Something else which the analysis, based as it is
upon Democratic proportions of the popular vote,
fails to highlight is the precipitous drop in
Southern voter turnout after the Bryan-McKinley
contest. In that election an average of about fifty-
five percent of the potential Southern electorate
ventured to the polls. Between 1904 and 1948 average
voter turnout among the fifteen states exceeded forty
percent only once (1916) and twice fell below thirty
percent (1924 and 1944). Such low turnouts deserve
explanation.

The agrarian radical threat of the 1890's shook the
Southern establishment by posing the possibility of a
united front between Republican blacks and Populist
whites. The national Democratic-Populist fusion of
1896 in fact generated confusion in the South where a
"cooperationist" Populist-Republican candidate had
won a seat in the United States Senate from North
Carolina in 1894 (Billington, 1975, p. 20). Similar
alliances mounted challenges for state offices in
such localities as Georgia and Texas between 1892 and
1898 (Kousser, 1974, pp. 185, 198, 216). The last
decade of the nineteenth century thus witnessed a
sharp example of Schattschneider's (1960) concept of
contesting political cleavages in which sectionalism
was used to successfully drive a wedge between
Western and Southern branches of the agrarian protest
movement. At national scale resurgent Republican
strength after 1900 in the North and West meant that
the GOP could turn away from potential Southern
support. This move was symbolized by the disappearance of a previously perennial plank in
Republican platforms calling for a fair election

count in the South after 1892 (Kousser, 1974, p. 31).
Within the South itself a "Southern System" of poll
taxes and literacy standards was solidified after
1896 (Rusk and Stucker, 1978). Thus was ushered in
the era of the solid South with its astonishingly low
voter turnouts and its astonishing high Democratic
proportions.

The geographical pattern associated with the Solid
South factor is shown in Figure 4.3(a). As expected,
the highest levels of Democratic support are in the
"deep South" where Democratic proportions in excess
of eight out of ten voters were recorded during the
era. Even Al Smith's candidacy in 1928 failed to
jolt these states into casting Republican electoral
ballots, although Hoover did capture support from
some border South states with their tradition of
mountain Republicanism.

While the average popular Democratic vote in the
South jumped more than twenty points from 1928 to
1932, the latter was scarcely a realigning election
in the region. Republicans were hardly less likely
to gain Southern electoral votes afterward than
before. As Nie, Verba and Petrocik (1979, p. 221)
recently explained, while the New Deal heightened
partisan cleavage along economic lines elsewhere, it
had virtually no impact on the South; within this
region "There was no Republican party to attract
upper status voters. Upper and lower status voters
were both in the Democratic party." And, they might
have added that most Southerners did not vote during
the era of the solid South.

1948 as the Critical Election in the South

The Truman-Dewey contest of 1948 has been as trouble-
some for later analysts as it was for the Chicago
Tribune's headline writers who mistakenly announced
"Dewey Defeats Truman" (Roseboom and Eckes, 1979,
p. 213). In the last chapter we noted that many
interpreters of electoral events do not view this as
an especially significant contest. Our analysis,
however, shows that it spelled the end of the
sectional normal vote which predominated at national
scale from 1880 to 1944. It also terminated the
solid South and this very likely accounts for the
demise of the sectional normal vote.

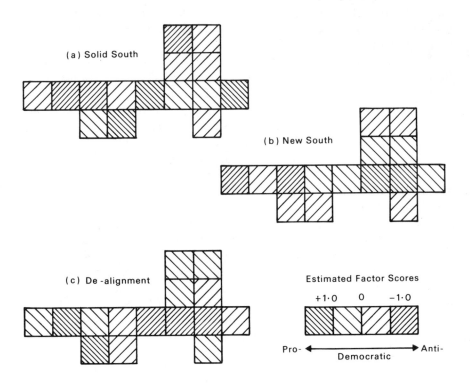

Figure 4.3   Estimated Factor Scores, Southern
             Periphery 1896–1980

This interpretation rests upon a point easily
overlooked by those who stress an individual level of
analysis; namely, realignment is a process which
involves both party organization and grass-roots
response. Thus, although the election of 1948 posed
a puzzle to social surveyors of the individual-
behavioral tradition, it was scarcely unmeaningful to
analysts of the group-ecological tradition. In what
has been described as a "brilliant study of the
unfolding of the New Deal parties" (Ladd and Hadley,
1978, p. 14), Samuel Lubell (1952, p. 5) also

pointed toward the dismemberment of the political
cleavage upon which those parties were based, noting,
even before the first Eisenhower-Stevenson contest,
that

> "The political crisis which wracks the United
> States today is largely a reflection of the fact
> that the nation no longer has an effective majority.
> So furiously divided is the Democratic coalition
> that it has lost all capacity for decisive
> political action. What is fundamentally at issue
> in 1952 is whether a new majority, capable of
> decision, can be formed, or whether today's
> stalemate is to drag on."

A "civil war inside the Democratic party" (Lubell,
1952, p. 9) was signaled by the Dixiecrat rebellion
of 1948. In four Southern states Thurmond's
Dixiecrat electors ran under the regular Democratic
Party label and won; elsewhere in the region they
ran competitively under a States' Rights label
(Roseboom and Eckes, 1979, p. 212). In national
popular terms Thurmond's vote was a miniscule 2.4
percent, but because of its regional concentration
this translated into 7.0 percent of the votes in the
Electoral College (Mazamian, 1974, p. 112).

The analyst's dilemma is thus obvious: were
Thurmond's thirty-nine electoral votes cast for a
Democrat or not? Since electors pledged to the
national Democratic ticket were not even listed on
the ballot in Alabama and lost in three other
Southern states, it is perfectly plausible to answer
no. Within the deep South voters faced with the
option rejected the national Democratic ticket,
though they did not at the same time accept the
Republican. This would have been too much of a step
in 1948. In the rim South, however, Dixiecrat and
Republican support tended to crop up in the same
areas and Eisenhower's performance in 1952 "often
correlated with the combined Republican-Dixiecrat
levels of 1948" (Phillips, 1970, p. 263).

The events of 1948 still echo. Before 1948, the
South held little if any appeal to candidates of the
"Grand Old Party" and Southern voters responded in

kind to politicans whose party label was the same as
Lincoln's. The Dixiecrat rebellion, however, showed
that national Democratic candidates could no longer
take the region's Electoral College votes for
granted to the extent that they were not even assured
of appearing on the popular ballot in some parts of
the South. Thus, "Since 1948 the Democratic Party
has been faced with a problem of how to cope with
local party insurgency"(Cotter and Bibby, 1980,
p. 25) and has undergone a series of internal upheavals
largely in response. Furthermore, since then there
has been a thirty percent decline in Democratic Party
identification among southern voters (Wayne, 1980,
p. 63).

The social surveyors may have been deceived by the
fact that Thurmond ran under the regular party label
in several southern states in 1948. Republican
strategists were not. Whereas Republican presidential candidates scarcely noticed the South after
Bryan's defeat in 1896, Eisenhower made more than ten
percent of his numerous campaign stops in the deep
South in 1952 (Tatalovich, 1979, p. 494). This
exceeded by nine points the proportion of Republican
campaign stops in the core South by a Republican
contender after Hoover lost to FDR in 1932. To an
observer narrowly concerned with party labels, 1948
may have seemed a "maintaining"election. It hardly
appears so when elections are viewed as contests
between competing political cleavages.

The Volatile South
If the South's voting structure is easy to interpret
up to 1944, this is not so afterwards. The election
of 1948 serves as a good case in point since not only
does it load negatively on the solid South factor but
also exhibits loadings of interpretable magnitude on
the remaining two factors. These are respectively
labelled Realignment and the New South. The
realignment factor is so termed because of a strong
negative correlation (-.48) with the solid South
factor. The New South fator's low correlation with
the solid South (.03 and the realignment factor
(-.23) also warrents its designation. As previously
noted, these correlations are to be regarded in

relative rather than in obsolute terms (see
Appendix A).

A striking feature unveiled by the analysis is that
the factor score maps associated with the realignment
and new South factors resemble the inverses one
another and in turn spark recollection of the pattern
geographically inscribed by the solid South factor
(Figures 4.3 (a, b, and c)). All three maps contrast
core and rim South. This poses the issue of how
volatility in electoral structure can be seemingly
unreflected in geographical outcomes. At national
scale different electoral structures were usually
found to pit different constellations of states; this
seems much less true of the South and consequently
deserves careful examination.

One of our constant themes has been that the
dynamic equilibrium tradition of American politics is
one of duopolistic competition between two opposing
major parties. The most distinguishing feature of
the solid South was the sectional disappearance of
this tradition for more than half a century.
Contemporary southern politics thus provide a
laboratory within which the resurgence of this
tradition can be examined. During the era of the
solid South one cleavage became so dominant that it
overshadowed all others. The ongoing rise of two-
party competition, however, poses the question of
which potential division or divisions will serve as
the basis for electoral mobilization within the
region. In some ways the issue is reminiscent of the
one which faced the American polity as a whole just
prior to the emergence of Van Buren's nonsectional
politics in the nineteenth century.

The factor pattern profiles for the realignment
and the new South factors show that there has been a
temporal oscillation between them since 1948 (Figure
4.2) even though they lack a strong correlation in
factor space. This generalisation, however, needs to
be qualified by pointing out that election loadings
on the new South factor are positive during the
post-1948 era while the realignment factor shows
strong loadings of both signs. This suggests an
analogy with a choral group singing separate

selections of which one is accompanied by its own
counterpoint.

Both election campaigns opposing Eisenhower and
Stevenson load strongly on the realignment factor.
In these elections the Republican Party experienced
success in the rim but not in the core South. This
factor, however, is dominated by contests between
1964 and 1972 which exhibit strong negative loadings.
Joining these is the election of 1948 with a
moderately strong negative loading on this factor.
During each of the later contests the national
Democratic candidate performed poorly in the core
South because of third-party southern revolts and
direct sectionally oriented southern challenges by
the Republican Party in varying combinations of
intensity. Since the 1948 revolt has been examined,
we will focus here upon the later ones.

The 1964 election is particularly interesting since
it pitted national candidates representing two
formerly secessionist jurisdictions for the first
time, namely Arizona and Texas. Four years earlier
Johnson had contributed to Kennedy's narrow victory
very directly as he "whistle-stopped his way across
the old Confederacy" emphasising his status as "the
grandson of a Confederate soldier" (Roseboom and
Eckes, 1979, p. 256). Many still regard this as the
margin of victory during a liberal national
Democratic campaign. After assuming the Presidency
subsequent to Kennedy's assassination, Johnson
maintained this liberal thrust through his "Great
Society Programs" and strong support for the 1964
Civil Rights Act and the 24th Amendment banning the
poll tax (Tarrance, 1978). Following reelection, he
achieved passage of the 1965 Voting Rights Act over-
turning literacy tests as a requirement for participation in federal elections (Wayne, 1980, pp. 69-71).
This completed the formal dismemberment of the
"Southern System," rigidified after McKinley's
victory in 1896, and symbolised that the Democratic
Party was no longer the hostage of its traditional
southern stronghold (Cotter and Bibby, 1980).

Goldwater's campaign tried to take advantage of
Johnson's weakened strength in the South by (Converse,
et.al., 1966, p. 241)

"appealing to southern whites on the civil rights issue....The power of this appeal is documented handsomely by the fact that for the first time since Reconstruction, the South cast a vote less Democratic than that of any other region of the country."

As will be recalled, Goldwater's drive into the core South was a tactical success and a strategic failure which in the short run produced a Democratic land-slide at national scale. In the equilibrium tradition of American politics, it also increased the momentum of a reversal of roles between the major parties since the Republican Party (Sale, 1975, p. 109):

"formed more than a century ago to transform the South has finally had to admit defeat; it is the South that has transformed the Republican Party. In fact, the most far reaching change in any political party in recent times has come about from the single fact of Republicans opening themselves to the new and increasingly powerful forces of the South."

To be sure, this is a bit of an exaggeration, since neither at national nor at sectional scale have party roles been entirely reversed. Nevertheless, some of the implications became manifest in 1968 when Nixon's successful second effort to gain the White House in the wake of national reaction against an incumbent Democratic administration nearly fell short in the face of Wallace's American Independent challenge to the two-party system. This placed a Republican "Southern Strategy" in grave jeopardy Wallace's 13.5 percent of the popular vote at national scale was the strongest third-party showing in half a century and reduced Nixon's plurality over Humphrey to a razor margin of 43.4 to 42.7 percent. The "winner-take-all" system of dividing electoral votes, however, amplified this to a strong 301 to 191 victory in the Electoral College and Wallace's dream of negotiating the outcome in the House failed to materialise. With Wallace out of the picture in 1972,

his supporters flocked to Nixon and a Republican
landslide resulted (Mazmanian, 1974).

The realignment factor thus joins two elections,
1964 and 1972, with vastly different national
results. Both Johnson and Nixon entered the White
House with popular mandates which rivalled
Roosevelt's at the height of the New Deal. In each
of the contests with negative loadings on the
realignment factor, the national Democratic standard
bearer did poorly in the core of the South. Thus, its
pattern of factor scores (Figure 4.3(b)) is direct
testimony to the realignment of the region and
indirect testimony, perhaps, to the realignment of
the parties. Interestingly, its intrasectional
period of strength corresponds with those of the
Southern revolt, liberal normal vote, and diluted
normal vote factors at national scale and shows a
particularly strong congruity with the last two of
these.

The realignment of the South has been recognised
by researchers of the individual-behavioral tradition
whose surveys have detected a decline in Democratic
identification from nearly eighty percent in the
early 1950's to fifty percent or below among southern
white Protestants during the 1970's (Nie, Verba and
Petrocik, 1979, 218). While many moved into the
independent column, a shift to Republican partisanship is noticeable among voters of higher socio-
economic status. This represents a second impetus to
two-party competition in the South reflecting
economic rather than civil rights issues. This
second impetus palusibly underlies the new South
factor which explains a portion of the variance
associated with elections from 1944 to 1964 and shows
prominent loadings for the most recent contests of
1976 and 1980.

Elections of the tumultous 1964 to 1972 period have
small or negligible loadings on the new South factor
(Figure 4.2). Notably, if southern states were to
exhibit an electoral structure reflecting their
variant levels of economic growth during the Southern
Rennaissance which has favored the southern periphery
over the southern core and thus to align with the
national economic stances of the two parties, then an

electoral pattern much like that associated with the
new South factor would be expected (Figure 4.3(c)).
These scores show a new South pattern of greatest
Democratic strength within the Southern core, a
pattern exactly opposite to that of the realignment
factor.

Two important trends lend credence to this interpretation. First, Republican strength in the
southern periphery, especially in Florida and the
Southwest, has been augmented during the past two
decades by sunbelt migration from the North. The
effect is particularly reinforced by the fact that
the members of this migration stream are not simply
a random sample from places of origin, but are often
older and higher in educational and occupa-
tional status than average. Thus, as Converse (1966,
p. 229) noted, "the nonSoutherner moving into the
South is actually more Republican than the non-
Southerners he leaves behind." This is highly
congruent with the finding that such states as
Florida, Texas and especially Arizona are less
Democratic than the southern norm under the domain of
the new South factor. The lower than average
Democraticness of Virginia may also reflect the
influence of spillover growth from Washington, D. C.
In Kentucky, there is the mountain Republican
heritage. New Mexico and Oklahoma also have stronger
than average Republican traditions as shown by new
South factor scores.

A second trend operates in the opposite direction
and exerts its greatest influence within the core of
the South. The Southern System, of course, greatly
reduced black electoral participation so that even as
late as the 1950's less than twenty percent of
southern blacks cast presidential ballots (Nie,
Verba, and Petrocik, 1979, p. 229). The destruction
of the legal foundations of this system and the
undertaking of an effort to bring southern blacks
into the electorate from the mid-1960's onward
increased this rate to fifty percent and above by the
1970's. Furthermore, up to the 1960's southern
balcks tended to identify with the Republican Party
to a greater extent than their northern counterparts.
In the wake of the Republican Southern Strategy

campaigns of the 1960's, this distinction vanished
(Nie, Verba and Petrocik, 1979, p. 227). Black
support was in fact crucial to Carter's success in
capturing southern electoral votes in 1976 when less
than fifty percent of southern whites, but more than
eighty percent of southern blacks, supported his
candidacy (Miller, 1978, p. 147). Although Carter
carried only Georgia in 1980, it is notable that this
election too loads on the new South factor.

The question now becomes a twofold one of whether
southern Republicanism will be dominated by an
economic cleavage or by a social cleavage and whether
Democrats will abandon efforts in the core South in
the wake of Carter's defeat in 1980 in the same way
that Republicans looked away from the area after
vanguishing Bryan in 1896. This question of
contesting cleavages is perhaps yet to be settled for
as Seagull (1980, p. 75 recently observed:

"In its more stable manifestation, new Republican
voting in the southern states has been based in the
counties with higher white-collar populations....
From 1952 to 1960 and again in 1968, the new
Republican vote in these states was concentrated
disproportionately in these white-collar counties.
But in 1964 and 1972 a different pattern prevailed.
...During these years, the southern states'
Republican votes were swelled by the temporary
support of groups and sectors not ordinarily
Republican."

Except for his view of the 1968 contest whose outcome in the South was clouded by Wallace's candidacy,
the interpretation which he offers aligns closely
with the picture presented here. The factor profile
for the new South factor which joins 1976 and 1980 to
the more stable phase, as he calls it, of new
Republican voting in the region is perhaps an
indication that the once solid South is truly of a
bygone era. The new South factor, it may be recalled,
is uncorrelated with the other two.

WESTERN PERIPHERY: FROM VOLATILITY TO STABILITY
The Mason-Dixon line surveyed in 1769 corresponds
with the sectional cleavage in voting structures
between the Northern Core and the Southern Periphery.
Another line is less well known, but also important
in American history. Passing through the central
prairie, this line supplies longitudinal positioning
where few cues are available from the landscape
itself. At roadside in North Dakota is a plaque
which proclaims:

"You are now on the 100° Meridian. Historically
that meridian is significant. For two generations
the Insurance Companies and other world-wide
lending agencies would not, as a matter of agreed
policy lend a shiny dime west of this line. Their
reason was that some geographer had labeled it the
EAST EDGE of the Great American Desert."

Whether or not the Great American Desert was a
misnomer, John Wesley Powell, one of the first
explorers of the western United States, insisted as
early as 1878 "that the political institutions and
farming methods of the humid regions--from which the
nation grew on the east coast--would have to be
modified west of the 100th meridian" (Hodge, 1963,
pp. 1-2). His prediction conforms with our analysis
since states traversed by the 100th meridian--North
and South Dakota, Kansas and Nebraska--are the
easternmost of those within the Western Periphery
established by the S-mode factor analysis of the last
chapter.
    Powell's statement directly linked political
institutions with the natural environment, a
practice which has been frowned upon by geographers
overly sensitive to the charge of environmental
determinism. Nevertheless, a recent "Analysis of the
Congressional Record reveals that in the House as
well as the Senate, westerners talked more about
water than about any other subject" (Nash, 1973,
p. 253), thus demonstrating that there are times
when the natural environment indeed impinges upon
politics. For those loath to this notion, there is
another attribute which distinguishes the West from

the rest of the country: its settlement generally
succeeded the great cleavage which shook the nation
to its foundation during the decade of the 1860's.
Nevertheless, it cannot be forgotten that the Civil
War was in part precipitated by the issue of western
settlement (see Chapter 2) and that some of the
earliest outbreaks of sectional violence pitted
Northern "Jayhawkers" against Southern "Kickapoo
Rangers" in the "Bloody Kansas" of the 1850's
(Morison and Commager, 1962, Vol. 1, p. 649).   But
because only three states were admitted to the Union
from west of the 100th meridan before the start of
the war, the region was by and large spared the
direct effects of its hostilities.   And, though
Kansas and Nevada were admitted during the fighting,
it was only after Appomatox that the Western
Periphery became an independent force in national
politics.

There are important physical variations among the
eleven states classed as Western.   East of the Rocky
Mountains the land is gently, almost imperceptibly
sloping, as befits its Great Plains designation.   The
rain shadow effect of the Rockies, however, creates
climatic differences to reflect those based upon
physiography.   In the so-called wet West, including
the states along the 100th meridian, rainfall is
adequate for dry farming methods although many
agriculturalists supplement current precipitation
with irrigation water drawn from the giant Ogallala
aquafer.   This has produced a unique landscape of
circular swatches of pivot irrigated green separated
by patches of red and brown when viewed from the air.
Unfortunately the withdrawal rate far exceeds the
recharge rate so that a coming crisis lurks beneath
the ever deepened wells of Kansas and Nebraska.   This
is one reason why Western Senators and Representatives talk so much about water.

In the dry West, which includes much of Oregon,
Idaho, Nevada, Utah, Colorado, Wyoming and Montana,
annual rainfall typically falls below 12 inches.   At
this level dry farming is unrewarding and irrigation
is essential for row and even fodder crops.   Except
for fortunate localities such as in the Salt Lake
Basin in Utah or Jackson's Hole in Wyoming, the

primary food producing activity is extensive grazing.
Some sixty percent of Western rangelands remain under
federal jurisdiction, although this has not prevented,
and in "Tragedy of Commons" fashion has perhaps even
encouraged, overstocking. As early as the 1930's a
government study of the Future of the Great Plains
warned that overgrazing may reduce the carrying
capacity of the land by more than half before the
middle of the twenty-first century (Patterson, 1979,
p. 262).

Drier than the rest of the country, the West is
also less densely populated. In 1975 the average for
the eleven states was only about thirteen persons per
square mile, only one-fourth the national figure.
The region is also less urbanized than the nation.
Wyoming, in fact, was nearly unique in 1970 in having
no metropolitan population at all; the only other
such state was Vermont in northern New England.

Ethnically, the region is predominately northern
European with English, German and Scandinavian stock
predominating. At 14 percent, the average proportion
of the population of foreign birth or parentage was
slightly less than that of the country as a whole in
1970 (16.5 percent). This is a level much above that
of the South, but well below that of the Northeast.

While the region has not been a subject of
political scrutiny to the same degree as the South,
its distinctiveness has not gone unnoticed. Perhaps
the most sensitive observer was Turner who asserted
the persistence of "the West's old initiative, its
love of innovation, its old idealism and optimism,
its old love of bigness, even its old boastfulness"
(Turner, 1932, pp. 254-255). However, as Nash (1973,
p. 44) recently commented, "The history of Western
politics since 1900 is still a virgin field." Thus
the section's electoral history, as captured by our
T-mode factor analysis of its voting patterns from
1896 to 1980, warrants attention.

Post-Frontier Instability

It is widely held that the political histories of the
South and West became closely intertwined toward the
close of the nineteenth century. It would be wrong
to infer, however, that the two peripheral sections
of the nation have followed parallel lines of

political development for several reasons. For one,
while the Southern System effectively, though sometimes extralegally, restricted popular suffrage in
the South during the first half of the twentieth
century, the West led the nation in bringing new
groups into the potential electorate. For example,
women became eligible to vote in several Western
states decades before this occurred nationally under
the 19th Amendment, ratified in 1920 (Brunn, 1974,
pp. 19-20). For another, a single cleavage did not
dominate in the West at the start of the modern
period as happened in the South so that actual
participation on a broad scale was encouraged, partly
as a result of the region's frontier heritage.
Between 1896 and 1980 Western presidential turnout
has ranged from fifty to seventy-five percent of the
electorate and in a slight majority of the contests
involved actually exceeded electoral turnout in the
Northern Core.

The absence of a single persistent political
cleavage in the West is echoed in its voting
structure. Following criteria adopted throughout
this study (see Appendix A) it has been found that
five distinct factors are necessary to describe the
West's electoral structure at a state level of
analysis for the period since 1896. In some ways
this complexity reflects, in addition to the characteristics of the section itself, its peripheral role
in national politics because of which national,
meaning mainly Northern Core, controversies have had
somewhat unpredictable implications for the West. Of
the five interpreted factors, four indeed pertain to
the pre-Eisenhower era implying great volatility in
the Western response to programs and candidates
offered by the major parties up to the end of the
Second World War. The West has also been a theatre
of strong third party activity as we observed in the
last chapter and need to elaborate upon here in an
intraregional context. In their temporal ordering
the Western factors can be identified as follows
(Figure 4.4).

Factor I because of its high loadings on elections
early in the period of study as well as its priority
of emergence from the analysis is called the Major

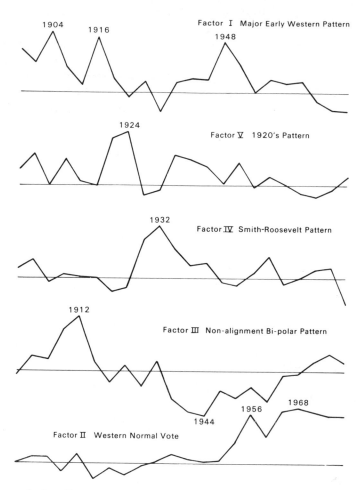

Figure 4.4   Factor Loading Profiles, Western
             Periphery 1896–1980

Early Western Pattern. Factor III appears to be
associated with lines of cleavage not greatly felt at
national scale and also exhibits strong loadings of
both positive and negative character in two distinct
phases, consequently it is labelled a Nonalignment
Bipolar Pattern. The first phase appears during the
Progressive era while the second, somewhat less
distinct phase appears during the New Deal. Factor V
is strongest during the early elections of the
"roaring twenties" and though it too shows a muted
resurgence in the late New Deal appears best

designated as a 1920's Pattern. Factor IV sharply
depicts a Smith-Roosevelt Pattern. Factor II
dominates the West's voting structure since World War
Two. None of the other four factors, in fact, make
any notable contribution to the Western electoral
response after 1952 which, by implication, was
perhaps a watershed contest in this section of the
nation.

In light of the conventional periodization of
American electoral behavior and the three phases of
the sectional normal vote at national scale, it seems
reasonable to combine discussions of the major early
western pattern, the first phase of the nonalignment
bipolar pattern and the 1920's pattern. Following
this, the Smith-Roosevelt pattern and the second
phase of the nonalignment bipolar pattern are
described. The western normal vote pattern deserves
separate attention because of its present
significance. Successively greater attention to
responses of greater recency is consistent with the
funnel of causality concept alluded to previously.

Except for an interlude leading to and contemporary
with the Progressive or "Bull Moose" schism in the
Republican Party, the major early western pattern
dominates between the elections of 1896 and 1916,
inclusively. It is thus coterminous with the period
dominated by the western revolt factor and the rise
of the second phase of the sectional normal vote at
national scale. It is notable, however, that whereas
the Bryan-McKinley contest is hence shown to exhibit
distinctive qualities from the larger perspective, it
does not do so from the perspective of the Western
Periphery alone. From this lesser perspective, it is
the elections of 1908 and especially 1912 which
breakout for separate identification, although it is
once again necessary to reiterate that the analytical
technique employed emphasises covariations in
geographical arrangement rather than similarities in
absolute levels of voting response (see Appendix A).
This caveat is significant because the elections of
1896, 1904 and 1916 exhibited great differences in
average levels of Democratic support in the West. In
1896, at the height of Bryan's popularity, an average
of almost 64 percent of Western voters supported his

candidacy. In 1904 less than one-third of the West's
voters preferred Democrat Alton Parker to Republican
Theodore Roosevelt or Socialist Eugene Debs. And, in
1916 Wilson received more than half of the West's
popular vote, considerably exceeding his popular
performance in the region four years earlier. After
this, however, Democratic voting in the West again
receded until the onset of the New Deal.

Certainly one of the elements contributing to the
volatility of the West's voting structure was the
impact of third-party candidates. In 1892 Populist
Weaver averaged 45 percent of the vote and won out-
right in four western states as we noted in the
previous chapter. He also received split electoral
votes from two others. Indeed, the national
Democratic ticket was not even on the ballot in
Colorado, Idaho, Kansas and North Dakota
(Congressional Quarterly Incorporated, 1975, p. 279).
In 1896 the Populist-Democratic fusion ticket
featuring the "Orator of the Platte" obviously did
not pose the same dilemma in the West that it did in
the South and potential third-party strength in the
region was mobilised behind a major party candidate
as a result. In this sense, 1896 was simply a
maintaining election in the Western Periphery.

Although Bryan's vote share in the West plummeted
from 64 to 48 percent between 1896 and 1900 his
candidacy once again preempted any significant
rejection of the two major parties. When easterner
Alton Parker headed the Democratic ticket in 1904,
however, this presaged a sequence of elections
culminating in that of 1924 in which third parties
polled an average of five percent or more of the
Western popular vote. In 1912 Socialist Eugene Debs
received an average of 9.8 percent in the region
and in 1924 La Follette's Progressive candidacy was
supported by an average of 29.5 percent of Western
voters compared with Davis' average Democratic
showing of 20.4 percent. These third party
proportions are obviously high enough to affect the
geographical pattern of Democratic support and to
thus add complexity to the voting structure uncovered
through the sectional T-mode factor analysis.
Consideration was given to the possible inclusion of

third-party proportions in the Western analysis, but
rejected on the grounds that this would disrupt
comparisons with the other analyses.

Before examining the maps associated with the major
early western, nonalignment, and 1920's factors, two
additional points deserve to be made. First,
although the Smith-Roosevelt and the Western normal
vote factors show negligible correlations (i.e. below
.20) with the others, the major early Western pattern
is strongly correlated (+.55) with the 1920's pattern
and weakly correlated (-.21) with the nonalignment
pattern. The 1920's and the nonalighment patterns,
however, are negligibly correlated. Again there is
the caveat that these correlations can only be
regarded as relative indicators (see Appendix A).
Second, both the elections of 1920 and 1924, which
load on the 1920's pattern, were associated with
comparatively low voter turnout in the West (i.e.
below 60 percent). This suggests that they were
viewed rather apathetically by the Western electorate,
perhaps not so surprisingly in the light of the
extent to which Core based interests dominated during
the second phase of the national sectional normal
vote.

The factor score map associated with the major
early Western factor (Figure 4.5(a)) at first glance
seems surprising in light of the stronger showing of
Democrats in mountain than in plains states. This,
however, can be explained in part as follows.
Although Bryan championed the cause of Western
agriculture, he was in fact even more popular in
silver mining states and indeed received a large
proportion of his financial campaign support from "a
group of wealthy silver mine owners" (Roseboom and
Eckes, 1979, p. 121). Similarly, the economic
recovery following 1896, while improving conditions
generally, was perhaps of greater benefit to grain
farmers than to ranchers, miners, and lumbermen
(Taylor and Johnston, 1979, p. 144). This impression
is reinforced by the fact that Socialist Eugene Debs
did much better in states such as Montana, Idaho and
Nevada than in states intersected by the 100th
Meridian.

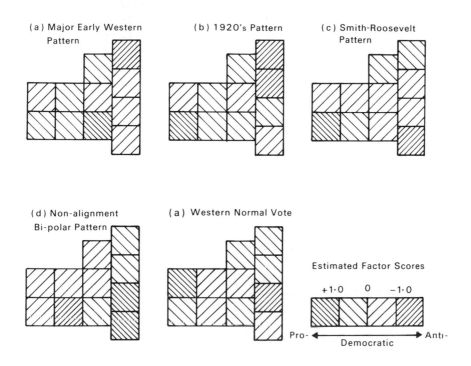

Figure 4.5   Estimated Factor Scores, Western
             Periphery 1896-1980

The factor score map for the 1920's factor (Figure
4.5(c)) is highly reminiscent of that for the major
early western factor. Since these factors are
strongly correlated, this should come as little of a
surprise. Once again, there is a rather direct
correspondence between topographic ruggedness and
Democratic support. Notably, during the election of
1924 which shows the strongest affinity with this
factor, La Follette scored most heavily within the
region in North Dakota (45.2 percent) and South

Dakota (36.9 percent). These states also show the
most negative values on the factor score map.

The nonalignment bipolar pattern almost exactly
reverses the relationship between terrain and
Democraticness so far observed (Figure 4.5(b)). The
plains now show stronger Democratic support than the
mountains. Since the election of 1912 is most
prominent on the factor profile, it may serve as the
vehicle for interpretation. In this election
Republican support was split between Theodore
Roosevelt and Taft. The response to Taft in the West
was symbolised by the fact that he did not even
appear on the ballot in South Dakota. Roosevelt
carried the state and out performed Taft in the
region (29 to 23 percent). But Wilson won the West
(38 percent) as he did the nation. As far as the map
of scores for Factor III is concerned, what seems to
have happened is that the third-party effects in a
sense reversed themselves with both Debs and
Roosevelt showing so strongly in the region that the
plains became relatively more Democratic than the
mountains almost by default.

The New Deal and the West
The Smith-Roosevelt factor, as we observed earlier,
serves as a break with the past in the region. This
factor is virtually uncorrelated with those preceding
it. But, the New Deal epoch as a whole did not
affect the area's voting structure in but one way
since the later New Deal, beginning about 1936, is
also associated in factor space with the nonalignment
bipolar pattern, though with negative loadings to
demonstrate a reversal of the Wilsonian pattern as
well.

The election of 1928 represented a resurgence of
Democratic performance in the West over that of four
years earlier. This was probably inevitable,
however, for the average Democratic vote was only 20
percent in the West in 1924, the lowest the party's
fortunes have ever reached in the region. Smith's 38
percent performance was scarcely a stirring one, but
it was a definite improvement in the face of what
were probably overwhelming odds; Al Smith, it will be
recalled, was the first Catholic ever to run for the
White House. He even caused Republican defections

from the border South. For him to do about as well
in the West as Wilson in 1912, at least in terms of
average popular vote proportions, is truly a cause of
wonderment. Indeed, this fact, plus the conjunction
between Smith and Franklin Delanore Roosevelt on the
Western factor profiles (Figure 4.4) calls into some
question Lubell's (1952, p. 38) classic depiction of
Al Smith's "brown derby and rasping East Side accent"
as athema to the West. To be sure, Bryan's
sonorous agrarian protest was more appealing to
Westerners than Smith's protest of Prohibition, but
it is too easily forgotten that his accent was
rejected by a shade smaller proportion of Western
voters than Wilson's cultivated professional accent
had been on his first try. In fact, Smith did rather
well in North Dakota with its German Catholic
minority and in Montana with its Irish Catholic
minority (Phillips, 1970, pp. 359 and 397). His
candidacy was also appealing to Mormans in Utah and
Nevada. One suspects, in fact, that the religiosity
issue accounts in part for the pattern of factor
scores associated with the Smith-Roosevelt factor
(Figure 4.5(d)) since these states show the highest
Democratic support for the period.

By 1932 the fact that Roosevelt, who had placed
Smith's name in nomination four years earlier, had
also been Governor of New York and had also
championed repeal of the 18th (Prohibition)
Amendment was no longer much of a campaign issue in
the West. Depression and drought had seen to that.
Protestant Kansas which had given Smith a paltry 27
percent of its popular vote rejected four more years
of Hoover and gave Roosevelt 54 percent of its vote.
Indeed, all of the region's electoral and an average
of 60 percent of its popular votes were rushed to the
challenger's aid, though probably mainly in desper-
ation, since the "New Deal" was yet to be configured
in a programmatic sense. Few now seem to recall, for
example, that the 1932 Democratic platform called for
reduced expenditures and a balanced federal budget
(Roseboom and Eckes, 1979, p. 160). But, Kansas
wheat was 36 cents a bushel and Wyoming sheep cost
more to ship than they were worth at the market so
that many were simply slaughtered to avoid holding

costs.   In North Dakota the value of farm products
sold plummeted from $200 million in 1929 to $80
million in 1932 (Nash, 1973, p. 158) and Protestants
joined Catholics to give Roosevelt 70 percent of the
state's popular vote, a substantial increase from
Smith's 45 percent four years earlier.   In 1932 and
again in 1936 the West voted its pocketbook to the
extent that the least Democratic state of the region,
Kansas, gave Roosevelt its electoral votes in both
elections.   The secular shift in voting proportions,
however, did not greatly alter the geographical
pattern of Democratic support in the region
(Figure 4.5(d)).

   As early as 1936, however, there were murmurings of
another change in the pattern of Democratic support.
Thus, whereas the 1928 and 1932 elections load almost
exclusively on the Smith-Roosevelt factor, the
variance of the 1936 election is spread over three,
including the 1920's factor and the nonalignment
bipolar factor (Figure 4.4).   This suggests that it
might not be unreasonable to regard the 1928 and 1932
elections as deviating ones in the West.   Nevertheless, the complexity of the loadings profiles for
the late New Deal period points our attention forward.
Two issues in particular warrant discussion; these
involve first, the significance of ethnic cleavages,
and second, recently uncovered evidence about the
impact of New Deal programs on the West.

   Although Roosevelt swept the West in 1936 as he had
in 1932, he lost the four Western states intersected
by the 100th Meridian in both subsequent contests.
He also lost Colorado in 1940 and both Colorado and
Wyoming in 1944.   Some have interpreted this as
simply a reversion to an earlier pattern, but it was
doubtless more complex than this, since cultural as
well as economic cleavages intertwined to produce
this outcome.   In The Future of American Politics
1952, p. 146) Lubell noted that:

   "The most isolationist of all Americans are
   unquestionably the 'Russian-German' farmers particularly numerous in the wheat country....Wherever
   their voting can be checked, in Nebraska, Kansas,

the Dakotas and the Big Bend region of Washington, the same pattern emerges."

Similarly, Phillips (1970, p. 372) has pointed to "a massive Republican tide" from counties" still German by culture and language, where memories of the First World War and its attendant strains made voters balk at a new and similar war." The intensity of the issue can be gaged by the fact that not only did voters in such states as South Dakota and Nebraska give a larger ballot share to Willkie than to Roosevelt, but the total number of ballots cast has never exceeded that of 1940 in either of these states. Finally, a recent statistical study found that in accounting for state-by-state changes in Democratic support nationwide from 1936 to 1940 "the percentage of German-Americans is the best single explanatory variable" (Wright, 1974, p. 37).

There thus would appear to be a full cycle of ethnic cleavages built into the New Deal epoch in the West. At the start of this cycle, Smith's Catholicism helped Democratic sentiment to break into the northern plains. This was reinforced by economic strains in 1932 and 1936. In 1940 and 1944, however, the direction of advantage associated with the Protestant-Catholic cleavage reversed itself. This is consistent with the factor score map for the 1920's factor (Figure 4.5(c)) which shows stronger anti-Democraticness in North and South Dakota as well as the factor score map for the nonalignment bipolar factor (Figure 4.5(b)) since there the shading is, in effect, inverted by the negative factor loadings involved. Thus, the complexity of the West's voting structure during the New Deal is explained by a tangled interweaving of economic and ethnic variations combined.

The second issue meriting attention involves the fact that the West benefited disproportionately from the economic programs of the New Deal. At the time of the Depression, the "nation's number one economic problem," in Roosevelt's words (Reading, 1973, p. 793), was the South where per capita income was only about half the national norm. Newly uncovered data on federal spending under the New Deal, however,

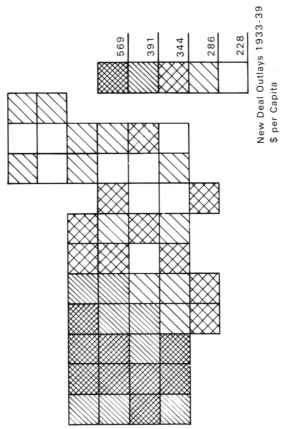

New Deal Outlays 1933-39
$ per Capita

569
391
344
286
228

Figure 4.6 New Deal Outlays Percapita, 1933–1939

shows that this was not the region which benefited
most from new federal spending (Figure 4.6). Indeed,
Reading's (1973, pp. 805-806) recent analysis yielded
an "insiginficant relationship between the level of
real per capita income and New Deal spending,"
suggesting that "the Roosevelt administration was
content with the modest goal of seeking to return
incomes to a pre-1929 level rather than striving to
equalize per capita income between states and
regions." Percent unemployment, it was found, was a
poorer predictor of the flow of newly expended funds
than either the length of federal highways or the
proportion of federal land in a state. Such
relationships may imply that "pump priming" efforts
followed regular channels in order to make their
influence felt most quickly. Since the West was then
as now rich in federal lands, it thus also became
rich in federal funds, especially on a per capita
basis.

Another study depicts a somewhat less charitable
picture, however. Recall that the South was
staunchly Democratic at the time. Indeed, Roosevelt
spent little time campaigning in the region
(Tatalovich, 1979, p. 494). He may also have pursued
a "vote buying" strategy (Johnston, 1979, p. 86;
Taylor and Johnston, 1979, pp. 314-320) in allocating
New Deal funds. Since the West's Democratic support
was questionable, this hypothesis too is consistent
with the observed pattern of outlays. Pertinently,
Wright's (1974, pp. 30-38) regression analysis for
the forty-eight contiguous states shows that a model
incorporating only "economic distress" variables fits
the pattern poorly (R^2 = .171). The most successful
model was found to be one which predicts per capita
New Deal spending from electoral votes, variability
in popular Democratic proportions between 1896 and
1932, and the closeness of the 1932 election in each
state (R^2 = .796). One can scarcely imagine a more
closely specified vote buying model than this one!
As Lee and Passel (1979, p. 392) recently observed:

"Roosevelt, then probably tried, and less probably
succeeded, in using New Deal spending to keep
Democrats in office. Economic goals were either

secondary or did not figure in decisions on how to allocate funds....But it would take an unreconstructed cynic to claim that FDR did not believe that his reelection and the election of New Deal Democrats would help the economy."

The New Republican Heartland

The Western Normal Vote which makes an appearance beginning in 1952 shows none of the volatility associated with the other Western factors, except for a brief dip corresponding with the Kennedy-Nixon contest of 1960. This election, which once again involved a Catholic on the Democratic ticket, and hence, no doubt rekindled an old cleavage, also shows up as a minor peak on the Smith-Roosevelt factor pattern (Figure 4.4). This, of course, adds credence to the earlier interpretation. With this exception, however, the western normal vote exhibits the almost linear solidarity of the solid South factor previously examined. A solid South, it would seem, has been replaced by a solid West.

Indeed, Democratic candidates received an average of only 40 percent of the West's popular vote between 1952 and 1980. Only once, in fact, has the average Democratic proportion for the eleven Western states been above fifty percent since the close of the Second World War. This occurred in 1964 when Johnson beat Goldwater in a national Democratic landslide. Significantly, Carter's 29 percent Western showing in 1980 rivals Republican performances in the South during the domain of the national sectional normal vote.

Eisenhower swept the West in 1952 and again in 1956. Since then the West has been a Republican stronghold, suggesting that 1952 was a watershed election in the region and perhaps even a realigning one in the strict usage of the term. Since 1952, even the most Democratic state on the factor score map for the western normal vote (Figure 4.5(e)), namely Oregon, has never failed to return a GOP popular margin, except in 1964 when it joined the rest of the region in treating Goldwater's candidacy as too extreme even for this conservative bastion. With the exception of Johnson, Democratic candidates

from Stevenson in 1952 to Carter in 1980, a period of
almost three decades in length, received a grand
total of three electoral votes from the eleven states
placed in the Western Periphery by the S-mode
analysis of the previous chapter. And in 1964 when
Johnson eclipsed Roosevelt's 1936 proportion of the
national popular vote with 61.1 percent, the Western
states gave him an average of 56.8 percent of their
popular support. This proportion has been bettered
by Republicans on five occasions since 1952. Even in
1968 when Wallace's average was 8.3 percent in the
area, Nixon did almost as well as Johnson with an
average of 53.4 percent of the West's popular vote.

The emergence of the solid West may have been
postponed in part by the vote-buying expenditure
allocations of New Deal strategists and in part by
the impact of American participation in a major
foreign conflict. But, to an observer familiar with
the writings of Frederick Jackson Turner, it might
have seemed inevitable. In "The West—1876 and 1926:
Its Progress in a Half-Century," he observed that
"This land of farm owners, this land trained in
pioneer ideals, has a deep conservatism, at bottom,
in spite of its social and political pioneering"
(Turner, 1932, p. 254).

There is always the possibility that a new crisis
will affect the region and that memories of the
"Orator of the Platte" and the "Bull Moose" will be
rekindled. As ever, moisture remains a cause for
constant concern, both among residents and representatives of the region. High energy costs already
demand serious reflection before throwing the switch
on a center pivot irrigation pump. As pleistocene
water, a resource hardly renewable on a scale of
human time, becomes even more scarce, what will be
the political response of the "Great American
Desert?" Will there be, at some future time, an
ironic footnote to history that in 1980 the candidate
so strongly supported in the Electoral College by the
West was once the announcer for a television serial
entitled "Death Valley Days?"

NORTHERN CORE: FROM REPUBLICAN TO DEMOCRATIC CENTER
The method of aggregating electoral votes has long
reinforced the influence of the Northern Core in

national politics. This can be seen directly in the
arithmetic of the Electoral College. The S-mode
analysis of the previous chapter classed twenty-two
states as exhibiting the voting structure of this
long dominant section. Including the two western
outliers of the region, these states together boasted
a total of 321 electoral votes as recently as 1980.
This was obviously in excess of the minimum winning
combination of 270 required for victory.

   Such arithmetic is by no means at odds with the
implications of the discussion engaged in at the
outset of this chapter involving the role of large
states. Of the nine states with more than fifteen
electoral votes in 1980, seven are to be found in the
Northern Core. These include (1980 electoral votes
in parentheses): California (45), New York (41),
Pennsylvania (27), Illinois (26), Ohio (25),
Michigan (21), and New Jersey (17). The remaining
two, Texas (26) and Florida (17), are in the Southern
Periphery. Thus, even were candidates to entirely
ignore sectional alliances and to allocate their
efforts strictly in terms of electoral votes, a
single minded strategy of dubious potential, they
would still be unable to ignore the Northern Core.

   Another indication of the region's importance can
be found in the geography of presidential origins.
"Probably nowhere is the notion that 'geography'
plays a role in the recruitment and selection of
politicans," according to Brunn (1974, p. 98),
"greater than the Presidential-Vice Presidential
teams nominated by the major parties." During the
heyday of the national sectional normal vote, for
example, nine of ten Presidents were natives of Core
states. The exception was Wilson, born in Virginia,
but nominated from New Jersey. Before 1860, it may
be recalled, eight of fifteen Presidents were natives
of the South. Since Truman in 1948, however, only
four of eight Presidents have been Core natives.
Loosing candidates also show similar patterns of
origin so that "both parties have viewed the
industrial Northeast and prosperous rural and urban
Midwest states as prime places to recruit or nominate
Presidential and Vice Presidential timber" (Brunn,
1974, p. 98). Most recently, however, the sunbelt

has offered stiff competition. For example, Carter
was the first native of the deep South to become
President in over a century in 1976. Thus, in this
as in other ways the influence of the Core has
diminished since the Second World War.

It would be wrong to view the Core as internally
undifferentiated. Indeed, several subsections
standout if the region is viewed with closer scrutiny.
These divisions, which often reflect culture as much
as economy, have exerted an impact upon intrasectional voting patterns. New England's stanchly
independent character extends back as far as the
Mayflower Compact and its distinctive moralistic
political culture has been regarded as one of the
most basic in America (Elazar, 1972). Today,
southern, more metropolitan New England displays a
mixture of the moralistic political culture and the
individualistic political culture which Elazar
envisaged as arising in the Middle Atlantic subregion
where it in turn is still dominant.

In 1961 Gottmann, (p. 13) pointed to "an almost
continuous stretch of urban and suburban areas from
New Hampshire to Northern Virginia and from the
Atlantic shore to the Appalachian foothills" which he
labelled Megalopolis. Transportation planners refer
to this heavily urbanized strip less eloquently as
the "Bos-Wash Corridor" but it has been and remains
the interior core of the Northern section whose
leading role in the national economy is indicated by
the fact that almost one-third of the Fortune 500
locate their head offices along this mainstreet of
the nation (Miller, 1975, p. 34). Equally impres-
sively, forty-two percent of the more than 13,600
national trade, professional, labor, fraternal and
patriotic associations in the country have Bos-Wash
postal addresses (Miller, 1975, p. 21). Indeed, even
the local street names have become national symbols:
Parkplace (Atlantic City), Wallstreet (New York) and
Pennsylvania Avenue (Washington, D. C.).

If megalopolis is the nation's nerve center, the
"American Manufacturing Belt" first identified by
De Geer (1927) is still the very heart of the
national economy. But, its former eminence has
dimmed as the current plight of the Detroit based

automobile industry testifies. Well into the 1960's
it was believed that the industrial centers of the
manufacturing belt would "always be prepared to pick
up new work in the early stages of the learning
curve--inventing, innovating, rationalizing"
(Thompson, 1968, p. 56). By the mid-1970's, it was
becoming clear that its populace and its politicians
would have to "face up to the basic and persisting
nature of industrial relocation and population
migration" (Thompson, 1978, p. 144). Between 1970
and 1975 the manufacturing belt grew less than half
as fast as the nation; at the same time, the South
and West grew twice as fast as the nation (Sternlieb
and Hughes, 1978, p. 94). Between the Civil War and
the Second World War, the manufacturing belt was "the
seedbed of the American system," an "American Rhur of
the New England, Mid-Atlantic and East North Central
Census Regions" (Rees, 1979, pp. 49 and 47). Since
then the Northeast has exhibited an "adverse
industrial structure" emphasising such lagging
industries as apparel, primary metals and motor
vehicles while the glamor industries of the postwar
period--electronics, computing equipment, scientific
instruments, and petrochemicals--have been nutured in
the sunbelt (Beyers, 1979).

Today in America there are fewer farmers and farm
laborers than there are teachers. Agricultural
influence is still strong, however, in the Midwestern
cornbelt which represents a fourth major subsection
of the Northern Core. Indeed, states such as Ohio,
Indiana and Illinois are at once included in both the
American manufacturing belt and the corn belt as
their histories of "up state-down state" political
rivalry testifies. This rivalry has been especially
intense in Illinois where remanents of boss Daley's
Cook County machine still creates sparks in
Springfield. Along the western margin of the
contiguous states of the Northern Core, however, corn
and hogs remain economic and political staples. In
1980 the defeat of such liberal Senators as Democrats
McGovern, Culver and Bayh had much to do with their
support of the Russian grain embargo, and presidential
campaign literature was careful to point out how the
candidates stood on agricultural trade with China.

The Midwest, it seems, is most selective in its
isolationism.

The Creation of the Republican Core
"Since the eighteenth century beginnings of the
United States the Northeast, as the seat of national
wealth, power, population and culture, has more often
than not dominated American politics," according to
Phillips (1970, p. 43). However, this long dominance
has corresponded with shifting patterns of cleavage
within the Core itself. Again following the by now
familiar strategy of extracting a maximal number of
interpretable factors, the voting structure of the
Northeast is found to require a total of six to
achieve a full description of its facets between 1896
and 1980 (Figure 4.7). These factors can be labelled
as follows.

Factor III which dominates from 1900 to 1924
clearly identifies the Old Republican North. Factor
V with the elections of 1928 to 1936 showing the
strongest loadings is titled the Democratic Challenge.
Factor VI joins elections from 1936 to 1944 and is
called the Late New Deal. Factor I with prominant
loadings between 1948 and 1956 is deemed the Post New
Deal Consolidation, even though it also exhibits an
impact of cleavages which existed before the old
Republican North at the time of the South-Western
revolt. Factors V, VI and I represent three
successive stages in the breakup of the formerly
dominant pattern. Factor II comes close to replacing
this pattern with another of some stability between
1960 and 1972 and is deemed the Liberal Normal Vote.
This factor, in fact looks strongly reminiscent of
the liberal normal vote factor at a national scale of
analysis (Figure 3.2). Beginning in 1976, however,
a replacement pattern termed the New North? is
established by Factor IV. A question mark is added
to this factor's label because it is still too early
to determine its permanency. Significantly, no
earlier election shows an appreciable loading on this
factor.

The interpretation of these factors is assisted by
examination of their intercorrelations (Figure 4.8).
The late New Deal and post New Deal consolidation
factors, for example, are strongly intercorrelated

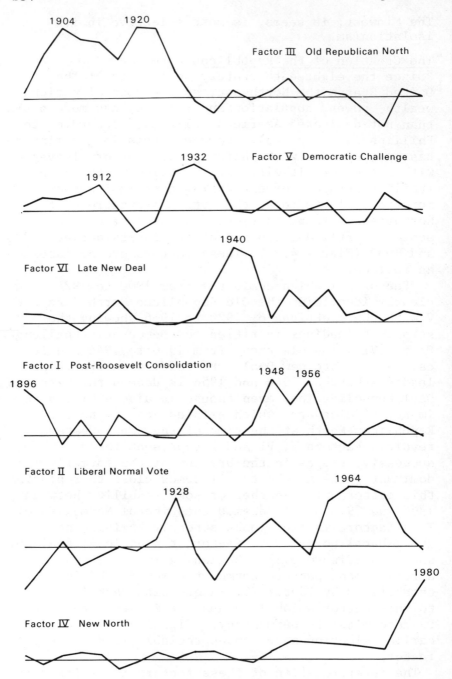

Figure 4.7   Factor Loading Profiles, Northern
Core 1896–1980

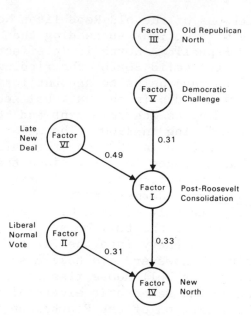

Figure 4.8   Factor Correlations, Northern
             Core 1896–1980

(+.49) and the new North factor shows moderate
correlations with each of these (+.34 and +.33
respectively) and the liberal normal vote (+.31).
Again it must be noted that the factor correlations
are only relative measures of correspondence. Nevertheless, it seems safe to suggest that in the North
as elsewhere new voting patterns have not totally
eradicated those established by previous generations.
   A puzzle has perhaps been posed by the treatments
given to the election of 1896 in previous discussion.
At national scale, this election was seen mainly as
deviating, rather than realigning, as has conven-
tionally been the case. Furthermore, it was seen to
fit rather well with the major early western pattern
which dominated, albeit with significant inter-
ruptions for the first two decades of the twentieth
century in the West and to impose scarcely a ripple
upon the solid South factor whose suffrage
restricting "Southern System" its wake reinforced.
The analysis for the North sheds considerable light
on the matter for in the factor profiles for this
region the election of 1896 is found to load, not

with the elections of the old Republican North, but
with two sets of elections succeeding the New Deal.
Since the old Republican North is in effect the
counterpart of the solid South, the finding for the
Northern section thus helps to account for why 1896
corresponded with a dip in the national sectional
normal vote leading to its resurgent and strongest
second phase beginning in 1900. The major question,
thus, is what happened in 1900 and thereafter in the
North, not what happened in 1896, since the
Republicans were so triumphant in the region from
Theodore Roosevelt to Herbert Hoover that the
Democrats could scarcely mount a believable challenge,
save for those during the Bull Moose fission and on
the eve of American entry into the First World War.
These were flukes, however. To take a specific case
in point, before the Bull Moose fission in 1912, Ohio
had cast exactly one Democratic electoral vote
following the formation of the Republican Party in
1856. In the region as a whole, the average
Democratic proportion of the popular vote exceeded
40 percent only once between 1900 and 1928, this
was in 1916 and perhaps in response to Wilson's
campaign slogan that "He kept us out of war"
(Roseboom and Eckes, 1979, p. 144). Even then,
however, sixteen of the twenty-two core states cast
Republican electoral votes to make the outcome a
highly sectional one, pitting the South and West
against the North.

What tends to be forgotten when the turn of the
century is viewed from a modern perspective is that
at the time the Democratic Party was "the party of
small towns and farms;" its base, in other words, was
mainly agrarian though there were some isolated
pockets of Democratic strength in urban ethnic
enclaves within the Northeast (Ladd and Hadley, 1978,
p. 37). But by and large, however, the Democrat's
Southern bastion projected an image of a "paternal-
istic and elitist conceptualization of...a substantially hierarchical society" (Elazar, 1972, p. 99).
The Republican Party, in contrast, tended to be
viewed as "the party of industrialization, as the
most likely instrument for national reform because
such reform could not come from those nostalgic for a

rural past" (Ladd and Hadley, 1978, p. 38). Events
at the turn of the century reinforced rather than
blurred these seeming differences in two ways. First,
the regular national Democratic and Republican
organizations were not all that far apart on a wide
range of social and economic issues. Cleveland, it
may be recalled, rebuffed requests for aid to
drought-stricken farmers with the stern comment that
"though the people support the government, the
government should not support the people" (Degler,
1974, p. 953). He also broke the Pullman strike with
federal troops (Morison and Commager, 1962, p. 242).

Contesting cleavages characterised the period.
When McKinley faced Bryan for the second time in 1900,
he did so after the nation had recovered from the
Panic of 1893 and with the slogan of a "full dinner
pail" (Roseboom and Eckes, 1979, p. 127). Four
years later Theodore Roosevelt demolished Parker as a
Progressive reformer offering a "square deal"
for labor (Morison and Commager, 1962, p. 466).

The second component contributing to the rise of
the old Republican North appears to have involved
ethnic rather than economic, cleavages although the
two were somewhat superimposed. Religious
differences aligned to some extent with partisan
differences in the urban core of the nation so that
groups dominated by a Catholic religious orientation
were more often than not the foundation of an urban
Democratic coalition (Kelley, 1979). As a
consequence, "Bryan's revivalist oratory might inflame
the Bible-belt—but in the city he was a repellent,
even comic figure" (Lubell, 1952, p. 38). Even those
major metropolitan dailies which were normally
Democratic in their editorial policies, and there
were admittedly not many, abandoned their party's
standard bearer and advised their readers to support
McKinley (Roseboom and Eckes, 1979, p. 122).

The national Populist-Democratic fusion created
intense cross-pressures in the North as it did in the
South. In the North those affected either swung
their electoral support to the GOP or stopped voting.
But, unlike in the South, withdrawal from the
electorate was a private rather than a public outcome.
Nevertheless, electoral participation in the region

edged downward from an average of more than eighty
percent in 1896 to low points of less than sixty
percent in 1920 and 1924. The last time Northern
participation had been this low was in 1836 when the
Whigs unsuccessfully fielded three regional candidates
in a futile effort to derail Van Buren's nonsectional
politics. The foundation of the old Republican North
now seems obvious: general economic prosperity and
Democratic agrarianism gave urbanites dissatisfied
with their circumstances nowhere else to go. Here is
another classic example of Schattschneider's
mobilisation of bias.

This argument is supported by the geographical
patterns revealed by the maps of estimated factor
scores. As previously observed, the election of 1896
loads most highly on Factor I although this factor is
more descriptive of much later alignments. Nevertheless, its pattern of estimated factor scores
(Figure 4.9(d)) shows greater Democratic strength in
western than in eastern subsections of the Northern
Core. Bryan's appeal was agrarian, not urban. In
marked contrast, the factor score map for the old
Republican North (Figure 4.9(a)) shows a tendency for
northeastern states to be moderately strong in their
Democratic voting by the standards of the era while
the western and midwestern states of the Core are
typically less Democratic although there are some
exceptions to this pattern. By far, however, the
strongest impression conveyed by the factor scores of
the old Republican North is that of cleavage along a
north-south axis: there is an almost unbroken line
of much heavier than average Democratic strength
along the section's juncture with the South. While
the point has been redundantly conveyed by now, this
adds further weight to the characterisation that the
second and most prominant phase of the national
sectional normal vote corresponds with the solid
South and the old Republican North at a sectional
scale of analysis.

Three Alternative Realignments

The breakup of the old Republican North occurred in
three phases which ultimately resulted in a near
reversal of the earlier tendency for this section to
be the least Democratically inclined of the three.

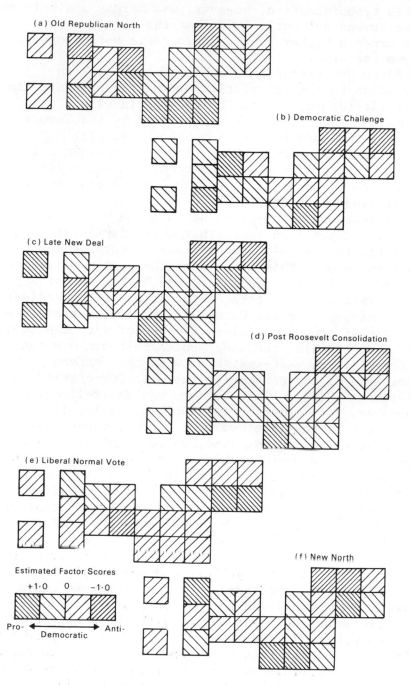

Figure 4.9   Estimated Factor Scores, Northern
              Core 1896–1980

This transformation, however, was hardly a simple one, for it was not until 1960 that the Northern Core returned a higher average Democratic vote proportion than the others.

Since our contentions are somewhat novel in relation to the description ordinarily presented in the literature, it will help to begin with a brief outline of the sequence as revealed by the T-mode factor analysis for the Northern Core. The Democratic challenge which arose to prominance in 1928, though with a minor antecedent suggestion of what was to come during the Bull Moose fission of 1912, and which continued in force through 1936 represented a cleavage so at variance with that of the old Republican North that there is virtually no correlation (+.14) between these factors (Figures 4.7 and 4.8). This break with the past was precipitated by Al Smith and reinforced by the second Roosevelt. The pattern of factor scores emphasises the change. Whereas Democratic strength before had been most pronounced along the border with the South (Figure 4.9(a)), the geographical pattern now tended to exhibit an east-west bias with the western portions of the core being the most Democratic (Figure 4.9(b)). This outcome was short-lived, however, for beginning in 1936, it was itself replaced by the late New Deal factor, especially prominent in 1940 and 1944, whereon the far western outliers, the southern border and the northeastern subregions, except for northern New England, were more Democratic than the Midwest (Figure 4.9(c)). A small correlation between this factor and that of the old Republican North (+.22) suggests a mild resurgence of older cleavages at this time. Beginning with the first post-World War II campaign, however, yet another pattern emerges. This is the post New Deal consolidation factor which is again essentially unrelated to the old Republican North (+.13), moderately associated with the Democratic challenge (+.31) and strongly linked to the late New Deal (+.49). At this time Democratic strength occurs in more southernly and more westernly sections of the Core (Figure 4.9(d)). The transformation is completed when the liberal normal vote emerges to

prominence. This factor, in turn, shows no correlation of substantial magnitude with the earlier ones
(i.e. of .20 or above). However, it is informative
that although too small to appear on the factor
correlation diagram, the correlations between this
factor and those of the old Republican North,
Democratic Challenge and post New Deal consolidation
were negative on the computer output. Let us now
examine the complexities of the transformation in
somewhat closer detail.

The last two elections of the old Republican North
(1920 and 1924) were also the most characteristic of
the era in that they exhibit the highest pair of
loadings on the factor profile involved and represent
perigees in the level of voter turnout in the region.
Between 1924 and 1928, however, average voter turnout
in the Core jumped nine percentage points to sixty-
eight percent and average Democratic support rose
even more strongly by nearly fifteen percentage
points to thirty-nine percent. Though obviously a
loosing margin in a two-party campaign—third party
effects were notably modest in 1928—this was still a
remarkable surge in Democratic strength in the region
and one most likely accounted for by the mobilisation
of new voting elements into the electorate.

It might be easy to dismiss this resurgence of
Democratic support in the Core as simply a rebound
toward a more normal reflection of the equilibrium
tradition of two-party politics. But if this is the
sole explanation, why does Smith load with Roosevelt
on the factor profile for the Democratic challenge?
This result is in fact heavily supportive of Lubell's
(1952, p. 35) comment that "Smith may be today's
'Forgotten Warrior' but the line he drew across the
map of American politics has never been erased." The
gist of Lubell's argument is this: before 1928 the
Democratic Party was no more and probably less urban
oriented than the Republican; after 1928 Democratic
candidates were increasingly successful in carrying
metropolitan areas, especially in the Northeast.
Smith was the Catholic son of Irish immigrant parents
whose rasping East Side accent, brown derby and
campaign theme song, "The Sidewalks of New York"
(Roseboom and Eckes, 1979, pp. 155-157; Lubell, 1952,

p. 38) emphasised and symbolised these origins. The
potential existed for galvanising the emergence of a
new set of electoral cleavages within the Core as a
shrill warning published by the Chicago Tribure
suggests (Merriam and Gosnell, 1940, p. 25):

> "If Al Smith is elected it will be due to three
> things: the Solid South, liquor and the foreign
> and Negro vote....In ten years Tammany would as
> completely dominate the United States as it now
> dominates New York."

It is doubtful that Smith received much support
from blacks who were still heavily committed to the
party of Lincoln, but he ran rather well in the
nation's major cities, including Chicago. In 1924
the Republicans beat Davis by one and a quarter
million votes in the nation's twelve largest cities;
Smith carried them by a slight plurality in 1928
(Lubell, 1952, p. 34). The urban Democratic margin
grew to nearly two million votes in 1932 and to more
than three and a half million in 1936. Smith, it
seems, can be given credit for bringing disenchanted
urbanites, often of Catholic immigrant stock, back
into the Northern electorate. This alone was not
sufficient to break the Republican hold on the
region, however. The Great Depression added the
remaining component.
     During the 1920's GNP increased at an average
annual rate of 4.7 percent as real per capita income
expanded by more than a quarter before the crash of
1929 (Lee and Passell, 1979, pp. 363-364. But from
an index of 216 in September, 1929, the stock market
collapsed to a bottom of 34 in June 1934. Bank
failures cost investors about $2.5 billion and the
stock market collapse wiped out a staggering $85
billion. By 1932 unemployment stood at nearly
twenty-three percent of the labor force. The cause--
over speculation in stocks, tight monetary policy,
crop failure, inadequate demand for durable goods,
excessive real estate speculation, and so on--
remains a puzzle to economic historians who still
have "no clean and quick explanation" (Lee and
Passell, 1979, p. 383). But whatever it was, "The

stock market crash in October 1929, and the spread of
the Great Depression changed the political picture,
as depressions always do" (Roseboom and Eckes, 1979,
p. 159).

As Merriam and Gosnell (1940, pp. 25-26) noted,
"one looks in vain in the platforms of the parties
or speeches of the candidates for the battle lines of
the 'new Deal'" in the contest of 1932 when both
candidates offered pledges of "economy and a balanced
budget," though both also "agreed on the desirability
of drastic farm relief and unemployment relief." The
outcome, therefore, was undoubtedly more a rejection
of Hoover than an acceptance of Roosevelt. But, the
Core's average Democratic proportion jumped another
fourteen points to fifty-three percent. It is
important to observe, however, that average Core
turnout in 1932 was sixty-eight percent, exactly what
it had been when Hoover faced Smith four years
earlier. This implies that a great deal of vote
switching took place between these two elections.
Nevertheless, there is evidence, undoubtedly known to
Lubell, that Roosevelt's pattern of support was
similar to Smith's. In their study of electoral
patterns in Chicago, for example, Gosnell and Gill
(1935, p. 972) found that "Roosevelt's highest votes
were obtained mainly in the same areas where Smith
obtained his highest votes." Their factor analysis,
apparently the first ecological use of the tool, in
fact yielded a "traditional Democratic vote" factor
with high positive loadings for Smith, Roosevelt,
Catholic origin, foreign birth, unemployment and
anti-prohibition sentiment on a referendum (Gosnell
and Gill, 1935, pp. 980-982).

In 1936 Roosevelt's average vote in the Core
reached nearly fifty-seven percent, the highest
achieved by any Democratic candidate up to that time.
This slight further increase also corresponded with
another spurt in turnout, to nearly seventy-three
percent, a level since exceeded only in 1940 and 1960
within the region. By the second Roosevelt campaign,
the programmatic configuration of the New Deal had
become apparent, and there is evidence that this had
an impact on certain segments of the electorate,
particularly among blacks and Jewish voters who had

formerly inclined toward the GOP (Merriam and Gosnell,
1940; Lubell, 1952; Ladd and Hadley, 1978). Campbell,
et.al.(1960, p. 92), for example, report that "During
the 1920's the vote in heavily Jewish districts of
Eastern metropolises ran as high as 80 percent
Republican" so that "the orientation of this group
toward the two parties was substantially altered
during the 1930's." By the 1950's about two-thirds
of Jewish survey respondents were classifying themselves as Democrats (Nie, Verber and Petrocik, 1979,
p. 230). In 1932 blacks apparently supported Hoover
by a margin of two to one in Chicago and Cincinnati,
but by 1936 they had switched to the same margin for
Roosevelt (Ladd and Hadley, 1978, pp. 59-60). This
is the same pattern uncovered by Lewis (1960, p. 384)
for a smaller community in Michigan; in his words,
"Flint's Negroes were relatively untouched by the
political upheaval of 1932," but four years later
"returned a Democratic landslide of eighty-one
percent" in one largely black precinct. The second
Roosevelt and the first truly New Deal election thus
seems to have exerted a converting influence in the
Northern black community (Nie, Verba and Petrocik,
1979, p. 226).

The composition of the Smith-Roosevelt coalition
altered between the first and second subperiods of
the New Deal, however. This is evidenced by the fact
that two distinct factors emerge for the period as a
whole in the Northern Core (Figure 4.7). The
transition year was 1936 when the Democratic
challenge and the late New Deal factors each account
for an appreciable proportion of election variance.
By 1940 and again in 1944 the latter factor is
clearly dominant. In some respects this reflected
the reappearance of older voting patterns in the
region as suggested by the correlation between the
late New Deal and the old Republican North factors.
This was also echoed in the mild resurgence of the
sectional normal vote at national scale at the same
time (Figure 3.2).

The change in the geographical locus of strongest
Democratic support away from the Midwest (Figure
4.9(b and c)) is indicative that ethnic forces
similar to those described for the Western section of

the nation were operating here as well. Iowa,
Wisconsin and Minnesota are states with moderately
strong German minorities and each shows a drop of at
least one level of relative Democratic strength from
the Democratic challenge to the late New Deal. As
Phillips (1970, pp. 372) suggests "Roosevelt
lost five farm states in 1940, principally because of
isolationist voting;" the shift was especially
strong in areas with large numbers of Germans where the
Republican vote rose 35 to 45 percent between 1936
and 1940.   Voter participation declined in the
Northeast between 1940 and 1944 and remained low in
1948. War-time mobilisation and the confusion
surrounding the Truman-Dewey contest are probably
responsible for this.

    Although 1948 did not apparently exert the same
powerful impact upon the North that it did upon the
South, it nevertheless signaled a shift from the late
New Deal to a post New Deal consolidation pattern
within the region. This contributed to the
distinctiveness of this election at national scale
(Figure 3.2). It did not usher in an entirely new
sectional normal voting pattern as it did in the West,
however. Instead, it aligns with the two succeeding
Eisenhower-Stevenson contests (Figure 4.7) to reflect
a third phase in the breakup of the old Republican
North when the geographical pattern of Democratic
strength once again shifted away from the New England
and Mid-Atlantic subsections of the Core toward the
southern and western margins (Figure 4.9(d)).

    What perhaps characterises the 1948 to 1956 era
from the vantage point of the Northern Core is that
its influence was strong within both major parties
at the time, producing a contest of moderates in the
final election campaigns. The core South, which at
first threatened to become the least Democratic
section of the nation, somewhat reverted to its
earlier stance by supporting Stevenson; at the same
time Democratic voting in the Core began to recede
toward pre-New Deal levels in a geographical pattern
somewhat reminiscent of that earlier period.
Consequently, the Core's reaction to changes in the
voting structures of the other two regions was somewhat delayed in time. In this regard, it is worth

recalling that the late New Deal and the post New Deal
consolidation factors are highly intercorrelated
(Figure 4.8).

The Democratic Core

The liberal normal vote factor presents a most interesting appearance in its profile (Figure 4.7).
Although this factor is essentially uncorrelated with
any of those preceding, its profile, nonetheless,
shows that the alignment involved had been presaged
by earlier individual elections, especially that of
1928. It is also of interest that negative loadings
for 1896 and 1936 make this the only Northern factor
to exhibit noticeable bipolarity. The profile also
shows evidence that the liberal normal vote pattern began
to emerge in the 1940's before being arrested by an
interlude during the Eisenhower era. Each of these
aspects deserves attention.

What is perhaps most impressive about this factor
is that aside from the old Republican North, it is
the only one to exhibit strength over a consecutive
sequence of more than three elections. It also
corresponds to a period during which Northern
Democratic voting was higher than that of any other
region of the country. Indeed, 1960 is notable as
the first time in history that this had happened,
although by only a slight margin. In each of the three
succeeding elections, the average Democratic vote for
the states of the Northern Core exceeded that of the
Western Periphery by more than five and that of the
Southern Periphery by more than ten percentage
points. This represents a complete reversal of
stance from that exhibited by the Core during the
first quarter of the twentieth century. The Core had
again become the most consistent supporter of the
more liberal of the two major parties as it had been
during the era of the old Republican North. It is
hard to avoid interpreting this as altogether
consistent with the declining fortunes of the region
relative to those of the sunbelt although the federal
role in encouraging expansion of the two peripheries
at the expense of the Core did not become a highly
polemical issue until near the end of the liberal
normal vote era (Pierce and Stanfield, 1976).

The congruent appearances of the liberal normal vote profile for the Northern Core (Figure 4.7) and the liberal normal vote profile for the nation as a whole (Figure 3.2) cannot excape notice. Both show dominant loadings for the four elections between 1960 and 1972. Indeed, the resemblance brings to mind the congruence which had existed early in the century between the sectional normal vote at national and the solid South and old Republican North factors at sectional levels. Although the voting structures of the era reflect both the pressures of an expanded electorate and the complexities of a metropolitan-industrial economy, there was thus a recent period during which the shifting cleavages of section and party once again rotated into close correspondence. In the West, the new western normal vote first appeared in 1952 and has been relatively to strongly apparent ever since (Figure 4.4). In the South, the realignment pattern prevailed during the period under discussion (Figure 4.2). What is perhaps most surprising is that the highly sectionalised politics of the 1960's has gone largely unremarked upon in the literature. Although the attention of observers was reveted upon the behavior of individual voters, the sections were indeed responding as a system of systems, to employ Elazar's cogent phrase.

As earlier mentioned, several preceding elections exhibit interpretably large loadings on the liberal normal vote factor. The strongest of these loadings is the one for the contest of 1928 in which a Catholic first received a major party's presidential nomination. The second time this happened was in 1960. Just as Smith had done, Kennedy succeeded in increasing both the level of voter turnout and the level of Democratic support within the Core, although by somewhat lesser amounts. But whereas Smith faced an electorate within which Republican partisanship was clearly in the majority, the opposite was true of Kennedy. Nevertheless, "the Democratic proportion of the two-party vote among Catholics across the nation skyrocketed from a rough 50 percent in the two Eisenhower elections to a vote of 80 percent for Kennedy" (Converse, et.al., 1966, p. 84). Though Southern Protestants shied away from his candidacy in

substantial proportions, the effect outside the South
was a net gain of nearly two percent of the normal
Democratic vote (Pool, Ableson, and Popkin, 1964,
pp. 117-118).

Thus, for the second time in a row a Catholic's
quest for the White House corresponded with a shift
in the voting structure of the Northern Core. This
time, the effect was even more persistent in duration.
Part of the credit for this doubtless goes to
Goldwater whose impact upon the Northern electorate
has been more or less ignored until recently. His
nomination was important for it represented a clear
challenge to Northern influence within the Republican
Party and contributed to a landslide victory for
Johnson. Indeed, "The 1964 election tore the
Republican Party loose from its Yankee roots" to
such an extent that "Several counties where the GOP
had not once dipped below 60 percent in presidential
races since 1920 gave Goldwater only 30 percent
support" (Phillips, 1970, pp. 101 and 100). In an
analysis based upon survey information it was
recently found that the proportion of New England and
Middle Atlantic voters who cast straight Republican
ballots plummeted from half to less than a quarter
between 1960 and 1964 (Hadley and Howell, 1980).
Moreover, it was found that the decrease was more
pronounced among upper rather than lower status,
among rural and suburban rather than urban, and among
Protestant rather than Catholic voters. In short,
Goldwater's candidacy was an exogenous shock to the
Northern Republican coalition. Whereas straight-
ticket Republican voting averaged 67 percent in the
eastern subsection of the Core between 1952 and 1960,
it averaged a mere 34 percent between 1964 and 1976
supporting the assertion that the Republican Party
is loosing its demographic base of support in the
Northeast (Hadley and Howell, 1980).

In 1968 and 1972 the patterns established by the
two preceding elections maintained within the core
although lower levels of Democratic voting were
manifested. Still, it is notable that even in the
Democratic debacle of 1972 McGovern's only electoral
votes came from within this section.

The negative loading for Bryan in 1896 on the
liberal normal vote factor at first poses a conundrum.
The mystery vanishes, however, when the geographical
distribution of factor scores associated with this
factor is examined (Figure 4.9(e)). Bryan's appeal,
it will be recalled, was greater in the agrarian
periphery than the urban-industrial heartland of the
Core. This pattern is almost perfectly mirrored by
the factor score map for the liberal normal vote which
shows above average Democratic strength concentrated
in a belt extending from Massachusetts to New York.
This establishes the locus of strongest pro-Democratic
orientation during the period as in northern
Megalopolis, though an outlying concentration is also
apparent in the upper Midwest, a reminder, perhaps,
of the penetration of the moralistic political
culture into this subsection. These are also
subsections of the Core within which Catholics have
long represented a potent political force. The
negative factor loading for 1936 is also something of
a puzzle until it is recalled that the late New Deal
factor (Figure 4.9(c)) upon which this election loads
most heavily was associated with a pattern of
increasing Democratic support toward the South and
West, a pattern which also mirrors that of the liberal
normal vote. The liberal normal vote thus identifies
the Core as the most Democratic section of the nation
with the epicenter of that sentiment to be found in
northern megalopolis. This is a complete turnabout
from the heyday of the old Republican North.

Jimmy Carter and the New North

A new pattern of electoral cleavage began to emerge
in 1976 and became dominant within the Northern Core
of the nation in 1980 (Figure 4.7). This is the
implication of the New North? factor which is
distinctive in that no election prior to 1976
exhibits a loading of interpretable magnitude. The
factor analysis results thus emphasise the fact that
the Northern pattern of Democratic voting across the
twenty-two states of the region in 1980 exhibits but
one correlation above point five with others included
in the analysis; this involves the preceding
electoral contest of 1976 (+.83). No other recent
election shows such tenuous links with previous

patterns of cleavage within the region, although it
should be noted that the new North? factor is not
entirely independent of temporally preceding ones,
since there are moderate positive correlations
between this and both the post New Deal consolidation
and the liberal normal vote factors (Figure 4.8).
These correlations are relatively modest, however,
(+.33 and +.31, respectively) and the absence of any
substantial loading for an election before 1976 on
the new North? factor is quite striking. Since only
two elections can be identified as associated with
this factor, caution needs to be exercised in
interpretation but there is certainly some indication
of structional change in the Northeastern voting
pattern during the latter half of the decade of the
1970's.

   With so few elections involved ideosyncratic short
term influences no doubt affected the geographical
distribution of varying intensities of Democratic
support within the Northeastern Core as shown by the
map of estimated factor scores (Figure 4.9(f)). As
one possibility, it seems likely that "native" state
advantages accrued to Ford in Michigan in 1976 and to
Reagan in Illinois in 1980, lessening otherwise to be
expected Democratic voting proportions in these
instances. On the other side of the two-party
division, it is highly probable that Carter's running
mate, Mondale, help to boost Democratic proportions
in Minnesota in both years. Nevertheless, there are
apparent subsectional variations.

   New England is perhaps the most divided of the
subsections under the regime of the new North voting
structure for while southern New England, with the
exception of Connecticut, is generally above average
in the level of Democratic support, the converse is
the case of the northern portion of this subsection.
Indeed, New Hampshire and Vermont are shown as the
least Democratic of the twenty-two states, thus
offering a reminder that Vermont has cast Democratic
electoral votes only once in the last century (during
the Democratic landslide of 1964). The middle-
Atlantic subsection, representing the core of
megalopolis, shows slightly above average Democratic
support although New Jersey fails to make this a

unified pattern. The upper-Midwest, with the
exception of Michigan, is also above or well above
average, thus completing several facets of a
correspondence between this pattern and that of the
liberal normal vote (Figure 4.9(e)). In marked
contrast to the liberal normal vote, however, there
is a tendency for states along the southern margin of
the section to be more or much more Democratic than
the norm. This may reflect Carter's Southern
origins, but it also brings to mind the most salient
aspect of the post New Deal consolidation voting
pattern (Figure 4.9 (d)). Moderately low levels of
Democratic support are seen in the corn belt Midwest
and the western outliers of the Core in a pattern
more reminiscent of the liberal normal vote than of
the post-New Deal consolidation.

It is of interest to note that each of the four
Core states to cast Democratic electoral ballots in
1980--Rhode Island, Maryland, West Virginia and
Minnesota--is shown as much more Democratic than the
norm for the new North? factor. The District of
Columbia was also tallied as Democratic in the
electoral College, but was excluded from our analysis
because it only recently became eligible to vote in
Presidential elections (in 1964). Outside the Core
only two states were recorded for Carter in 1980,
Georgia and Hawaii.

Although the new North pattern of factor scores is
novel in its overall appearance, it shares elements
of resemblance to earlier ones. In particular, there
is a tendency for northern megalopolis and the upper
Midwest to be more than typically Democratic in
keeping with the distribution for the liberal normal
vote, and a tendency for Democratic support to
increase along the southern margin of the region in
keeping with the post New Deal consolidation pattern.
These geographical similarities with the past prompt
a question as to whether the new North cleavage is a
transitory deviation from what recently seemed a
relatively stable liberal normal vote within the
core, reflecting perhaps the novelty of a Southerner
at the head of the Democratic ballot, or whether the
outcomes of the two most recent elections will form
a new baseline of divisions with the region.

Adding intrigue to this question is the fact that
the election of 1980 brought with it signs that
voters of the Core may be susceptible to a third-
party rebellion of their own if the two major parties
again field candidates and adopt strategies
reflecting the rise of the sunbelt. Although John
Anderson only slightly exceeded the five percent
national cutoff required by the Federal Election
Commission for eligibility for federal campaign funds,
he did much better than this in parts of the Core.
In the Northeast as a whole he averaged eight and a
half percent of the popular ballot and exceeded ten
percent in all six New England states where the
moralistic political culture remains strong. He also
exceeded ten percent of the vote in Minnesota,
Colorado and Washington which Elazar (1972) also
classed as partially moralistic in tone. Indeed,
this pattern would seem to make Anderson, rather than
Reagan, Lincoln's true electoral heir.

CHAPTER 5
Section and Party

A decade ago Walter Dean Burnham (1970, p. 3)
lamented that our understanding of American elections
was being hindered by "an annoying incompleteness in
certain key ranges of data analysis; this often
leaves us in controversy, not only as to the implications of the facts of change, but even as to the
structure of those facts themselves." By careful
application of factor analytic techniques to
electoral returns for presidential contests since
1828, we have been able to delineate 'structure'
within these 'facts' so as to be able to claim to
have made a significant contribution to eliminating
Burnham's 'annoying incompleteness.' This inductive
purpose constituted the initial stimulus for
producing this monograph, but as the work progressed,
it became much more than a simple 'factorial ecology
of elections.' A large proportion of our text is
devoted to the context within which the factor
analysis results are interpreted. Quite simply it
became apparent at a very early stage that the
geography of American presidential elections could
only be adequately understood within a framework
which emphasized the political role of both section
and party. Hence, the title of this volume.
   The sections are interpreted as the geographical
expression of broad materialist interests within the
evolving American state. The sections and the
interests being reflected change over time, but this
geographical basis for economic conflict has been

remarkably resilient over two hundred years. This is
the product of both the spatial organization of
presidential elections through state-based Electoral
College arrangements and its interaction with the
spatial organization of the American economy
responding to both specialization and integration
processes. As recognised by Turner many years ago,
the sheer continental scale of the United States will
produce a sectional politics that is largely missing
from the much smaller European states. Sectional
strategy has, therefore, always been a fundamental
element of presidential politics from the very first
geographically 'balanced ticket' in 1789.

But what is the political institution that actually
utilizes this sectional strategy? After an inhospi-
table beginning, political parties have come to
dominate presidential politics. This was certainly
evident by 1800 and was generally accepted after
1836. Parties became indispensable mobilizers of
public opinion for their chosen candidates. In this
way sectionalized economic interests could only
aspire to control the American state through use of
the political party. Parties consequently tended to
become sectionalized as particular economic interests
dominated particular parties. This was not always a
simple process, however, and our analyses show that
there was not a smooth evolution in the matching of
economic forces to political parties. In fact, much
of the interest in the history of presidential
politics comes from the mismatches and challenges to
dominant economic interests. Nevertheless, the
overall conclusion must be that parties have been
major tools in the manipulation of public opinion for
the benefit of the dominant classes and sections in
America. This Schattsneider based view of political
parties as 'the mobilization of bias' reached its
apogee in 1980 as the parties limited the
electorate's choice to a very small range in the
political spectrum.

This context is vital for our analyses as we aim
toward a 'new' electoral geography, but it does
remain based upon secondary sources--Turner, Key,
Schattsneider, et.al.--and, therefore, within the
broader realm of electoral studies the major interest

in this monograph will be the primary research
findings from the factor analyses. We conclude,
therefore, with a brief review of the more interesting results from the inductive parts of our study.
This is organised into two parts, the first
considering some general results of the analyses and
the second highlighting several of the more specific
findings.

POLITICAL SECTIONALISM: SOME GENERAL RESULTS
By 'general results' we mean ideas derived from more
than a simple analysis. Three such sets of ideas are
briefly enumerated here.

The relationship between our analyses and previous
ideas concerning critical elections, realignments and
party systems has been a recurrent theme throughout
the study. Our analyses are interesting because in
part they support existing models and at the same
time suggest important modifications. Although the
critical elections and realignment periods of earlier
studies are identifiable within our analyses, they
do not appear to be of equal importance. This has
led us to utilize a different three-fold classification of presidential politics: sectional competition to 1860, sectional dominance to 1944 and
sectional volatility since then.

This largely maintains the realignment of the Civil
War era, but reduces the importance of the other two
critical periods, the 1890's and 1928-1932. In our
reinterpretation, these merely define 'phases' within
one era of sectional dominance. The most original
suggestion of our classification is the identification of 1948 as initiating the current era of
politics. Most previous researchers seem to have
chosen to underplay the importance of the Dixiecrat
revolt of that year whereas in our analysis it
represents the first major sign of the breakup of the
politics of sectional dominance. We may even suggest
that its neglect by previous researchers reflects a
sectional dominance within political science. We may
also suggest that excessive preoccupation with the
voting behavior of individuals has obscured the joint
dependence of party appeal and voter response.
Despite self descriptions of waining partisan

attachment, the election of a President is still a
duopolistic mobilization of bias and a contest of
competing cleavages.

The second general result that we choose to
emphasise here is the way in which our analyses pick
up patterns of voting and not overall levels of
voting. Our discussion is about sectional conflicts
and sectional alliances and these exist for an
election irrespective of whether a particular
strategy is successful or not. For instance, the
nonsectional politics of pre-Civil War days produced
alternating party victories while the underlying
pattern of alliances remained relatively constant
from 1836 to 1852. This property of our analyses to
emphasise pattern is particularly pertinent in the
twentieth century since, for example, the vast
differences in the outcomes of the 1928 and 1932
elections do not hide their basic similarities in
pattern. Even more striking is the finding regarding
the set of elections from 1960 to 1972. Two of these
were landslide victories; one for the Democrats in
1964 and one for the Republicans in 1972. Nevertheless, they all show a basic similarity of underlying sectional alliances. McGovern in 1972 tended
to do better in those places where Johnson had done
better in 1964, although nowhere did he do as well.
In some ways, this finding is counter-intuitive (and,
hence, especially interesting). It warrants further
investigation, particularly in the way it relates to
differential turnout between groups and states over
time.

The third general point relates to the relationship
between the analyses at national and sectional
scales. These exhibit both interesting similarities
and important differences. Most important, of
course, is the fact that the sections are not simple
mirror images of the nation as a whole. This is
what makes sectional strategies so vital for
presidential politics. Nevertheless, salient
features of the national pattern can be found
replicated in the sectional patterns. These
relations suggest changing sectional politics within
the national polity. The most obvious coincidence
is between the national and southern analyses in
identifying 1948 as a key election. This emphasises

the basic role of the South in the old sectional
alignment. In contrast the North analysis coincides
with the national analysis most notably from 1960 to
1972 which we have interpreted as reflecting a
liberal core lead within the national polity.
Finally, the most recent elections suggest that
perhaps we will be entering a period when what
happens in the West becomes particularly important
for national politics.

POLITICAL SECTIONALISM: MORE SPECIFIC FINDINGS
Our more specific findings relate to factor analytic
results for particular elections or groups of
elections. We would not claim that any single one
was particularly original or new, but all are
explicitly generated by our analyses and warrant
further consideration in future researches. We
highlight twelve specific findings here in approximately their chronological order.
    1. The nonsectional normal vote from 1836 to 1852
neatly describes a very unusual set of elections.
Our findings on the matter are consistent with
several recent studies which emphasise the importance
of Martin Van Buren. Although this period is often
referred to as 'Jacksonian,' our analysis clearly
supports the view that the electoral politics of this
era only develops fully after 1836 under the
influence of Van Buren.
    2. Previous researchers have been uncertain in
their treatment of the period between the nonsectional politics and the sectional politics that
followed. The third party system is typically
initiated in the mid-1850's with the emergence of the
Republican Party. Although it has not been suggested
that this was a smooth transition, our analysis does
emphasise the complexity of the process. In
particular, the elections of 1856 and 1860 do not
seem to presage a new pattern of sectional politics
despite their explicit sectional nature. Rather
these two elections form their own singular pattern
of sectional politics. In fact this part of our
analysis throws into doubt the notion of a
distinctive ongoing third party system from 1854-1856
to 1892-1896.

3. One part of the analysis of this period that is consistent with that of other recent researchers is to be found in the timing of the Reconstruction factor. In particular, this pattern of voting does not abruptly end with the withdrawal of troops from southern states, but recedes gradually through to the 1890's. That the effects of Reconstruction outlasted Federal occupation and delayed the formation of the 'solid South' is now generally accepted, and our factor neatly calibrates these effects on presidential voting.

4. A dominant finding of our analyses is that of a sectional normal vote beginning in the third party system, covering all the fourth party system, and concluding within the fifth party system. Hence, our analyses emphasise similarities across these often strongly differentiated party systems. But, interestingly enough they do emerge as 'phases of intensity' within the sectional normal vote which dominated the national voting structure from 1884 to 1944. This suggests that while the critical elections previously identified do represent changes in sectional relations, they do not signal fundamental alterations of the sectional cleavages underlying the era as a whole.

5. That the sectional basis of American politics does consist of three distinct sections is conclusively shown through our regionalization by S-mode factor analysis. This inductive exercise produced several interesting elements, particularly the assignment of California and Washington to the northern group of states. However, the results are more than just a regionalization since the factor loadings measure the 'degree' to which each state belongs to each section. This explicitly identifies border states between sections and even states with electoral elements of all three sections such as Missouri and New Mexico.

6. The election of 1896 represents an unsuccessful challenge to the sectional normal vote. In fact the treatment of 1896 in our analyses is perhaps the most original contribution of our findings. The 1896 election dominates its own factor and does not relate to the sectional normal vote. In this sense, it is

neither the end of an era, nor the beginning of a new
one; instead, it is a deviating election par
excellence. It represents the failure of the
Democrats to forge a peripheral alliance to defeat
the core. As it was a failure, it does not
contribute to future patterns—South and West
immediately diverged again in 1900. Hence, to understand the Republican dominance of the early twentieth
century, we need to place more emphasis upon the
election that reinaugurated that particular pattern
of sectional alliances: namely, the election of 1900
not that of 1896.

7. One finding that does agree with several recent
studies is the close relationship between 1928 and
1932 despite the massive differences in their overall
results. In several of our analyses at national and
sectional scales, 1928 and 1932 load at similar
levels on the same factor. Interestingly the main
difference between them is that the 1928 election of
Al Smith more often relates to the more recent past
than Roosevelt's more famous victory. If any pattern
of voting survived into the 1960's, it was an Al
Smith coalition, not a Roosevelt New Deal coalition.
This is largely because Smith briefly showed, before
1948, that the South need not be so solidly
Democratic. Roosevelt's first two campaigns created
a slight retreat from the old politics of sectionalism, but this did not last into the latter half of
his administration. In hindsight, therefore, it is
Roosevelt who represents the end of an electoral era
while Smith represents a glimpse into the future.

8. This point is emphasised by our finding that
1948 was a key election in national politics. This
has been mentioned above as a general point, but
warrants repeating, since it is so at variance with
all other viewpoints on recent American presidential
politics. Quite simply, 1948 marks the end of the
most dominant factor we identify—the sectional
normal vote. It does not, however, directly point
the way to a new sectional pattern and, therefore,
should be seen, like 1896, as an important deviating
election.

9. The two elections of the 1950's provided a
laboratory for the first sustained investigation of

American elections using survey methods. In some
way, it is unfortunate, therefore, that they emerge
from our analyses as fairly distinctive, a 'diluted'
throwback to the pre-1948 era. This result can be
found in the national analysis and to varying degrees
in the sectional analyses.

   10. Much more important is the finding that the
period from 1960 to 1972 shows the nearest we have
come to a consistent pattern to replace the old
sectional normal vote. If these analyses had been
carried out before the 1976 dlection, we would have
confidently written of a new normal vote transcending
landslide victories for each party. Surprisingly
perhaps, this pattern of just four elections has
disappeared. However, it is certainly something to
look out for in 1984, especially if the Democrats
nominate a northern politician such as Edward
Kennedy.

   11. One particularly topical finding is the
distinctiveness of the last two elections culminating
in the defeat of Carter in 1980. At the national
level the uniqueness of this pattern of sectional
alliances is represented as an inverse of 1896,
making Ronald Reagan the heir apparent of William
Jennings Bryan! The bible-agrarian belt of the past
is today's sun belt, a metamorphosis which has
perhaps precipitated a realignment of parties of
equal importance to a realignment of voters.
However, this phenomena is more than a new South-West
sectional alliance. Within the North, 1976 and 1980
appear to constitute a new pattern of voting which we
suggest may be the first strivings of a 'New North,'
a northern revolt to complement earlier southern and
western revolts as this former dominant section, and
especially its northeastern subsection, adjusts to
new patterns of sectional alliance.

   12. Finally the reversals that have taken place in
the stability of sectional responses to presidential
elections is worthy of note. It seems that the
'solid South' has been replaced by a 'solid West.'
Whereas the West was once the most volatile of the
three sections, it now provides the Republican Party
with a new heartland. Meanwhile, the Democratic
South has crumbled to such an extent that even a

native Democratic southerner could not win it for his
party in 1980. While one of the issues that
perplexed Republicans in the past was how to counter-
act an antagonistic solid South, in the future the
Democrats must begin to devise a strategy for
tackling an antagonistic solid West in presidential
elections.

In recent years much has been written on both the
decline of party and the lessening of the relevance
of section in American politics. In 1980 both the
complete rout of John Anderson as an independent
and the explicitly sectional strategy of both party
campaigns suggests section and party are not dead,
but are alive and kicking. What is true is that
the relationships between party and section become
much more subtle as American elections become more
volatile affairs. Many commentators have confused
these important, but subtle changes, with notions of
the emergence of a new independent and nationalized
electorate. No such beast has more than fleetingly
emerged. That section and party have had crucial and
interdependent roles to play in the evolution of the
American state has been abundantly documented by this
study. We see no fundamental reason why they should
not continue as vital components of the American
state in the future for there is still, in Turner's
phrase, "a geography of American politics."

Appendices

Appendix A   FACTOR ANALYTIC PROCEDURES

The factor analytic procedures used in this investigation are outlined in Chapter One. This appendix
expands upon that discussion for those interested in
more technical aspects of our analysis.   In
particular, it examines the rationale for adopting
the common factor model with oblique direct oblimin
rotation and factor-based scales in the cross-
temporal analyses of Chapters Two through Four, as
well as the use of the common factor model with
orthogonal varimax rotation in the regionalizing
analysis of Chapter Three. It also offers background
on the terminology employed and the use of factor
analysis in ecological electoral research.

   All factor analyses share the aim of representing
a set of observed patterns in terms of a smaller set
of hypothetical variables called factors. There are,
however, a wide range of rather distinctive
techniques which fall under the same general label so
that the term factor analysis is probably better
thought of as referring to a family of techniques
rather than to a single one. This appendix makes no
attempt to cover the entire spectrum; it focuses upon
the specific operational procedures which we have
adopted. Readers wishing a more comprehensive
coverage of the subject are encouraged to consult one
of the many available references on factor analysis
and related multivariate statistics. Some, such as
Harman (1967) or Morrison (1967) require a background

in statistics and matrix algebra for comprehension.
Others, such as Cattell (1952), Fruchter (1954), or
Rummel (1970), are less demanding in these respects.
A wide choice of substantive settings is also
available: some treatments are oriented toward
psychology (e.g. Harmon, 1967; Cattell, 1952), others
toward educational testing and measurement
(e.g. Fruchter, 1954), and yet others toward
political and social science (e.g. Rummel, 1970). In
geography, a number of texts in spatial analysis
incorporate sections on factor analysis including
King (1969), Johnston (1978), and Taylor (1977).
Since the factor analyses for this research were
undertaken using the SPSS algorithm, it needs to be
noted that Kim's (1975) discussion of the algorithm
incorporates a brief introduction to the general
subject.

Background
The concept of latent factors was first developed in
the late nineteenth century (Galton, 1888, cited in
Morrison, 1967, p. 260) and soon thereafter applied
to operationalize the psychological notion of
"general intelligence" (Spearman, 1904, cited in
Morrison, 1967, p. 260). The bifactor model first
developed for this task posited that the performance
of a group of people on a series of tests can be
accounted for by one general underlying dimension
plus a set of minor or specific dimensions for each
included variable (Rummel, 1970, pp. 330-332).
Criticisms that intelligence is not unidimensional
led to the development of the more flexible multifactor model capable of handling several general
factors at once (Thurstone, 1945; Cattell, 1952).
  With the emergence of multifactor techniques factor
analysis became attractive to researchers beyond
psychology and educational testing. One of the
earliest applications, in fact, was the use of
Thurstone's multiple factor model by Gosnell and Gill
(1935) to investigate the outcome of the 1932
presidential election in Chicago. More recent uses
of factor analysis in electoral research include
MacRae and Meldrum (1960; 1969), Reynolds and Archer
(1969), Dykstra and Reynolds (1978), Taylor and
Johnston (1979), and Downing, et.al. (1980). By far

the most widespread application of factorial methods
to areal data analysis, however, has been in the
field of urban factorial ecology where many studies
have derived the familiar trilogy of socio-economic
rank, family status, and ethnicity as the basic
dimensions of census tract data (Schwirian, 1972;
Johnston, 1976). Interestingly, both streams of
research could trace their antecedents back to the
Gosnell and Gill (1935) study which combined
electoral and ecological data within the same correlation matrix, although contemporary researchers
might frown on thus mixing different causal levels
within the same factor array.

Data Cube

The aim of factor analysis is to derive a smaller set
of basis vectors or factors from a larger collection
of data. The results obtained necessarily reflect
both data operationalization and analysis operationalization. As Schwirian (1976, p. 139) recently
observed in the context of factorial ecology,
"different inputs lead to different resulting factor
structures" so that in Johnston's (1976, p. 23) words,
"Perhaps more concern should be expressed about the
nature of the material fed into factorial ecologies
than with the method itself." Indeed, so-called
"modes" of analysis are differentiated, not in
relation to the methodology used for extracting
factors, but in relation to the data array examined.

Six alternative factor analytic modes exist. Using
notation first suggested by Cattell (1952) and later
adopted by Rummel (1970) and Johnston (1978), these
modes can be denoted using the letters R and Q, P and
O, and T and S. The modes are paired since each
member of a pair represents one or another transpose
of a single slice through a data cube whose axes for
present purposes may be regarded as constituencies,
offices, and elections. This idea of a data cube is
similar to Berry's (1964) notion of a geographic
matrix. An entry into this data cube is the
proportion of the electorate of a constituency
casting ballots for the Democratic candidate for a
specific office in a given election. For example,
one entry might be the proportion of Iowa's popular
vote received by Culver who sought reelection to the

Senate in 1980. Another might be Wilson's proportion
of the vote cast in Vermont in 1912, and so on.
Using this framework, three sets of potential
electoral factor analysis can be suggested, depending
upon alternative transposes of three data cube slices,
as follows:

I.   Cross-section analyses with election year fixed:
     R-mode analysis of correlations between
     candidates for different offices in terms of
     support over constituencies. This yields the
     general structure of Democratic voting in a given
     election with respect to locations. Q-mode
     analysis of correlations between constituencies
     in terms of their support for candidates for
     different offices. This yields the regional
     structure of Democratic voting in a given
     election.

II. Time-series analyses with constituency fixed:
     P-mode analysis of correlations between
     candidates for different offices over election
     years. This yields patterns of similar voting
     behaviour for different offices over time in a
     given jurisdiction. O-mode analysis of corre-
     lations between election years in terms of
     support for candidates seeking different offices.
     This yields a temporal categorisation of
     elections in terms of similar support levels for
     different offices.

III. Geographic-series analyses with office fixed:
     T-mode analysis of correlations between elections
     over jurisdictions. This yields the structure of
     Democratic voting for one office over time.
     S-mode analysis of correlations between juris-
     dictions over elections. This yields a regional-
     ization of Democratic voting for a period of
     investigation.

     Not all of these alternatives have been represented
in the literature, for as Rummel (1970, p. 202)
recently noted, the six possible modes of analysis
"have not been fully appreciated" by researchers.
Downing, et.al.'s (1980) study of patterns of support
for Democratic candidates across Massachusetts cities
and towns during the gubernatorial, senatorial and
otherwise general election of 1978 in Massachusetts

exemplifies R-mode electoral analysis. Q-mode
electoral analysis is pertinently, though not
perfectly, exemplified by Russett's (1969) derivation
of supranational regions on the basis of the 18th
U. N. General Assembly roll call voting. No example
of P- or O-mode analysis comes readily to mind,
although correlation based studies focusing on office
seeking activity at different governmental levels
within the United States as a whole or within
specific states over time suggest these as plausible
(e.g. Burnham, 1970; Campbell and Trilling, 1980).
Several precedents exist for T- and S-mode analyses,
including MacRae and Meldrum's (1960; 1969)
investigations of Illinois electoral history, Dykstra
and Reynold's (1978) effort to test the thesis of a
continuous geographical locus of agrarian radical
voting in Wisconsin and Taylor and Johnston's (1979,
pp. 88-92) exploratory analysis of patterns of
presidential voting among the nine major Census
divisions between 1952 and 1976. Of course, there
are also a number of studies using a T-mode framework
but without employing the synoptic power of factor
analysis to examine correlations between elections
over states or lesser jurisdictions across time
(e.g. Pomper, 1967; Burnham, 1970; 1974; Campbell and
Trilling, 1980).

Factor Indeterminancy

A basic distinction among the various methods which
loosely fall under the general factor analysis
terminology is that between the principal components
and the common factor models. Components analysis
first arose as a method for fitting planes by
orthogonal least squares (Pearson, 1901, cited in
Morrison, 1967, p. 222), but was later proposed by
Hotelling (1933, cited in King 1969, p. 166) as a
method for analysing correlation matrices. The
objective is a parsimonious description of the system
identified by the correlation matrix in terms of new
orthogonal variates which are, in a sense, 'means' of
the original ones (Johnston, 1978, p. 136). In
principal components analysis these mean variates are
extracted in their order of importance in relation to
the overall variation of the correlation matrix under
an assumption that all such variation is of intrinsic

interest through eigenvalue-eigenvector techniques.
These techniques are beyond the scope of our
discussion, but are well described in Morrison (1967,
pp. 222-230). In essence, the principal components
model involves a straightforward and invariant transformation of the original correlation matrix.

   In contrast to the mathematical closure of the
unrotated principal components model which assumes
that all of the information of interest is included
in the correlation matrix, the common factor model
requires additional outside constraints for
successful implementation. This has surrounded the
common factor model in controversy virtually since
its inception. The foundation of the controversy is
the assumption underlying factor analysis that
observed patterns are composed of both common and
specific variance with the latter not of interest.
Thus, whereas principal components analysis is
concerned with the total variance of the space
containing the observed variates, factor analysis is
concerned only with the common subset of that space
(Morrison, 1967, pp. 260-262; Rummel, 1970, p. 112;
Kim and Mueller, 1978, p. 11). This leads to what
has been referred to as a basic indeterminancy in
the common factor model since factoring cannot
proceed until estimates of this common variance have
been supplied for each variable which is included.
These estimates are typically referred to as
communalities. Yet, how can communalities be known
until after the factoring is complete? As Rummel
(1970, p. 105) has observed, "This dilemma has yet to
be satisfactorily solved within the confines of the
model." The problem first surfaced in a review of
Spearman's efforts to identify an empirical referent
for the concept of general intelligence (Wilson,
1928, cited in Steiger and Schonemann, 1978, p. 143)
and after a period of abatement in the 1940's and
1950's has reverberated through the 1960's and 1970's
(Steiger, 1979). Since the controversey has
mathematical, epistomological, and substantive
aspects, it is unlikely to be soon resolved even in
the technical literature. Recent synopses are to be
found in reviews by Steiger and Schonemann (1978),
Steiger (1979) and Elffers (1980).

There is hardly concensus in the literature about the pragmatic significance of the theoretical debate over the distinction between common and specific variance underlying the common factor model. Some writers advise avoiding it entirely via use of the alternative and mathematically closed principal components model (e.g. Steiger, 1979, p. 157). Others, while acknowledging the existence of the debate, advise employing the common factor model as a way of giving substantive researchers a more flexible set of tools with which to work (e.g. Kim and Mueller, 1978a, p. 48). In the end, it would seem to be a matter for informed choice. One illusory solution, it may be noted, is the use of the principal components model with factor rotation. Unrotated components are in fact mathematically unique in that they are variance maximizing basis vactors of a variable space. But since the components model posits that all of the variance in the original correlation matrix (indicated by unities in the main diagonal before factoring) is of interest, rotation of fewer than the complete set of components involves implicit, though often unacknowledged, acceptance of the common factor premise. Since (assuming more observations than variables) the rank of a correlation matrix with unities in the diagonal is equal to the number of variables, rotation of fewer factors than there are variables involves retention of less than the total variance and implies that there are a lot of slightly less than candid "principal components" studies about in the literature.

On a more promising note, operational investigations tend to suggest that the practical significance of adopting the premise of the common factor rather than the principal components model is rather minimal for many types of data sets provided that the principal axis variant of the common factor model is adopted at the prerotation stage of analysis (Morrison, 1967, p. 274; Velicer, 1972, cited in Steiger and Schonemann, 1978, p. 173). The reason is, in part, that as the number of variables in an analysis increases, the overall impact of the values inserted into the main diagonal of the correlation matrix tends to decline, at least empirically

(Rummel, 1970, pp. 318-320). Furthermore, when the
data exhibit rather strong intercorrelations, a
condition which is likely to promote interest in the
power of factor analysis in the first place, then
high communality estimates will approximate the
diagonal unities of principal components analysis
yielding a convergence of the two techniques (Rummel,
1970, p. 112). In a comparative study by Morrison
(1967, p. 274) meeting these conditions, for example,
it was found that "The interpretations of the factors
are similar to those given for the original principal
components." This comparison, by the way, was prior
to rotation.

In the current investigation, the maximum column
correlations employed as communality estimates were
typically in the .80 and above range. For the 1872
to 1980 T-mode analysis, for instance, the average
maximum column correlation for the twenty-eight
elections was a positive .87; for the corresponding
S-mode analysis, the average maximum column correlation for the forty-eight states was a positive .93.
Such values strongly suggest that prerotation
solutions involving the common factor assumptions
employed should not differ more than marginally from
solutions which might have been obtained under
principal components assumptions.

Missing Data

Before going on to consider the rotation methods
selected, it is necessary to mention that a problem
with missing observations was encountered during the
course of the research. This problem was quite
unavoidable since the last of the contiguous Western
states to be admitted to the Union did not cease to
be territories until after the turn of the twentieth
century. Consequently, the number of available
observations varied from twenty-four in 1828 to
forty-eight subsequent to 1912. While the SPSS
factoring algorithm employed in the analyses (Kim,
1975, pp. 503-504) offers seemingly painless methods
for coping with missing observations, there are
distinctive hazards involved as Rummel's (1970,
pp. 258-267) discussion of the subject amply
demonstrates. Skirting technicalities as much as
possible, the immediate impact of missing

observations is to cause the correlations upon which
a factor analysis necessarily proceeds to depend upon
varying numbers of observations. This in turn
results in the association of negative eigenvalues
with the original variation during the course of
factoring, producing what is sometimes known as
imaginary variance. The significance of this is that
the positive roots of the correlation matrix are
somewhat inflated as a result. Indeed, when iterative
refinement of communality estimates is attempted in
such a situation, the effect can be to make the
imputed common variance of some variables exceed
unity, a conceptually absurd and computationally
debilitating condition.

One typical approach to the problem of missing data
in practical applications of the common factor model
(or for that matter the principal components model)
is to try to substitute numerical values for the
missing entries via either guesswork or such seemingly more refined means as least-squares extrap-
olation. Such approaches would appear to have some
merit when missing data arise for reasons of noncom-
pliance or nonreporting as sometimes happens in
survey research. But, when the missing entries in
the data matrix are due to structural constraints,
such arbitrary "filling in" would seem to rest on
dubious grounds, indeed. How, for example, might one
defend inputting such and such an electoral response
to what was at the time a nonexistent state? Another
alternative is to entirely disregard cases which
involve missing entries, an option sometimes referred
to as listwise deletion. Since this would have been
tantamont to an assumption that entities such as, say,
Oklahoma, never existed, it too was rather unappealing,
to say the least.

The option elected was pairwise deletion of missing
cases (Kim, 1975, p. 504). This involves omitting
a case only when the data for that case is missing,
thus retaining as much of the original information
as possible. Unfortunately, this does not banish the
problem of imaginary variance. This problem, in turn,
was minimised in its impact by partitioning the data
set into the twenty-five state sample for the eastern
1828 to 1920 analysis and the forty-eight state

sample for the 1872 to 1980 analysis. The overlap
permitted the influence of the partitioning to be
assessed in terms of the results obtained. Since the
amount of imaginary variance produced during the
course of the factoring was in each of these cases
below one percent this gave a posteriori confirmation
of its success. Iterative improvement of the initial
maximum column correlation estimates of communality
was also employed in both of these instances.

Rank of Matrix

A problem closely related to missing cases for
particular variables in its impact upon factor
analytic procedures is that of the total number of
variables versus the total number of cases. This
issue arises because the rank of a data matrix can be
no higher than the lesser of these two (Rummel, 1970,
p. 219). The maximum number of factors, in turn, is
restricted to the rank of the data matrix. Factoring
when the rank of the data matrix is restricted by the
number of cases rather than the number of variables
is generally not a recommended procedure and is, in
fact, unallowable when the aim of a study is to
generalize from sample results to universal factors
(Johnston, 1978, p. 181). But, "When the interest is
only in describing data variability, then a factor
analysis will yield such a description regardless of
variables exceeding cases in number" (Rummel, 1970,
p. 220). Since twenty-eight elections were conducted
between 1872 and 1980, this condition was encountered
during the S-mode analysis. At first glance, it
might seem that extending the S-mode analysis back to
1828 would have brought the number of cases and the
number of variables into closer correspondence.
However, this would also have increased the problem
of missing observations. Hence, in a strict
technical sense the results of the 1872 to 1980
S-mode analysis must be viewed as a descriptive,
rather than as an inferential use of the common
factor model. Since there was but one United States
during this period, doing otherwise would rest upon
dubious epistomological grounds anyway. Furthermore,
there are two operational checks which can be used to
test the sensitivity of the results to the existence

of more variables (viz. states) than observations
(viz. elections).

Since the number of factors is restricted in this
instance by the number of cases rather than the
number of variables, one reasonable test of the
importance of this limitation in a descriptive application of the factor model is the question of the
number of important and interpretable factors
extracted from the data matrix. For, if the number
of interpretable factors approaches the rank of the
matrix as set by the number of cases, then this might,
though it would not necessarily, imply that inclusion
of additional cases would yield additional important
factors in the domain of investigation. Because but
three sectional S-mode factors are sufficient to
account for 92.5 percent of the variance in the data
matrix while the theoretical maximum number of
extractable factors is twenty-eight (the number of
elections), this check would seem to be passed with
ample room to spare. It ought to be noted, nevertheless, that an imaginary variance problem amounting
to 6.1 percent of variance was encountered during the
course of the S-mode factoring, making it impossible
to employ iterative improvement of original
communality estimates since the "refined" communality
of particular variables (viz. states) exceeded unity
when such improvement was attempted. This has two
implications. First, the prerotation model used for
the S-mode analysis is a common factor model, but
without iteration for improvement of communality
estimates. Second, the relative importance of the
three interpreted factors may have been somewhat
inflated by the imaginary variance. However, the
amount of inflation could not have been much, even in
the most unlikely circumstance that the first three
factors absorbed all of the impact of the imaginary
variance, since there were quite a number of other
smaller, uninterpreted factors with positive
eigenvalues.

The 1896 to 1980 span was chosen for the sectional
T-mode analyses for several reasons. One was to give
emphasis to the contemporary era at this more focused
stage of the analysis. Another was to keep the
missing observations and the more variables than

than cases problems within reasonable bounds.
Success in achieving these technical objectives was
considerable. In the twenty-two state analysis for
the Northeastern Core, the number of variables
(elections) and the number of cases (states) were the
same and the standard common factor model with
iterations could be used. In the analyses for the
Southern Periphery with fifteen states so classed and
for the Western Periphery with eleven states so
classed, however, the number of variables exceeded
the number of cases and iteration could not be
employed. Missing observations for three states
(Arizona, New Mexico and Oklahoma) also posed a
difficulty for the Southern analysis until the 1912
election. There were no missing observations for the
other sections at this stage of the analysis. Once
again, the discoveries that well fewer factors than
cases were adequate to account for the electoral
patterns and that imaginary variance was insub-
stantial (6.9 percent for the South, 12.2 percent for
the West and 0.0 percent for the Northeast) gave
confidence in the results. There is again the
caution that the T-mode analyses for the sections
must be viewed as descriptive, rather than
inferential efforts, but even without the technical
rationale for this involving fewer cases than
variables doing otherwise would require a rather
strange sophistry anyway, for the results reflect the
historically contingent circumstances of the 1896 to
1980 era.

Factor Rotation

Extraction of the unrotated factors was only a
preliminary stage of the factor analytic procedures
used in this research. The reason is that the
unrotated principal axis factors derived at this
early stage identify maximum variance vectors within
the common variance space. This somewhat contradicts
the objective of obtaining factors which categorise
elections into normal voting periods (on this general
point, see Johnston, 1978, p. 162). In the 1872 to
1980 T-mode analysis, for instance, the first
unrotated factor exhibited substantial or fairly
substantial loadings for most of the twenty-eight
elections involved. Under such circumstances, what

is desired are factors which establish the so-called
simple structure of the common variance space. The
concept of simple structure has been attributed to
Thurstone (1945, cited in Morrison, 1967, p. 263) and
involves selecting a set of factors which are most
meaningful and interpretable in subject matter terms.
Attainment of simple structure is achieved by
rotating the factors until each is maximally colinear
with a distinct cluster of variables. Thus, there is
a shift "from factors maximizing total variance to
factors delineating separate groups of highly intercorrelated variables" (Rummel, 1970, p. 377).
Although the major goal of simple structure is "to
make our model of reality as simple as possible"
(Rummel, 1970, p. 381), there are numerous
alternative rotation schemes for achieving this. The
question of which is best has no undisputably best
answer except, perhaps, in the context of a given
substantive purpose.

In some respects, the rotation problem is merely
the common factor indeterminancy problem under a
different guise. Since alternative rotations are
simply different, but mathematically equivalent
factor solutions, "the only good reason to stick at
some rotational method is," in Elffers' (1980,
pp. 321-322) words:

"the interpretability of the result within our
underlying theory. All current rotation methods
have that as their goal, but it has to be checked
anew in every individual case whether this goal is
reached. So, every a priori plea for a rotational
method should be understood merely as a recommend-
ation to try that method, as it has proved to be of
value in some other problems. If we are not
satisfied with the result in our case, we need not
hesitate to try another method."

In the instance of the S-mode analysis for which
the objective was to derive a political sectional-
ization of the United States, the choice of rotation
method was quite straightforward since this goal is
altogether consistent with the widely used varimax
criterion. This criterion involves maximizing the

variances of the squared loadings and implies
obtaining as many large and small, but as few intermediate loadings as possible for a given correlation
matrix (Morrison, 1967, pp. 284-286). Not surprisingly, orthogonal varimax rotation has become
standard among studies designed to obtain uniform
regions. It is, however, exceedingly rare for the
regionalizations so obtained to demarcate contiguous
classes of places to the extent achieved in this
study. Needless to say, this gave us very little
incentive indeed to experiment with alternative
rotation strategies for the S-mode analysis.

Selection of a rotational strategy appropriate to
the T-mode objective of identifying different normal
voting patterns over time was somewhat less straightforward. Here, the pertinent literature offered
fewer relevant guidelines because of the paucity of
T-mode analyses which have been reported. Although
we considered and experimented with orthogonal
varimax rotation at this stage, the implied
independence of the electoral patterns of different
epochs which this involved seemed hardly consistent
with the redundant emphasis in the literature of the
subject domain on the stability of partisan attitudes
in the electorate. While it might indeed be found
that the electoral patterns of one epoch little
resembled those of another, it appeared quite
unreasonable to impose this as an analytical
assumption. The advantage of oblique rotation
schemes "over orthogonal rotations is that, after
making oblique rotations, if the resulting factors
are orthogonal, one can be sure that the orthogon-
ality is not an artifact of the method of rotation"
(Kim and Mueller, 1978b, p. 37).

The oblique rotation option of the SPSS program
involves what is called direct oblimin (Kim and
Mueller, 1978a, p. 61). This is a simple structure
technique based upon simplifying loadings on the
primary axes and should not be confused with the
similarly named indirect oblimin technique which
involves loadings on the reference axes (Kim and
Mueller, 1978b, pp. 37-39). The importance of this
is examined below under the subject of oblique
factor interpretation. Under the direct oblimin

criterion, first proposed by Jennrich and Sampson
(1966, cited in Kim and Mueller, 1978b, p. 39), "the
factors are allowed to be correlated if such correlations exist in the data" (Kim, 1975, p. 486).
However, the researcher has some degree of control
over the degree of factor correlation via the
parameter delta which can be manipulated to make the
solution more or less oblique. To be on the safe
side, we experimented with different values to assess
the impact on our results, in one instance, trying
as many as twenty-one alternative values of delta
for one of our data sets. After this experimentation,
we concluded that the degree of imposed obliqueness
had little effect on either the patterns of
relationships between the factors or upon the interpretations of the factors themselves except in most
extreme cases. This is not an altogether uncommon
finding and "usually appears to be the case in
practice," according to Rummel (1970, p. 411). In
the end, we settled upon the default value for delta
of zero offered by the SPSS program. Since this
value is known to produce a fairly oblique solution
(Kim, 1975, p. 486), this suggests that in our
substantive interpretations of the factor correlations we are erring on the conservative side in
instances in which the normal voting patterns of one
eopch are found to be relatively uncorrelated with
those of another. Nevertheless, it must be stressed
that these correlations do not permit interpretation
in any absolute sense. This is necessarily the case
with any particular oblique operationalization of
the common factor model.

Number of Factors

Another somewhat subjective element in the use of the
common factor model is the selection of the number of
factors to rotate. Although the issue seems to be
little appreciated outside of psychology, the number
of factors rotated can exert nearly as much influence
on the final outcome as the selection of the rotation
procedure itself. Indeed, many factor analytic
studies have been published without even noting the
relevance of the issue (Rummel, 1970, p. 351). One
reason, perhaps, is that like the questions of which
methods of rotation and communality estimation are

to be preferred, there is probably no universally
acceptable answer on technical grounds alone so that
many would doubtless like to ignore its existence.

There are several common guides as to the number of
factors to rotate with an eigenvalue equal to one
probably being the most usual one employed, although
this is obviously very arbitrary. As an alternative,
a visual guide is offered by the use of graphs
showing cumulative variance accounted for by successively larger numbers of factors. Either a leveling
off toward the tail or a sharp drop-off in the graph
is then regarded as identifying an appropriate place
to stop factoring if such occurs. Expert opinion
seems to imply that rotation of too many factors is
less hazardous than rotation of too few. Thus, in
addition to inspection of the pattern of variance
accounted for at the prerotation stage, we also
employed Catell's (1958, cited in Rummel, 1970,
p. 365) strategy of overfactoring. But, instead of
simply leaving the trivial factors uninterpreted, as
he suggested, we added factors at the rotation stage
until we encountered one which was uninterpretable
in the sense that none of the elections exhibited a
substantial loading upon it; then, we adopted the
solution with the previously smaller number of
rotated factors. Furthermore, we adopted the
convention that each election should exhibit a
cumulative communality of at least .6 among the
factors which were rotated. This helped to ensure
that there would not be any conspicuously neglected
elections in the final results. Our approach perhaps
tends to produce more factors than is usual for the
number of variables examined, but in our view, is
warranted by the degree of variation in the data set
which we have chosen to analyse and consistent with
our overall objective of deriving a time-space framework aimed at an understanding of a century and a
half of American electoral competition.

Interpretation of Oblique Factors

Oblique rotation yields two sets of factor loadings
rather than one. With primary axis techniques, the
factor pattern loadings are essentially regression
weights of the variables on the factors; the
structure loadings in turn are correlations between

the factors and the variables (Rummel, 1970,
pp. 396-409). With reference axis techniques,
exactly the converse is the case, so that caution
must be exercised in noting which type of solution is
being presented. As a point in passing, the
discussion of oblique rotation in Johnston's Multivariate Statistical Analysis in Geography (1978,
pp. 166-171) apparently pertains to reference axis
solutions, although this does not seem to be
explicit.

With direct oblimin the factor pattern matrix
delineates more clearly the grouping or clustering of
variables than the structure matrix (Kim, 1975,
p. 476). "The pattern matrix, therefore, defines the
simple structure configuration and is basic for
substantively interpreting the oblique factors"
(Rummel, 1970, p. 401). To be sure, the structure
loadings cannot be ignored, and we, in fact, employ
them in conjunction with the derivation of estimated
factor scores. However, their interpretation
involves the easily overlooked hazard that the correlations of the variables with the factors can be in
a sense spuriously due to the correlations between
the factors themselves. In other words, the
structure loadings combine both direct and indirect
effects (Kim, 1975, p. 477) while "The pattern
loadings may be interpreted as measures of the unique
contribution each factor makes to the variance of
the variables" (Rummel, 1970, p. 397).

Although as correlations, the structure loadings
are bounded by plus and minus one, this is not
entirely true of the patten loadings which may on
occasion exceed unity when a particular variable is
especially important to the make-up of a given
factor. Thus, the reader should not be excessively
alarmed that some values slightly above unity are
found in Appendix Tables B.1 through B.5. Table B.1
shows the pattern loadings for the 1828 to 1920
analysis for the East, Table B.2 does the same for
the national 1872 to 1980 analysis, and Tables B.3
to B.5 do the same for the 1892 to 1980 sectional
analyses for the South, West and Northern Core,
respectively. These values are the basis for the
T-mode factor pattern profiles shown at various
points in the text.

In orthogonal analyses, it is quite proper to form
sums of squared loadings as estimates of the
importance of each factor because such loadings
combine the roles of pattern and structure loadings
in oblique analysis and the factors are independent
of another (Johnston, 1978, p. 166). In oblique
analysis, however, the variance of a variable
accounted for by the common factors is no longer
given by the sum of the squares of the pattern
coefficients because of the intercorrelations of the
factors (Kim, 1975, p. 476). Nevertheless, such sums
can be cautiously formed as relative estimates of the
importance of the factors, a procedure recommended by
Rummel (1970, pp. 148 and 520) and followed here.

    Clearly use of the oblique case of the common
factor model involves a considerable increase in the
complexity of the analysis and the interpretation of
the results. Nevertheless, "It is," in Sundquist's
(1973, p. 10) words, "hardly conceivable that any
political force could arise that would obliterate all
the reasons for attachment by members of the
electorate to the existing parties." Thus, the
duopolistic competition between the Democratic and
Republican parties is far better expressed via
oblique rotation than it would be via orthogonal
rotation. The independence assumption behind
orthogonal rotation is simply inconsistent with the
substantive context of our research.

Estimated Factor Scores

The last of the matrices employed in our research
establish the geographical arrangements associated
with each of the normal voting patterns identified
through the oblique T-mode analyses. Once again, it
needs to be noted that there is a mathematical
indeterminancy associated with the common factor
model because of the distinction between common and
specific variance in this context as well (Kim and
Mueller, 1978b, pp. 60-72; Johnston, 1978, pp. 172-
174). Although this is a problem which has only
recently been brought to the attention of geographers
(Elffers, 1980), and many others have chosen to
conspicuously overlook its existence (Steiger, 1979,
p. 157), its identification in fact goes all the way
back to Wilson's (1928, cited in Steiger and

Schonemann, 1978, p. 147) review of Spearman's Models of Man (1927). In that review, it was "pointed out that different sets of factor scores could fit Spearman's model equally well, for the same set of data" (Steiger and Schonemann, 1978, p. 147). Rummel (1970, p. 444) recently made essentially the same point in a more general fashion by noting that "distinctly different common factor score matrices can exist for the same data, correlation, and common factor loading matrices." Although the components model is often suggested as an alternative when factor scores are of interest, this is not an entirely helpful suggestion when missing data and oblique rotation are involved since it is no longer possible to compute exact factor scores in these instances either.

Rummel also points to another difficulty which is rarely, in his view, faced in psychology. In particular, he poses this question (Rummel, 1970, pp. 442-443):

"Should the researcher compute exact factor scores or estimates for relatively unknown factors that are only arithmetical combinations of the variables, or should he take a well known variable as representative of the factor even though the variable gives a comparatively poor estimate?"

When the original variables of an analysis are themselves of great and longstanding interest with many books and research articles having been published regarding them, it is probably best, in his view, to employ these rather than factor scales to convey the observational implications of the research, for in his words (Rummel, 1970, p 443):

"Basic variables usually communicate more meaning than other estimates. To make a known variable a central representation of a factor can make the factor more understandable and useful to the interested scientific and policy community."

It would be hard indeed to find a more appropriate context for this view than a study involving patterns

associated with United States presidential elections,
as we remarked in the opening chapter. Consequently,
after considerable thought we decided to employ basic
variable estimates in order to identify the
geographical arrangements associated with the normal
voting patterns which we have uncovered. Another
justification for thus selecting factor-based scales
is that given the long time frame of the analysis, it
is quite possible that minor associations at distant
points in time could disrupt full scale factor score
estimation. When such circumstances are encountered,
as Kim and Mueller (1978b, p. 72) recently remarked,
"factor-based scales have a legitimate place in
practical research" despite their disparagement by
mathematically inclined purists.

Our procedures for deriving factor-based scales for
the composite basis variable factor score estimates
which we have used deserve discussion, for they were
incorporated into an original computer program to
perform the following operations. First, Democratic
proportions of the popular vote were transformed to
z-scores computed from the cross-state means of each
election. States with above average Democratic
support were thus assigned values greater than zero
and conversely for states with below average
Democratic support for a given election. Since
z-scores have unit standard deviations, the election
proportions were also standardised in the process.
Then for each state, the z-scores were summed across
elections with pattern loadings above .4 and
structure loadings above .5 on a given factor.
Although most of the factors derived were unipolar
with few negative loadings , the exceptions required
that negative and positive unit weights be employed
in the summation process to account for this when the
occasion arose.

These sums were then converted to mean values on a
state by state basis. Although this increased the
number of intermediate computations which were
necessary, it evaded a problem which is intrinsic to
the SPSS factor score routine. In the SPSS routine,
the problem of missing data is handled at the stage
of factor score computation by inserting the means of
variables into the cells with missing cases (Kim,

1975, pp. 489-490). After some reflection, it became clear that this approach would pull states with missing values toward the means of the resulting scales and, thereby, distort the geographical patterns which were of interest. In allowing the estimated scores to be based upon differing numbers of elections for different states during the period before all contiguous forty-eight states were admitted to the Union, this problem was entirely avoided. Finally, after mean values were derived for each state on a given factor, these values in turn were standardised to zero mean and unit variance through a z-score transformation and classed into categories for the cartograms presented in the text.

Thus, although our composite basis variable factor scores, referred to simply as estimated factor scores in the text, are somewhat novel, they have several advantageous properties. First, since they are simply standardised averages of Democratic election proportions for contests which load highly on a given factor, they are readily comprehended, even by those with only a modicum of experience with the subtleties of factor analysis. Second, and for the same reason, they are readily relatable to patterns documented in an existing and voluminous literature on American presidential elections as fully estimated factor scores would not be. Third, they do not scatter the influences of elections with trivially low loadings on all but a few factors throughout the array of estimated factor scores, a point of more than slight importance in light of the oblique variant of the common factor model employed in the T-mode analyses. Indeed, all but a few of the elections contribute to the estimated scores of but one factor because of the criteria selected. Finally, the estimated scores can be interpreted in a most straightforward manner: states with above zero scores for a factor gave greater than average support to the Democratic Party during an electoral epoch and conversely for states with below zero scores. Because of this, visual comparisons between factor score maps are quite proper and reasonable. In essence, the scales represent the average level of Democratic support during the domain of a specific normal voting pattern.

Appendix B.   FACTOR PATTERN MATRICES

Table B.1   Factor Pattern: East, 1828–1920 (N=25).

Election	I	II	III	IV	V
		Factor Pattern Loadings			
1828	.04	.03	.01	.87	.14
1832	.22	.14	-.18	.84	.08
1836	.03	.91	-.10	-.26	.10
1840	-.18	.87	-.06	.20	.04
1844	.22	.74	-.02	.27	.03
1848	.02	.65	.23	.17	-.24
1852	.39	.53	.20	.20	.01
1856	.15	.39	.23	.28	-.43
1860	.03	.08	.08	.08	.83
1864	-.43	.01	.55	-.23	.27
1868	.03	-.08	.69	-.10	.04
1872	.05	.15	.62	.39	-.08
1876	.32	.04	.31	.42	-.24
1880	.62	.11	.28	.14	-.22
1884	.57	.02	.38	.26	-.16
1888	.94	-.03	.21	.05	.07
1892	1.06	.08	.09	-.16	.07
1896	.79	.07	-.05	.20	.01
1900	.97	-.02	.02	.09	.05
1904	.96	-.07	-.05	-.02	-.09
1908	.95	.00	-.06	.02	-.03
1912	.85	-.06	-.07	.11	-.13
1916	.95	.03	-.16	-.05	-.09
1920	.74	.01	-.07	.06	-.30
Sum of P^2	8.89	3.78	1.78	2.36	1.32

Factor	I	II	III	IV	V
		Factor Correlations			
I	1.00	.26	.12	.56	-.59
II		1.00	.12	.42	-.01
III			1.00	.17	-.01
IV				1.00	-.46
V					1.00

Table B.2   Factor Pattern: U. S. A., 1872–1980 (N=48)

Election	Factor Pattern Loadings					
	I	II	III	IV	IV	VI
1872	−.15	−.07	.93	.02	−.02	.22
1876	.03	−.03	.80	−.01	.26	−.07
1880	.44	.08	.62	.13	.01	−.13
1884	.57	.02	.43	.04	.07	−.08
1888	.61	.10	.28	.06	.14	−.21
1892	.47	.23	.33	−.39	−.01	−.24
1896	.27	−.06	.27	.70	.06	−.10
1900	.74	−.02	.07	.29	.06	−.11
1904	.93	.01	.13	−.11	−.06	−.08
1908	.88	−.08	.04	.06	−.04	−.12
1912	.86	−.06	.06	−.07	.04	−.10
1916	.84	−.02	−.03	.25	.07	−.07
1920	.96	−.14	.01	−.07	.03	.04
1924	1.02	−.11	.04	−.19	−.01	.09
1928	.70	.28	−.10	.10	.09	−.30
1932	.67	−.05	−.04	.24	.30	.01
1936	.56	.04	.09	.36	.31	−.07
1940	.74	.07	.03	.10	.24	−.06
1944	.66	.10	.01	.08	.32	−.14
1948	.01	.09	.15	.05	.07	.93
1952	.29	.11	.22	−.16	.58	.03
1956	−.10	−.07	.11	.04	.98	.03
1960	.20	.62	.01	−.06	.28	.30
1964	−.17	.49	−.01	−.19	−.38	.43
1968	−.39	.69	−.08	−.10	−.23	.01
1972	−.53	.63	−.11	−.09	−.01	−.03
1976	.22	.25	.13	−.36	.51	.08
1980	.14	.21	.14	−.59	.44	−.17
Sum of p^2	9.71	1.84	2.51	1.65	2.50	1.54

Factor	Factor Correlations					
	I	II	III	IV	V	VI
I	1.00	−.07	.50	.15	.59	−.47
II		1.00	.00	−.39	.13	.14
III			1.00	−.03	.48	.05
IV				1.00	.18	−.13
V					1.00	−.12
						1.00

Table B.3 Factor Pattern: South, 1896-1980 (N=15).

Election	Factor Pattern Loadings		
	I	II	III
1896	.89	-.28	.04
1900	.98	-.21	-.04
1904	.99	-.33	-.03
1908	1.06	-.20	-.19
1912	.94	.17	.02
1916	.98	.14	.00
1920	.91	.17	.07
1924	.95	.24	.00
1928	.90	.07	.03
1932	.86	.25	.07
1936	.90	.19	.09
1940	.87	.24	.15
1944	.80	.16	.29
1948	-.61	.40	-.34
1952	.05	.55	.66
1956	-.14	.50	.74
1960	.09	.79	-.17
1964	-.37	.31	-.72
1968	-.03	-.03	-.87
1972	-.16	.18	-.82
1976	.03	.89	.17
1980	.21	.71	.27
Sum of p^2	11.79	3.35	3.34

Factor	Factor Correlations		
	I	II	III
I	1.00	.03	.48
II		1.00	.23
III			1.00

Table B.4   Factor Pattern: West, 1896–1980 (N=11).

| Election | __Factor Pattern Loadings__ | | | | |
	I	II	III	IV	V
1896	.70	−.01	−.08	.17	.25
1900	.48	.11	.26	.30	.51
1904	.98	.11	.19	−.08	.03
1908	.41	−.13	.67	.07	.42
1912	.13	.16	.90	.02	.07
1916	.90	−.27	.14	.00	−.02
1920	.21	−.09	−.18	−.21	.75
1924	−.11	−.17	.10	−.17	.85
1928	.18	−.05	−.25	.71	−.18
1932	−.30	.03	.17	.85	−.11
1936	.15	.15	−.46	.48	.49
1940	.23	.08	−.65	.22	.42
1944	.22	.04	−.73	.25	.30
1948	.82	.06	−.31	−.07	.03
1952	.47	.34	−.43	−.13	.38
1956	.02	.83	−.25	.09	−.01
1960	.22	.46	−.49	.36	.15
1964	.14	.88	−.05	−.09	.02
1968	.18	.92	−.02	.00	−.14
1972	−.17	.86	.17	.15	−.18
1976	−.29	.80	.30	.19	−.08
1980	−.29	.79	.14	−.43	.15
Sum of P^2	4.15	4.81	3.40	2.18	2.60

| Factor | __Factor Corrleations__ | | | | |
	I	II	III	IV	V
I	1.00	−.05	−.21	.15	.55
II		1.00	−.09	.12	−.04
III			1.00	−.19	−.10
IV				1.00	−.06
V					1.00

Table B.5 Factor Pattern: North, 1896-1980 (N=22).

			Factor Pattern Loadings			
Election	I	II	III	IV	V	VI
1896	.61	-.58	.04	.07	.09	.13
1900	.42	-.25	.59	-.06	.17	.13
1904	-.13	.09	.93	.08	.17	.06
1908	.23	-.26	.79	.13	.21	-.11
1912	-.14	-.10	.76	.09	.34	.10
1916	.28	.01	.52	-.14	.03	.32
1920	.09	-.04	.96	-.03	-.31	.04
1924	-.03	.12	.95	.10	-.16	-.02
1928	-.03	.68	.34	.02	.53	-.04
1932	.39	-.09	-.06	.12	.61	.05
1936	.18	-.44	-.23	.13	.49	.52
1940	-.10	-.04	.10	.02	-.02	1.00
1944	.13	.21	-.05	-.03	-.04	.87
1948	.73	.37	.09	.14	.12	.04
1952	.41	.11	.24	.25	-.10	.44
1956	.72	-.11	-.05	.24	.00	.19
1960	.02	.62	.09	.20	.08	.46
1964	-.17	.79	.04	.20	-.20	.11
1968	.05	.80	-.20	.16	-.18	.16
1972	.19	.70	-.40	.12	.22	.02
1976	.13	.20	.12	.69	.05	.15
1980	-.03	-.05	.03	1.06	-.04	.11
Sum of P^2	2.25	3.55	4.98	1.95	1.81	2.71

			Factor Correlations			
Factor	I	II	III	IV	V	VI
I	1.00	-.12	.13	.33	.31	.49
II		1.00	-.06	.31	-.05	.13
III			1.00	.14	.14	.22
IV				1.00	.18	.34
V					1.00	.18
VI						1.00

BIBLIOGRAPHY

Abler, R., Adams, J. S., and Gould, P. (1971) _Spatial Organization_. Prentice-Hall, Englewood Cliffs, New Jersey.

Abrams, B. A. (1980) "The Influence of State-Level Economic Conditions on Presidential Elections," _Public Choice_ 35, 623-631.

Alker, H. R. (1969) "A Typology of Ecological Fallacies," in Dogan, M., and Rokkan, S. (editors) _Quantitative Ecological Analysis in the Social Sciences_. M.I.T. Press, Cambridge, Massachusetts, 69-86.

Anderson, K. (1979) "Generation, Partisan Shift and Realignment: A Glance Back to the New Deal," in Nie, N. H., Verba, S. and Petrocik, J. R., _The Changing American Voter_. Harvard University Press, Cambridge, Massachusetts, Enlarged Edition, 74-95.

Archer, J. C. (1979) "Incrementalism and Federal Outlays Among States, _Geographical Perspectives_, 44, 5-14.

Archer, J. C. (1980) "Congressional-Incumbent Reelection Success and Federal-Outlays Distribution," _Environment and Planning,_ 12, 263-277.

Asher, H. (1976) _Presidential Elections and American Politics: Voters, Candidates, Campaigns Since 1952_. Dorsey Press, Homewood, Illinois.

Baggaley, A. R. (1959) "Patterns of Voting Change in Wisconsin, 1952-1957," _Western Political Quarterly_, 12, 141-144.

Beard, C. A. (1914) _An Economic Interpretation of the Constitution of the United States_. MacMillan, New York.

Beard, C. A., and Beard M. (1937) _The Rise of American Civilization_. MacMillan, New York, Revised Edition.

Beard, C. A. and Beard, M. (1944) _A Basic History of the United States_. Doubleday and Doran, New York.

Berelson, B., Lazarsfeld, P. F., and McPhee, W. H. (1954) _Voting_. University of Chicago Press, Chicago.

Bernhard, W. E. A. (1973) _Political Parties in American History, Volume 1: 1789-1828_. Putnams, New York.

Berry, B. J. L. (1964) "Approaches to Regional Analysis: A Synthesis," _Annals of the Association of American Geographers_, 54, 2-11.

Berry, B. J. L. (1970) "The Geography of the United States in the Year 2000," _Transactions, Institute of British Geographers_, 51, 21-54.

Berry, B. J. L., and Horton, F. E. (1970) _Geographic Perspectives on Urban Systems_. Prentice-Hall, Englewood Cliffs, New Jersey.

Beyers, W. B. (1979) "Contemporary Trends in the Regional Economic Development of the United States," _Professional Geographer_, 31, 34-44.

Billington, M. L. (1975) _The Political South in the Twentieth Century_. Charles Scribner's Sons, New York.

Billington, R. A. (1960) _Westward Expansion_. MacMillan, New York, Second Edition.

Birdsall, S. S. (1969) "A Preliminary Analysis of the 1968 Wallace Vote in the Southeast," _Southeastern Geographer_, 9, 55-66.

Blair, D. H. (1979) "Electoral College Reform and the Distribution of Voting Power," _Public Choice_, 34, 201-215.

Bogue, A. G. (1968) "United States: The 'New' Political History," _Journal of Contemporary History_, 3, 5-27.

Bonadio, F. A. (1974) Political Parties in American History, Volume 2, 1828–1890. Putnams, New York.

Boorstin, D. J. (1965) The Americans: The National Experience. Random House, New York.

Brahms, S. J. (1978) The Presidential Election Game. Yale University Press, New Haven, Connecticuit.

Brams, S. J., and Davis, M. D. (1974) "The 3/2's Rule in Presidential Campaigning," American Political Science Review, 68, 113–134.

Broder, D. S. (1972) The Party's Over; The Failure of Politics in America. Harper and Row, New York.

Broh, C. A., and Levine, M. S. (1978) "Patterns of Party Competition," American Politics Quarterly, 6, 357–384.

Brown, R. E. (1960) Middle-Class Democracy and the Revolution in Massachusetts, 1691–1780. Princeton University Press, Princeton, New Jersey.

Brown, R. H. (1948) Historical Geography of the United States. Harcourt, Brace, and World, New York.

Brunn, S. D. (1974) Geography and Politics in America. Harper and Row, New York.

Brunn, S., and Ingalls, G. (1972) "The Emergence of Republicanism in the Urban South," Southeastern Geographer, 12, 133–144.

Buchanan, J. M., and Tullock, G. (1962) The Calculus of Consent. University of Michigan Press, Ann Arbor, Michigan.

Burnham, W. D. (1967) "Party Systems and the Political Process," in Chambers, W. N., and Burnham, W. D. (editors) The American Party Systems. Oxford University Press, New York, 277–307.

Burnham, W. D. (1970) Critical Elections and the
  Mainsprings of American Politics. Norton, New York.

Burnham, W. D. (1974) "The United States: The
  Politics of Heterogeneity," in Rose, R. (editor)
  Electoral Behavior: A Comparative Handbook. Free
  Press, New York, 653-725.

Burnham, W. D. (1975) "American Politics in the
  1970's: Beyond Party?," in Chambers. W. N., and
  Burnham, W. D. (editors) The American Party
  Systems. Oxford University Press, New York, Second
  Edition, 308-357.

Burnham, W. D., Clubb, J. M., and Flanigan, W. H.
  (1978) "Partisan Realignment: A Systemic
  Perspective," in Silbey, J. H., Bogue, A. G., and
  Flanigan, W. H. (editors) The History of American
  Electoral Behavior. Princeton University Press,
  Princeton, New Jersey, 45-77.

Burstein, P. (1979) "Electoral Competition and
  Changes in the Party Balance in the U. S. Congress,
  1789-1977," Social Science Research, 8, 105-119.

Calleo, D. R., and Rowland, V. M. (1973) America and
  the World Political Economy. Indiana University
  Press, Bloomington, Indiana.

Campbell, A., Converse, P. E., Miller, W. E., and
  Stokes, D. A. (1960) The American Voter. Wiley,
  New York.

Campbell, A., Converse, P. E., Miller, W. E., and
  Stokes, D. A. (1964) The American Voter: An
  Abridgement. Wiley, New York.

Campbell, A., Converse, P. E., Miller, W. E., and
  Stokes, D. E. (1966) Elections and the Political
  Order. Wiley, New York.

Campbell, A., Gurin, G., and Miller, W. E. (1954) The
  Voter Decides. Row-Peterson, Evanston, Illinois.

Campbell, B. A., and Trilling, R. J. (1980)
Realignment in American Politics: Toward a Theory.
University of Texas Press, Austin, Texas.

Cattell, R. B. (1952) Factor Analysis: An Introduction for the Psychologist and Social Scientist.
Harper and Brothers, New York.

Cattell, R. B. (1957) Personality and Motivation:
Structure and Measurement. World Book, Yonkers-on-
Hudson, New York.

Cattell, R. B. (1958) "Extracting the Correct Number
of Factors in Factor Analysis," Educational and
Psychological Measurement, 22, 667-697.

Ceaser, J. W. (1979) Presidential Selection: Theory
and Development. Princeton University Press,
Princeton, New Jersey.

Chambers, W. N. (1964) The Democrats: 1789-1964.
Van Nostrand, Princeton, New Jersey.

Chambers, W. N. (1966) "Parties and Nation-Building
in America," in La Palombara, J., and Werner, M.
(editors) Political Parties and Political
Development. Princeton University Press, Princeton,
New Jersey, 79-106.

Chambers, W. N. (1967) "Party Development and the
American Mainstream," in Chambers, W. N. and
Burnham, W. D. (editors) The American Party Systems.
Oxford University Press, New York, 3-32.

Chambers, W. N., and Burnham, W. D. (1967) The
American Party Ststems. Oxford University Press,
New York.

Chambers, W. N., and Burnham, W. D. (1975) The
American Party Systems. Oxford University Press,
New York, Second Edition.

Chase-Dunn, C. (1980) "The Development of Core
Capitalism in the Antebellum United States," in

Bergesen, A. (editor) Studies of the Modern World System. Academic Press, New York, 189-230.

Clubb, J. M., and Allen H. W. (1971) Electoral Change and Stability in American Political History. Free Press, New York.

Colantoni, C. S., Levesque, T. J., and Ordeshook, P. (1975) "Campaign Resource Allocation Under the Electoral College," American Political Science Review, 68, 141-154.

Colby, C. C. (1922) Sourcebook for the Economic Geography of North America. University of Chicago Press, Chicago.

Congressional Quarterly, Inc. (1975) Congressional Quarterly's Guide to U. S. Elections. Congressional Quarterly, Inc., Washington, D. C.

Congressional Quarterly, Inc. (1979) Presidential Elections Since 1789. Congressional Quarterly, Inc., Washington, D. C., Second Edition.

Converse, P. E. (1966a) "The Concept of a Normal Vote," in Campbell, A., Converse, P. E., Miller, W. E., and Stokes, D. E. Elections and the Political Order. Wiley, New York, 9-39.

Converse, P. E. (1966b) "Information Flow and the Stability of Partisan Attitudes," in Campbell, A., Converse, P. E., Miller, W. E., and Stokes, D. E. (1966) Elections and the Political Order. Wiley, New York, 136-157.

Converse, P. E., et.al. (1966) "Stability and Change in 1960: A Reinstating Election," in Campbell, A. Converse, P. E., Miller, W. E., and Stokes, D. E. Elections and the Political Order. Wiley, New York, 78-95.

Cosman, B. (1966) Five States for Goldwater. University of Alabama Press, University, Alabama.

Costain, A. N. (1978) "An Analysis of Voting in
American National Nominating Conventions, 1940-
1976," American Politics Quarterly, 6, 95-120.

Cotter, C. P., and Bibby, J. F. (1980) "Institutional
Development of Parties and the Thesis of Party
Decline," Political Science Quarterly 95, 1-29.

Cox, K. R. (1969) "The Voting Decision in a Spatial
Context," Progress in Geography, 1, 81-117.

Cox, K. R. (1970) "Residential Relocation and
Political Behavior: Conceptual Model and Empirical
Tests," Acta Sociologica, 13, 40-53.

Cox, K. R. (1976) "American Geography: Social Science
Emergent," Social Science Quarterly, 57, 182-207.

Cox, K. R. (undated) "The Spatial Evolution of
National Voting Response Surfaces: Theory and
Measurement," Department of Geography, Ohio State
University, Discussion Paper No. 9, Columbus, Ohio.

Crisler, R. M. (1952) "Voting Habits in the United
States," Geographical Review, 42, 300-301.

Dahl, R. A. (1961) Who Governs? Yale University Press,
New Haven, Connecticut.

Dahl, R. A. (1966) "The American Oppositions:
Affirmation and Denial," in Dahl, R. A. (editor)
Political Opposition in Western Democracy. Yale
University Press, New Haven, 34-69.

David, P. T. (1972) Party Strength in the United
States, 1872-1970. University of Virginia Press,
Charlottesville, Virginia.

DeGeer, S. (1927) "The American Manufacturing Belt,"
Geografiska Annaler, 9, 233-259.

Degler, C. (1974) "American Political Parties and
the Rise of the City" in Murphy, P. L. (editor)

*Political Parties in American History, Volume 3,
1890-Present*. Putnams, New York, 949-968.

Degraza, A. (1951) *Public and Republic*. Knopf, New
York.

Dogan, M., and Rokkan, S. (1969) *Quantitative
Ecological Analysis in the Scoial Sciences*. M. I. T.
Press, Cambridge, Massachusetts.

Downing, B., et.al. (1980) "The Decline of Party
Voting: A Geographical Analysis of the 1978
Massachusetts Election," *Professional Geographer*,
32, 454-461.

Downs, A. (1957) *An Economic Theory of Democracy*.
Harper and Row, New York.

Duverger, M. (1959) *Political Parties*. Methuen,
London, Second Edition.

Dye, T. R. (1966) *Politics, Economics and the Public*.
Rand McNally, Chicago.

Dykstra, R. R., and Reynolds, D. R. (1978) "In Search
of Wisconsin Progressivism, 1904-1952: A Test of
the Rogin Scenario," in Silbey, J. H., Bogue, A. G.,
and Flanigan, W. H. (editors) *The History of
American Electoral Behavior*. Princeton University
Press, Princeton, New Jersey, 299-326.

Edwards, E. E. (1938) *The Early Writings of
Frederick Jackson Turner*. University of Wisconsin
Press, Madison, Wisconsin.

Eidelberg, P. (1968) *The Philosophy of the American
Constitution: A Reinterpretation of the Intentions
of the Founding Fathers*. Free Press, New York.

Elazar, D. J. (1970) *Cities of the Prairie: The
Metropolitan Frontier and American Politics*. Basic
Books, New York.

Elazar, D. J. (1972) American Federalism: A View
From the States. Crowell, New York, Second Edition.

Elazar, D. J. (1978) "The Generational Rhythm of
American Politics," American Politics Quarterly,
6, 55-94.

Elffers, H. (1980) "On Uninterpretability of Factor
Analysis Results," Tractions, Institute of British
Geographers, 5, 318-329.

Eulau, H. (1976) "Understanding Political Life in
America: The Contribution of Political Science,"
Social Science Quarterly, 57, 112-153.

Eulau, H., Eldersveld, S. J., and Janowitz, M. (1956)
Political Behavior. Free Press, Glencoe, Illinois.

Fifer, J. V. (1976) "Unity By Inclusion: Core Area
and Federal State at American Independence,"
Geographical Journal, 142, 402-410.

Fishel, J. (1978) Parties and Elections in an Anti-
Party Age. Indiana University Press, Bloomington,
Indiana.

Flanigan, W. H., and Zingale, N. H. (1979) Political
Behavior of the American Electorate. Allyn and
Bacon, Boston, Fourth Edition.

Friedman, J., and Weaver, C. (1979) Territory and
Function: The Evolution of Regional Planning.
University of California Press, Berkeley.

Fruchter, B. (1954) Introduction to Factor Analysis.
Van Nostrand, New York.

Gaither, G. H. (1977) Blacks and the Populist Revolt:
Ballots and Bigotry in the 'New South.' University
of Alabama Press, University, Alabama.

Galton, F. (1888) "Co-relations and Their
   Measurement, Chiefly from Anthropometric Data,"
   Proceedings of the Royal Society, 45, 135-140.

Gerston, L. N., Burstein, J. S., and Cohen, S. J.
   (1979) "Presidential Nominations and Coalition
   Theory," American Politics Quarterly, 7, 175-197.

Ginsberg, B. (1972) "Critical Elections and the
   Substance of Party Conflict: 1844-1968," Midwest
   Journal of Political Science, 16, 603-625.

Goodman, P. (1967) "The First American Party System,"
   in Chambers, W. N., and Burnham, W. D. (editors)
   The American Party System. Oxford University Press,
   New York, 56-89.

Gordon, D. M. (1978) "Capitalist Development and the
   History of American Cities," in Tabb, W. K. and
   Sawers, L. (editors) Marxism and the Metropolis.
   Oxford University Press, New York.

Gosnell, H. F., and Gill, N. N. (1935) "An Analysis
   of the 1932 Presidential Vote in Chicago,"
   American Political Science Review, 29, 967-984.

Gottmann, J. (1961) Megalopolis. M. I. T. Press,
   Cambridge, Massachusetts.

Grant, P. A. (1980) "Establishing a Two-Party
   System: The 1932 Presidential Election in South
   Dakota," Presidential Studies Quarterly, 10, 73-79.

Grantham, D. W. (1967) The South and the Sectional
   Image: The Sectional Theme Since Reconstruction.
   Harper and Row, New York.

Gudgin, G., and Taylor, P. J. (1979) Seats, Votes
   and the Spatial Organization of Elections. Pion,
   London.

Hadley, C. D., and Howell, S. E. (1980) "Partisan
   Conversion in the Northeast: An Analysis of Split

Ticket Voting, 1952–1976," American Politics Quarterly, 8, 128–135.

Hamilton, A., Jay, J., and Madison, J. (1937) The Federalist. Modern Library, New York.

Harman, H. H. (1967) Modern Factor Analysis. University of Chicago Press, Chicago, Revised Edition.

Hart, J. F. (1976) The South. Van Nostrand, New York, Second Edition.

Hartshorne, R. (1935) "Recent Developments in Political Geography," American Political Science Review, 29, 943–966.

Haveman, J., Pierce, N. R., and Stanfield, R. L. (1976) "Federal Spending: The North's Loss is the Sunbelt's Gain," National Journal, 8, 878–891.

Hess, S. (1972) "Foreign Policy and Presidential Campaigns," Foreign Policy, 8, 3–22.

Hess, S. (1980) "Does Foreign Policy Really Matter?," Wilson Quarterly, 4, 96–111.

Hodge, C. (1963) "Aridity and Man: An Interpretive Summary," in Hodge, C., and Duisberg, P. C. (editors) Aridity and Man. American Association for the Advancement of Science, Washington, D. C., 1–19.

Hofstadter, R. (1948) The American Political Tradition. Knopf, New York.

Hofstadter, R. (1968) The Progressive Historians Alfred A. Knopf, New York.

Hofstadter, R. (1969) The Idea of a Party System: The Rise of Legitimate Opposition in the United States, 1780–1840. University of California Press, Berkeley.

Hofstadter, R. (1973) "A Constitution Against
    Parties," in Bernard, W. E. A. (editor) Political
    Parties in American History, Volume 1, 1789-1928.
    Putnams, New York, 34-58.

Hollingsworth, J. R. (1963) The Whirligig of Politics.
    University of Chicago Press, Chicago.

Hotelling, H. (1933) "Analysis of a Complex of
    Statistical Variables into Principal Components,"
    Journal of Educational Psychology, 24, 417-441,
    498-520.

Hunter, F. (1953) Community Power Structure.
    University of North Carolina Press, Chapel Hill
    North Carolina.

Huntington, E. (1963) The Human Habitat. Norton,
    New York.

Ingalls, G. L., and Brunn, S. D. (1979) "Electoral
    Changes in the American South, 1948-1976," South-
    eastern Geographer, 19, 80-90.

Jahnige, T. P. (1971) "Critical Elections and Social
    change," Polity, 3, 465-500.

Jennrich, R. I., and Sampson, P. F. (1966) "Rotation
    for Simple Loadings," Psychometrika, 31, 313-323.

Jensen, M., and Becker, R. A. (1976) The Documentary
    History of the First Federal Elections, 1788-1790,
    Volume 1. University of Wisconsin Press, Madison,
    Wisconsin.

Jensen, R. (1969a) "History and the Political
    Scientist," in Lipset, S. M. (editor) Politics and
    the Political Scientist. Oxford University Press,
    New York, 1-28.

Jensen, R. (1969b) "American Election Analysis: A
    Case History of Methodological Innovation and
    Diffusion," in Lipset, S. M. (editor) Politics and

the Political Scientist. Oxford University Press,
New York, 226-243.

Johnston, R. J. (1976) "Residential Area Characteristics: Research Methods for Identifying Urban
Sub-areas—Social Area Analysis and Factorial
Ecology," in Herbert, D. T., and Johnston, R. J.
(editors) Social Areas in Cities: Spatial Processes
and Form. Wiley, London.

Johnston, R. J. (1978) Multivariate Statistical
Analysis in Geography. Longman, London.

Johnston, R. J. (1979a) Political, Electoral and
Spatial Systems. Oxford University Press, London.

Johnston, R. J. (1979b) Geography and Geographers:
Anglo-American Human Geography Since 1945. Edward
Arnold, London.

Johnston, R. J. (1980) "Electoral Geography and
Political Geography" Australian Geographical
Studies, 18, 37-50.

Jones, G. S. (1970) "The Specificity of U. S.
Imperialism," New Left Review, 60, 59-86.

Kasperson, R. E., and Minghi, J. V. (1969) The
Structure of Political Geography. Aldine, Chicago.

Kelley, R. (1977) "Ideology and Political Culture
from Jefferson to Nixon," American Historical
Review 82, 531-563.

Kelley, R. (1979) The Cultural Pattern in American
Politics: The First Century. Alfred A. Knopf,
New York.

Key, V. O. (1949) Southern Politics in State and
Nation. Alfred A. Knopf, New York.

Key, V. O. (1955) "A Theory of Critical Elections,"
Journal of Politics, 17, 3-18.

Key, V. O. (1959) "Secular Realignment and the Party System," Journal of Politics, 21, 198–210.

Key, V. O. (1961) Public Opinion and American Democracy. Alfred A. Knopf, New York.

Key, V. O. (1964) Politics, Parties and Pressure Groups. Crowell, New York, Fifth Edition.

Key, V. O. (1966) The Responsible Electorate: Rationality in Presidential Voting 1936–1960. Belknap, Cambridge, Massachusetts.

Key, V. O., and Munger, F. (1959) "Social Determinism and Electoral Decision: The Case of Indiana," in Burdick, E., and Brodbeck, A. J. (editors) American Voting Behavior. Free Press, Glencoe, Illinois, 281–299.

Kim, J. (1975) "Factor Analysis," in Nie, N. H., et.al., SPSS: Statistical Package for the Social Sciences. McGraw-Hill, New York, Second Edition, 468–514.

Kim, J., and Mueller, C. W. (1978a) Introduction to Factor Analysis. Sage, Beverly Hills, California.

Kim, J., and Mueller, C. W. (1978b) Factor Analysis. Sage, Beverly Hills, California.

King, L. J. (1969) Statistical Analysis in Geography. Prentice-Hall, Englewood Cliffs, New Jersey.

Kleppner, P. (1979) The Third Electoral System: 1853–1892. University of North Carolina Press, Chapel Hill, North Carolina.

Kneeland, D. E. (1980) "Reagan Backs States' Rights in Visit to Mississippi Fair," Valley News, August 4, 1980, p. 18

Kollmorgen, W. (1936) "Political Regionalism in the United States--Fact or Myth," Social Forces, 15, 111–122.

Kousser, J. M. (1974) The Shaping of Southern
Politics: Suffrage Restriction and the
Establishment of the One-Party South, 1880-1910.
Yale University Press, New Haven, Connecticut.

Kramer, G. H. (1971) "Short-Term Fluctuations in
U. S. Voting Behavior, 1896-1964," American
Political Science Review, 65, 131-143.

Ladd, E. C., and Hadley, C. D. (1975) Transformations
of the American Party System: Political Coalitions
from the New Deal to the 1970's. Norton, New York.

Ladd, E. C., and Hadley, C. D. (1978) Transformation
of the American Party System: Political Coalitions
From the New Deal to the 1970's. Norton, New York,
Second Edition.

Lanouette, W. J. (1980) "Turning Out the Vote--Reagan
Seeks Larger Share of Blue-Collar Vote," National
Journal, 12, 1832-1835.

Lazarsfeld, P. F., Berelson, B., and Gaudet, H. (1944)
The People's Choice. Duell, New York.

Lazarsfeld, P. F., Lipset, S. M., Barton, A., and
Linz, J. (1954) "The Psychology of Voting," in
Lindzey, G. (editor) Handbook of Social Psychology.
Addison-Wesley, Cambridge, Massachusetts, 1124-1170.

Lebowitz, M. A. (1968) "The Jacksonians: Paradox
Lost?," in Bernstein, B. J. (editor) Towards a New
Past. Random House, New York, 65-89.

Lee, S. P., and Passell, P. (1979) A New Economic
View of American History. Norton, New York.

Lewis, P. F. (1969) "Impact of Negro Migration on the
Electoral Geography of Flint, Michigan, 1932-1962:
A Cartographic Analysis," in Kasperson, R. E., and
Minghi, J. V. (editors) The Structure of Political
Geography. Aldine, Chicago, 384-406.

Libby, O. G. (1894) "The Geographical Distribution of
the Vote of the Thirteen States on the Federal
Constitution, 1787-1788," Bulletin of the
University of Wisconsin, 1, 1-116.

Libby, O. G. (1912) "A Sketch of the Early Political
Parties in the United States," Quarterly Journal of
the University of North Dakota, 2, 205-242.

Lichtman, A. J. (1976) "Critical Election Theory and
the Reality of American Presidential Politics,
1916-1940," American Historical Review, 81,
317-348.

Link, A. S. (1973) Crucial American Elections.
American Philosophical Society, Philadelphia,
Pennsylvania.

Lipset, S. M. (1960) Political Man. Doubleday, New
York.

Lipset, S. M. (1969) Politics and the Social Sciences.
Oxford University Press, New York.

Lipset, S. M., and Rokkan, S. (1967) Party Systems
and Voter Alignments. Free Press, New York.

Lowi, T. J. (1967) "Party, Policy, and Constitution
in America," in Chambers, W. N., and Burnham, W. D.
(editors) The American Party Systems. Oxford
University Press, New York, 238-276.

Lubell, S. (1952) The Future of American Politics.
Harper, New York.

Lubell, S. (1965) The Future of American Politics.
Harper, New York, Third Edition.

Lynd, S. (1970) "Beyond Beard," in Bernstein, B. J.
(editor) Towards a New Past: Dissenting Essays in
American History. Chatto and Windus, London, 46-64.

MacRae, D., and Meldrum, J. A. (1960) "Critical
Elections in Illinois: 1888-1958," American
Political Science Review, 54, 669-683.

MacRae, D., and Meldrum, J. A. (1969) "Factor Analysis
of Aggregate Voting Statistics," in Dogan, M., and
Rokkan, S. (editors) Quantitative Ecological
Analysis in the Social Sciences. M. I. T. Press,
Cambridge, Massachusetts.

McCormick, R. P. (1967) "Political Development and the
Second Party System," in Chambers, W. N., and
Burnham, W. D. (editors) The American Party Systems.
Oxford University Press, New York, 90-116.

Main, J. T. (1965) The Social Structure of Revolutionary America. Princeton University Press,
Princeton, New Jersey.

Maisel, L., and Cooper, J. (1977) The Impact of the
Electoral Process. Sage, Beverly Hills, California.

Margolis, M. (1977) "From Confusion to Confusion:
Issues and the American Voter (1952-1972),"
American Political Science Review, 71, 31-43.

Mayo, E. O. (1979) "Republicanism, Antipartyism, and
Jacksonian Party Politics: A View From the
Nation's Capital," American Quarterly, 31, 3-20.

Mazmanian, D. A. (1974) Third Parties in Presidential
Elections. Brookings, Washington, D. C.

Merriam, C. E. (1925) New Aspects of Politics.
University of Chicago Press, Chicago.

Merriam, C. E., and Gosnell, H. F. (1940) The
American Party System: An Introduction to the
Study of Political Parties in the United States.
MacMillan, New York.

Miller, A. H. (1978) "Partisanship Reinstated? A
Comparison of the 1972 and 1976 U. S. Presidential

Elections," British Journal of Political Science, 8, 129-152.

Miller, D. C. (1975) Leadership and Power in the Bos-Wash Megalopolis. Wiley-Interscience, New York.

Mitchell, W. C. (1970) The American Polity. Free Press, New York.

Morison, S. E., and Commager, H. S. (1962) The Growth of the American Republic. Oxford University Press, New York.

Morison, S. E. , Commager, H. S., and Leuchtenburg, W. E. (1980) The Growth of the American Republic. Oxford University Press, New York, Seventh Edition.

Morrison, D. F. (1967) Multivariate Statistical Methods. McGraw-Hill, New York.

Munro, W. B. (1930) The Makers of the Unwritten Constitution. MacMillan, New York.

Murphy, P E. (1974) Political Parties in American History, Volume 3, 1890-Present. Putnams, New York.

Nash, G. D. (1973) The American West in the Twentieth Century: A Short History of an Urban Oasis. Prentice-Hall, Englewood Cliffs, New Jersey.

Nie, N. H., Verba, S., and Petrocik, J. R. (1979) The Changing American Voter. Harvard University Press, Cambridge, Massachusetts, Enlarged Edition.

Oh-Ra, J. (1978) Labor at the Polls: Union Voting in Presidential Elections, 1952-1976. University of Massachusetts Press, Amherst, Massachusetts.

Oldendick, R., and Bennett, S. E. (1978) "The Wallace Factor," American Politics Quarterly, 6, 469-484.

Parker, G. R. (1979) "Trends in Party Preferences: 1949-1976," American Politics Quarterly, 7, 132-146.

Paterson, J. H. (1975) North America. Oxford
University Press, New York, Fifth Edition.

Person, K. (1901) "On Lines and Planes of Closest Fit
to Systems of Points in Space," Philosophical
Magazine, 2, 559-572.

Patterson, S. C. (1968) "The Political Cultures of
the American States," Journal of Politics, 30,
187-209.

Peirce, N. R., and Hagstrom, J. (1980) "The Voters
Send Carter a Message: Time for a Change--to
Reagan," National Journal, 12, 1876-1878.

Pennock, J. R. (1979) Democratic Political Theory.
Princeton University Press, Princeton, New Jersey.

Perloff, H. S., Dunn, E. S., Lampard, E. E., and
Muth, R. F. (1960) Regions, Resources and Economic
Growth. University of Nebraska Press, Lincoln,
Nebraska.

Petersen, S. (1963) A Statistical History of the
American Presidential Elections. Frederick Ungar,
New York.

Peterson, M. D. (1973) "The Election of 1800," in
Link, A. S. (editor) Crucial American Elections.
American Philosophical Society, Philadelphia, 1-13.

Phillips, K. P. (1970) The Emerging Republican
Majority. Anchor Books, Garden City, New York.

Polsby, N. W., Dentler, R. A., and Smith, P. A.
(1963) Parties and Social Life: An Introduction to
Political Behavior. Houghton Mifflin, Boston.

Pomper, G. M. (1967) "Classification of Presidential
Elections," Journal of Politics, 29, 535-566.

Pomper, G. M. (1968) Elections in America: Control
and Influence in Democratic Politics. Dodd, Mead
and Co., New York.

Pomper, G. M.(1972)"From Confusion to Clarity: Issues and American Voters, 1956-1968," American Political Science Review, 66, 415-428.

Pomper, G. M. (1975) Voter's Choice: Varieties of American Electoral Behavior. Dodd, Mead and Co., New York.

Pomper, G. M.(1977) The Election of 1976. David McKay, New York.

Pool, I. S., Abelson, R. P., and Popkin, S. L. (1964) Candidates, Issues and Strategies. M. I. T. Press, Cambridge, Massachusetts.

Pounds, N. (1972) Political Geography. McGraw-Hill, New York, Second Edition.

Pred, A. (1977) City Systems in Advanced Economies: Past Growth, Present Processes and Future Developments. Wiley, New York.

Prescott, J. R. V. (1959) "The Functions and Methods of Electoral Geography," Annals of the Association of American Geographers, 49, 296-304.

Prescott, J. R. V. (1969) "Electoral Studies in Political Geography," in Kasperson, R. E., and Minghi, J. V. (editors), The Structure of Political Geography. Aldine, Chicago, 376-383.

Prescott, J. R. V. (1972) Political Geography. Methuen, London.

Reading, D. C. (1973) "New Deal Activity and the States, 1933-1939," Journal of Economic History, 33, 792-811.

Rees, J. (1979) "Technological Change and Regional Shifts in American Manufacturing," Professional Geographer, 31, 45-54.

Reiner, T. A. (1974) "Welfare Differences Within a Nation," Papers: Regional Science Association, 32, 65-82.

Reynolds, D. R. (1974) "Spatial Contagion in Political Influence Processes," in Cox, K., Reynolds, D. R., and Rokkan, S. (editors), Locational Approaches to Power and Conflict. Halsted, New York, 233-274.

Reynolds, D. R., and Archer, J. C. (1969) "An Inquiry into the Spatial Basis of Electoral Geography," Department of Geography, University of Iowa, Discussion Paper Series No. 11, Iowa City, Iowa.

Rice, S. A. (1928) Quantitative Methods in Politics. Appleton, New York.

Rifkin, J., and Barber, R. (1978) The North Will Rise Again: Pensions, Politics and Power in the 1980's. Beacon Press, Boston.

Roberts, C. A. (1979) "Interregional Per Capita Income Differentials and Convergence: 1880-1950," Journal of Economic History, 39, 101-112.

Rokkan, S. (1970) Citizens, Elections, Parties. McKay, New York.

Rose, R. (1974) Electoral Behavior: A Comparative Handbook. Free Press, New York.

Rose, R. and Urwin, D. (1975) Regional Differentiation and Political Unity in Western Nations. Sage, Beverly Hills, California.

Roseboom, E. H., and Eckes, A. E. (1979) A History of Presidential Elections. Collier, New York, Fourth Edition.

Rossi, P. (1959) "Four Landmarks in Voting Research," in Burdick, E., and Brodbeck, A. J. (editors) American Voting Behavior. Free Press, Glencoe, Illinois, 5-54.

Rubinson, R. (1978) "Political Transformation in
Germany and the United States," in Kaplan, B. H.
(editor) Social Change in the Capitalist World
Economy. Sage, Beverly Hills, 39–73.

Rummel, R. J. (1970) Applied Factor Analysis.
Northwestern University Press, Evanston, Illinois.

Rusk, J. G. and Stucker, J. J. (1978) "The Effect of
the Southern System of Election Laws on Voting
Participation: A Reply to V. O. Key, Jr.," in
Silbey, J. H., Bogue, A. G., and Flanigan, W. H.
(editors) The History of American Electoral
Behavior. Princeton University Press, Princeton,
New Jersey, 198–250.

Russett, B. (1969) "Discovering Voting Groups in the
United Nations," in Kasperson, R. E., and Minghi,
J. V. (editors) The Structure of Political
Geography. Aldine, Chicago, 407–418.

Sale, K. (1976) Power Shift: The Rise of the
Southern Rim and Its Challenge to the Eastern
Establishment. Vintage Books, New York.

Sartori, G. (1969) "From the Sociology of Politics to
Political Sociology," in Lipset, S. M. (editor)
Politics and the Social Sciences. Oxford University
Press, New York, 65–100.

Sayre, W. S., and Parris, J. H. (1976) Voting for
President: The Electoral College and the American
Political System. Brookings, Washington, D. C.

Schafer, J. (1941) "Who Elected Lincoln," American
Historical Review, 47, 51–63.

Schattschneider, E. E. (1960) The Semi-Sovereign
People. Holt, Rinehart and Winston, New York.

Schwirian, K. P. (1972) "Analytical Convergence in
Ecological Research: Factorial Analysis, Gradient,
and Sector Models," in Sweet, D. C. (editor) Models

of Urban Structure. Lexington Books, Lexington,
Massachusetts.

Seagull, L. M. (1980) "Secular Realignment: The
Concept and its Utility," in Campbell, B. A., and
Trilling, R. J. (editors) Realignment in American
Politics: Toward a Theory. University of Texas
Press, Austin, Texas, 69–81.

Shade, W. L. (1973) Social Change and the Electoral
Process. University of Florida Press, Gainesville,
Florida.

Sharkansky, I. (1969) The Politics of Taxing and
Spending. Bobbs–Merrill, Indianapolis, Indiana.

Sharkansky, I. (1970) Regionalism in American
Politics. Bobbs–Merrill, Indianapolis, Indiana.

Shortridge, R. M. (1980) "Voter Turnout in the
Midwest,; 1840–1872," Social Science Quarterly,
60, 617–629.

Silbey, J. H. (1973) Political Ideology and Voting
Behavior in the Age of Jackson. Prentice–Hall,
Englewood Cliffs, New Jersey.

Silbey, J. H., and McSeveney, S. T. (1972) Voters,
Parties, and Elections: Quantitative Essays in the
History of American Popular Voting Behavior. Xerox
College Publishing, Lexington, Massachusetts.

Silbey, J. H., Bogue, A. G., and Flanigan, W. H.
(1978) The History of American Electoral Behavior.
Princeton University Press, Princeton, New Jersey.

Simpson, W. (1978) Vision and Reality: The
Evolution of American Government. Murray, London.

Singer, J. W. (1980) "Unions Hard at Work for
Carter's Reelection," National Journal, 12,
1836–2839.

Smith, H. R. and Hart, J. F. (1955) "The American
Tariff Map," Geographical Review, 55, 327-346.

Spearman, C. (1904) "General Intelligence Objectively
Determined and Measured," American Journal of
Psychology, 15, 201-293.

Spearman, C. (1927) The Abilities of Man. MacMillan,
New York.

Stanwood, E. (1928) A History of the Presidency from
1788 to 1897. Houghton Mifflin, Boston.

Steiger, J. H. (1979) "Factor Indeterminacy in the
1930's and the 1970's: Some Interesting Parallels,"
Psychometrica, 44, 157-167.

Steiger, J. H., and Schonemann, P. H. (1978) "A
History of Factor Indeterminacy" in Shye, S.
(editor) Theory Construction and Data Analysis in
the Behavioral Sciences. Jossey-Bass, San
Francisco, 136-178.

Sternlieb, G., and Hughes, J. W. (1978) Revitalizing
the Northeast. Center for Urban Policy Research,
Rutgers University, New Brunswick, New Jersey.

Sundquist, J. L. (1973) Dynamics of the Party System:
Alignment and Realignment of Political Parties in
the United States. Brookings, Washington, D. C.

Sutton, R. L., and Wilson, L. A. (1978) "Opinion-
Policy Congruence: State Regimes and State Regime
Differences," Political Methodology, 5, 127-144.

Swauger, J. (1980) "Regionalism in the 1976
Presidential Election," Geographical Review, 70,
157-166.

Tarrance, V. L. (1978) "Suffrage and Voter Turnout in
the United States: The Vanishing Voter," in
Fishel, J. (editor) Parties and Elections in an

<u>Anti-Party Age</u>. Indian University Press, Bloomington Indiana, 77-85.

Tatalovich, R. (1979) "Electoral Votes and Presidential Campaign Trails, 1932-1976," <u>American Politics Quarterly</u>, 7, 489-497.

Taylor, P. J. (1973) "Some Implications of the Spatial Organization of Elections," <u>Transactions, Institute of British Geographers</u>, 60, 121-136.

Taylor, P. J. (1977) <u>Quantitative Methods in Geography</u>. Houghton Mifflin, Boston.

Taylor, P. J., and Johnston, R. J. (1979) <u>Geography of Elections</u>. Penguin Books, Harmondsworth.

Thompson, W. R. (1968) "Internal and External Factors in the Development of Urban Economies," in Perloff, H. S., and Wingo, L. (editors) <u>Issues in Urban Economics</u>, Johns Hopkins Press, Baltimore, 43-62.

Thompson, W. R. (1978) "Aging Industries and Cities: Time and Tides in the Northeast," in Sternlieb, G., and Hughes, J. W. (editors) <u>Revitalizing the Northeast</u>. Center for Urban Policy Research, Rutgers University, New Brunswick, New Jersey, 144-152.

Thurstone, L. L. (1928) "Attitudes Can be Measured," <u>American Journal of Sociology</u>, 33, 529-554.

Thurstone, L. L. (1945) <u>Multiple Factor Analysis</u>. University of Chicago Press, Chicago.

Trewartha, G. T. (1953) "A Case for Population Geography," <u>Annals of the Association of American Geographers</u> 43, 71-97.

Tullock, G. (1976) <u>The Vote Motive</u>. Institute of Economic Affairs, London.

Turner, F. J. (1914) "Geographical Influences in
  American Political History," Bulletin of the
  American Geographical Soceity, 46; reprinted in
  Turner, F. J. (1932) The Significance of Sections
  in American History. Holt, New York, 183-192.

Turner, F. J. (1920) The Frontier in American History.
  Holt, New York.

Turner, F. J. (1926) "Geographic Sectionalism in
  American History," Annals of the Association of
  American Geographers, 16; reprinted in Turner,
  F. J., The Significance of Sections in American
  History. Holt, New York, 193-206.

Turner, F. J. (1932) The Singificance of Sections in
  American History. Holt, New York.

U. S. Bureau of Census (1976a) Historical Statistics
  of the United States, Colonial Times to 1970,
  Bicentennial Edition. U. S. Government Printing
  Office, Washington, D. C.

U. S. Bureau of Census (1976b) Statistical Abstract
  of the United States. U. S. Government Printing
  Office, Washington, D. C. Ninety-seventh Edition.

Velicer, W. (1972) "An Empirical Comparison of
  Factor Analysis, Image Analysis, and Principal
  Component Analysis," Unpublished Ph.D. Dissertation,
  Purdue University, Lafayette, Indiana.

Wallerstein, I. (1974) "The Rise and Future Demise of
  the Capitalist World System: Concepts for Comparative Analysis," Comparative Studies in History and
  Society, 16, 387-418.

Ward, D. (1971) Cities and Immigrants. Oxford
  University Press, New York.

Wayne, S. J. (1980) The Road to the White House: The
  Politics of Presidential Elections. St. Martin's,
  New York.

Whittlesey, D. (1957a) "The United States: The
Origin of a Federal State," in East, W. G. and
Moodie, A. E. (editors) The Changing World:
Studies in Political Geography. World Book,
Yonkers-on-Hudson, 239-260.

Whittlesey, D. (1957b) "The United States: Expansion
and Consolidation," in East, W. G., and Moodie, A.
E. (editors) The Changing World: Studies in
Political Geography. World Book, Yonkers-on-Hudson,
261-284.

Williams, W. A. (1966) The Contours of American
History. Quadrangle Books, Chicago.

Williams, W. A. (1969) The Roots of the Modern
American Empire. Vintage, New York.

Williamson, J. G. (1965) "Regional Inequalities and
the Process of National Development," Economic
Development and Cultural Change, 13, 3-45.

Wilson, E. B. (1928) "Review of 'The Abilities of Man,
Their Nature and Measurement' by C. Spearman,"
Science, 67 244-248.

Wright, G. (1974) "The Political Economy of New Deal
Spending: An Econometric Analysis," Review of
Economics and Statistics, 51, 30-38.

Wright, J. K. (1932a) "Sections and National Growth,
Geographical Review, 22, 353-360.

Wright, J. K. (1932b) "Voting Habits in the United
States; A Note on Two Maps," Geographical Review,
22, 666-672.

Yeates, M., and Garner, B. (1976) The North American
City. Harper and Row, New York, Second Edition.

Zelinsky, W. (1973) The Cultural Geography of the
United States. Prentice-Hall, Englewood Cliffs,
New Jersey.

INDEX